Conflict and Change in the Russian Industrial Enterprise

Conflict and Change in the Russian Industrial Enterprise

Edited by Simon Clarke
Professor of Sociology
Centre for Comparative Labour Studies
University of Warwick
Coventry, UK

MANAGEMENT AND INDUSTRY IN RUSSIA SERIES

Centre for Comparative Labour Studies, Warwick
Institute for Comparative Labour Relations Research, Moscow

Edward Elgar

Published by
Edward Elgar Publishing Limited
8 Lansdown Place
Cheltenham
Glos GL50 2HU
UK

Edward Elgar Publishing Company
Old Post Road
Brookfield
Vermont 05036
US

British Library Cataloguing in Publication Data

Conflict and change in the Russian industrial enterprise. –
(Management and industry in Russia ; v. 2)
1. Labor economics – Russia 2. Trade-unions – Russia
3. Industrial relations – Russia
I. Clarke, Simon
331'.0947

ISBN 1 85898 340 1

Printed and bound in Great Britain by
Hartnolls Limited, Bodmin, Cornwall

Contents

The Authors

Vladimir Ilyin was born in 1950 in the North Caucasus. He went to Nalchik to study history in 1968, continuing his studies in Leningrad from 1972, where he wrote his dissertation on 'the social psychology of the American student movement of the 1960s', which enabled him to gain access to the writings of the New Left. On graduation in 1975 he was offered the choice of working as a prison officer in Leningrad, or as a lecturer in American history at Syktyvkar State University. He chose the latter, although he switched his specialism to the History of the CPSU in order to gain access to the Party archives. In 1977 he returned to Leningrad for postgraduate study, researching the management structure of enterprises for three years, returning to Syktyvkar as reader in history until 1986, when he switched to reader in Philosophy and Scientific Communism in order to be able to teach sociology. Since 1993 he has been a senior researcher in the university. Volodya returns to the Caucasus every two years, where, when a student, he worked as a mountaineering instructor. His mountaineering has led to more troubles than his dissidence: he has twice been arrested on the borders of the Soviet Union, with Finland and with Iran, once got lost in the mountains of Abhazia for two weeks, and got frostbite when caught in a blizzard descending Mount Elbrus. In 1993 he introduced his son to the Caucasus with a tour of the war zones of Chechnya and Ingushetia. His wife Marina does not encourage such adventures.

Irina Tartakovskaya was born in 1964 in Samara. She graduated with distinction from the Historical Faculty of Samara University in 1987, having written a sociological dissertation. She worked in the Sociology Laboratory of Samara University and, since 1992, has been a researcher in the Samara branch of the Institute for Comparative Labour Relations Research. In 1994 she defended her Candidate's dissertation in the sociology of literature. Her scientific interests, apart from industrial sociology, include political sociology and the sociology of culture, but more recently she has been working primarily in the sociology of gender, and particularly the position of women in the system of labour relations. Her hobbies are journalism and literary criticism, and she is interested in the ideas of feminism. She has a husband and a dog.

Irina Kozina was born in 1957 in Samara. She graduated from the Historical Faculty of Samara University. At university she was drawn to archaeology and ancient history, but found contemporary problems of social life more interesting and after graduation began to work as a sociologist in an industrial enterprise. After a year she was invited to head the sociology laboratory of Samara Pedagogical University, where she established a collective which has worked on a wide range of sociology projects over the past nine years. For the last four years the laboratory has specialised on problems of labour relations. Since 1994 she has combined her scientific work with the post of director of the Samara branch of the Institute for Comparative Labour Relations Research (ISITO). She has just completed her dissertation for the Institute of Sociology of the Russian Academy of Sciences on 'Methodology and Methods of Sociological Research'. She married a fellow student while still at university. Her husband, fortunately, works as a businessman, not as a scientist. They have a thirteen year old son, who is at school.

Vadim Borisov was born in 1961 in Chelyabinsk, pollution capital of the world. He finished school in 1978, working for a year as a setter of printing equipment in the Chelyabinsk Metallurgical Factory before becoming a student of philosophy in the Department of Scientific Communism of Ural State University in Sverdlovsk. While a student he worked as a member of the *corps de ballet* at the Lunacharsky Theatre in Sverdlovsk. On graduation in 1984 he went to work as a prison officer, only escaping from a life contract by feigning insanity. In 1987 he became a teacher of 'Scientific Communism' at the Chelyabinsk Medical Institute, where he soon became a leader of the informal movement, in 1988 organising the first gathering of informal leaders and the first mass demonstration in Chelyabinsk, where his main opponent was his uncle, then head of the City Party Committee (now he is the 'democratic' head of the regional administration). The local Party suggested that he establish a Popular Front in Chelyabinsk but, instead, he returned to Sverdlovsk as a postgraduate student. He moved to Moscow in 1990, where he continued his informal activity, while studying sociology and then working as a freelance journalist and sociologist. He was awarded his candidate's degree in sociology in 1993 and became a member of the Journalists' Union in 1994. He is now a research fellow in the Centre for Comparative Labour Studies at the University of Warwick, and Director of the Institute for Comparative Labour Relations Research (ISITO) in Moscow.

Galina Monousova was born in 1959 in the Moscow region. She graduated as a labour economist from the Institute for National Economy in Moscow in 1980. After graduation she worked for several years as an economist in the Centre for Health Care Economics of the Ministry of Health. From 1986 to 1991 she worked as a researcher at the Institute for the International Labour Movement of the Academy of Sciences, where she studied the development of the new independent trade unions and the development of strikes in Russia. In 1990 she was awarded her Candidate's degree with a dissertation on the brigade system in industry in Eastern Europe. In 1991 she moved, with the rest of her research team, to the new Institute for Employment Studies, continuing her research on the same themes. Since 1993 she has been a research fellow in the Institute for World Economy and International Relations. Since 1992, in addition to our collaborative research programme, she has been involved in a number of international research projects, including those directed by A. Touraine (1992–3) and A. Schleifer (1994), covering various topics including social movements, industrial relations, privatisation and corporate governance.

Elain Bowers was born in Cardiff in 1959. She worked as a nurse for several years before going to university as a mature student, graduating from the University of Wales, College of Cardiff in sociology with first class honours in 1990. After working as a sociological researcher, she went as a graduate student to the University of Warwick, being awarded an MA with distinction in Labour Studies in 1992 with a dissertation on women and work in Russia, and immediately began work on a doctorate on the same subject, following an intensive Russian language course. She conducted her fieldwork in Samara, Moscow and Syktyvkar, working closely with our Russian collaborators and participating in our research seminars. She does not have a dog or a husband, but she likes cats.

Pavel Romanov was born in 1964 into a family of office workers in the metallurgical complex. Before he became a sociologist he was involved in a range of very different activities. He worked as an unskilled labourer and as a fitter in a factory and worked in a Siberian national park. After a five-year break to study for a degree in biology at Samara University, when he was first drawn to sociology, he became one of the founders of the independent sociological centre Sotsio, where he worked on various political and socio-economic themes, and later worked in the Laboratory of the Samara Pedagogical University. He was initially a specialist in the statistical analysis of questionnaire data, but more recently has concentrated on qualitative methods. His interests include management of industrial enterprises and the specific socio-cultural features of Russian industry.

Veronika Kabalina had a passion for knowledge and high grades as a student, graduating from high school as a gold medallist, and from university with a 'red diploma'. Her first experience of scientific work, and of the organisation of conferences and seminars, was as a student in the economics faculty of Moscow State University from which she graduated in 1978. On graduation she was faced with the choice between becoming a graduate student and working as an economic adviser in embassies aboad. To the astonishment of her friends and her teachers she chose to have and to bring up two children. She began work in 1982 and, for the next three years, taught political economy in an aviation institute. Following this she researched and wrote her candidate's dissertation on the professional training of industrial workers in Eastern and Central Europe, which she defended in 1988 in the Institute of the International Workers' Movement in Moscow. With perestroika it became possible for her to research areas of social life which had formerly been closed and forbidden and to exchange ideas and experience with Western colleagues through joint research. In 1991–2 she participated in an international project on trade unions and industrial relations in former socialist countries and worked on a project on new social movements in Russia, directed by Alain Touraine, in the course of which she became familiar with the methodology of interview research. Since 1992 her research interests have concentrated on the processes of transformation of enterprises: privatisation, the restructuring of management and employment relations, working within the framework of our collaborative research programme.

1. Conflict and Change in the Russian Industrial Enterprise

Simon Clarke

This book is the second volume in a series on the Russian industrial enterprise in transition which has been produced within the framework of a collaborative programme of case study research that has been under way in industrial enterprises in Russia continuously since 1991.[1] The first volume brought together a collection of papers around the theme of 'formal and informal relations' in the Russian industrial enterprise. This volume brings together a collection of papers around the theme of 'conflict and change', and a third volume will contain papers around the theme of 'labour in transition', focusing on the restructuring of wages and employment and on strikes. A fourth volume will present a selection of detailed case studies of particular industrial enterprises. We hope to publish further volumes as the research programme develops. Annette Robertson translated the paper by Irina Kozina and Vadim Borisov. All the other papers have been translated and edited by Simon Clarke, in consultation with their authors.

The theme of this volume, conflict and change, lies at the heart of our research programme. According to the ideology of Marxism-Leninism social antagonism had no place in the society of 'developed socialism', and change took place according to the programme of the Communist Party of the Soviet Union, the formation of which was guided by the scientific research of myriad institutes, and the implementation of which was monitored by Party bodies at all levels. Conflict might arise, but since the Party programme was the embodiment of right and reason, such conflict could only be the irrational result of human ignorance, venality or weakness, to be corrected by

[1] The programme has been directed by Simon Clarke and Peter Fairbrother, and has involved research teams in the Komi Republic, Kuzbass, Samara and Moscow, coordinated since 1994 by the Moscow-based inter-regional Institute for Comparative Labour Relations Research. This programme has been funded by the University of Warwick Research and Innovations Fund, the British Economic and Social Research Council and INTAS.

punishment, re-education, or even some small corrections to the Party programme in the light of the further findings of science. Of course conflict existed, indeed conflict was pervasive, but the Soviet system had very effective institutional mechanisms for the fragmentation, dissipation and suppression of conflict which gave it the appearance of enormous stability — until those institutional mechanisms decayed and were dismantled and the system fragmented.

The ideological structures of the state ideology of Marxism-Leninism were by no means dissolved with the collapse of the Soviet Union, but they were filled with a new content, that of neo-liberalism, many of whose most ardent proponents in Russia in the 1990s were precisely those who had previously been most thoroughly immersed in Marxism-Leninism. Neo-liberalism, like Marxism-Leninism before it, provides an inviolable truth, impervious to rational or empirical evaluation, backed by the divine morality of the market, the beacon that lights the way to the radiant future of 'developed capitalism'. The neo-liberals recognise that their revolutionary programme of moral purification through '-isation' — destatisation, privatisation, marketisation, monetisation — will lead to conflict and resistance, but since the neo-liberal programme is the embodiment of right and reason, such conflict could only be the irrational result of human ignorance, venality or weakness, to be corrected by punishment, re-education, or even some small corrections to the reform programme in the light of further advice from divine messengers from the World Bank.

Although Russia is being flooded with consultants, bearing new values and new techniques to modernise the Russian economy, their plans retain a central feature of the Soviet system: the authoritarianism of management structures backed up by the certainty of dogmatic ideological absolutism. They seek only to replace the legitimation of managerial authority on the basis of class and collective interest, enforced by the Party, with its legitimation on the basis of the rights of property enforced by the courts, and backed up by mass unemployment. Recognising that the Soviet institutions of social and industrial democracy were a hollow sham, but fearing that they might be filled with content by the democratic aspirations of the people, they demand their abolition as barriers to the realisation of their Utopian fantasies. This is the basis of the alliance between the most reactionary elements of East and West, who try to build a new Russia by combining the worst elements of both systems.

Despite the twin myopias of Marxism-Leninism and neo-liberalism, conflict did and does exist, and it was not and is not irrational. Without understanding the rational foundations of conflict in objective differences of interest one cannot understand the patterns or directions of change in Russia, nor can one provide any predictions of or prescriptions for the future. Although the papers in this volume are all based on small-scale ethnographic and case study research, at the same time they all address aspects of these fundamental issues of conflict and change and the future development of Russian society.

The two papers by Volodya Ilyin provide an analytical framework within which to understand the parameters of conflict and change in the transitional period, and in particular to theorise the apparent contradiction between the extremely high levels of discontent recorded at all levels of post-Soviet society and the relatively very low levels of industrial and political unrest, with very little organised resistance to the path or pace of 'reform', despite its devastating impact on living standards and on living and working conditions.

Volodya's first paper, 'Social Contradictions and Conflicts in State Enterprises in the Transition Period', develops a theoretical analysis of the relationship between social contradictions and conflict, which is substantiated by the results of his own empirical research in a passenger transport enterprise since 1989. In my view this is an extremely important paper within the context of our research programme, both theoretically and methodologically. It is theoretically important because Volodya manages to explain, within a consistent analytical framework, a number of apparently paradoxical phenomena which remain inexplicable within what Volodya characterises as the 'functionalist' and the 'conflict' paradigms of sociology, but which equally remain inexplicable for any empiricist sociology which is content to remain at the level of superficial phenomena. Volodya therefore demonstrates in practice the necessity of distinguishing between the theoretical analysis of objective contradictions which exist at various levels of the social system, and the explanation of the particular manifestations of these contradictions in the form of specific social conflicts.

Methodologically the paper is important in clearly bringing out the justification for the case study method of research, which lies at the heart of our research programme. The passenger transport enterprise which is the focus of Volodya's study was not chosen because it was by any means 'typical', but precisely because it was atypical — we initially selected it for intensive study because it was the one enterprise that we could find in the first stage of our research in which the trade union appeared to be locked in conflict with management as representative of the workforce. In fact, as the struggle unfolded and Volodya penetrated more deeply, it became clear that the enterprise was not fundamentally different from any other Soviet enterprise, but was one in which the underlying contradictions manifested themselves in the sharpest form, thus providing, as Volodya argues, a privileged insight into the reality of those contradictions.

Volodya argues that we can characterise objectively the internal and external contradictions of interest which are embedded in the Soviet and post-Soviet enterprise, and from this point of view every enterprise is alike. However, enterprises differ from one another very considerably in the forms in which different social groups perceive or misperceive these contradictions, and so in the patterns of conflict that arise. On the other hand, these perceptions and misperceptions are in turn not purely subjective, although they always involve a subjective element, but are to some degree an expression of the articulation and intersection of the various objective contradictions. In particular, Volodya argues that in most post-Soviet enterprises it is the external contradiction, between the 'labour collective' of the enterprise as a whole and the market and/or political and bureaucratic environment, that is dominant and that enables the enterprise management, under the leadership of the director, to repress or divert conflicts arising on the basis of the internal contradictions.

While the external contradiction remains a dominant factor in the development of conflict in the passenger transport enterprise studied by Volodya, the enterprise is exceptional in the pervasiveness and duration of internal conflicts affecting in differing ways and to differing degrees all levels and sub-divisions of the enterprise. Study of this enterprise therefore provides a unique opportunity to characterise the complexity and inter-relations of the various contradictions within the Soviet and post-Soviet enterprise not only on the basis of theoretical speculation, but with a firm grounding in empirical research. This research both enables us to explain why conflicts developed in the way they did in the enterprise in question, and why conflicts develop in different ways in other enterprises.

This same theoretical framework informs Volodya's second paper, which in essence deals with the other side of the same coin, explaining the persistence of the passive and conciliatory character of Soviet trade unionism in the post-Soviet era. It is easy to attribute this to the persistence of old institutional structures and to the continued domination of the former 'official' trade unions by the same conservative bureaucrats who controlled the unions in the Soviet period. However, as Volodya notes in his paper, the trade unions have in fact undergone quite fundamental institutional changes, with the collapse of Communist Party control and the decentralisation of trade union structures. Moreover, there has been a very substantial turnover of personnel at all levels, with many trade union officials having emerged from the rank-and-file in the conflicts of the late perestroika period. These changes led some on the left to revise their former negative view of the official trade union structures, and to seek to work more closely with the 'official' Federation of Independent Trade Unions of Russia (FNPR) as the only significant mass opposition force to the 'reformist' policies of the Yeltsin regime.[2] However, it was difficult to maintain these illusions for long, as it became clear that FNPR remained as attached to bureaucratic machine politics as it had ever been in the past, more concerned to court the employers than to organise the workers.

The persistence of this form of trade unionism cannot be explained by the personal or intellectual failings of the trade union leadership, but has to be related to its objective foundations, in the persistence of the traditional relationship between management and workers, between the enterprise director and the labour collective, which rests in turn on the dominance of the external relations of the enterprise as objective determinants of the fate of the enterprise and its employees. This means that the ultimate subordination of the trade union to management continues to express the collective interests of the employees of the enterprise, within the limits of the system.

This argument is reinforced by examination of the fate of the 'new' trade unions which have emerged with the collapse of the Soviet system, trade unions which originally emerged with a strongly anti-Communist and anti-managerial orientation, but which have been compelled by force of circumstance increasingly to converge with the established patterns of traditional trade unionism. The leaders of these new trade unions understood only too well that the condition for

2 This was particularly the case with the intellectuals associated with the 'Party of Labour', Andrei Isaev, Boris Kagarlitskii and Aleksandr Buzgalin, whose backgrounds lay in anarcho-syndicalism, 'New-Leftism', and Fourth International Trotskyism respectively, and who are much better-known in the West than in Russia. Kagarlitskii broke with FNPR in 1994, as he and Buzgalin moved closer to the Russian Communist Party.

effective trade unionism was the complete destruction of the system, within which management could otherwise always use the workers as shock troops in fighting its own bureaucratic–redistributive battles. But they also soon discovered that, while the system persisted, they had no choice, if they were to retain their members and their influence, but to play the traditional game. The progressive weakening of reformist forces at the political level, which was a manifestation of the parallel inability of reformist politicians to establish a significant social base for their programme, appeared to the new union leaders as a betrayal by their former political allies, and reinforced their growing convergence with the traditional patterns of trade unionism.[3]

This analysis is by no means undermined by examples of trade union militancy and radicalism, such as that of the Independent Miners' Union, the air traffic controllers, or the trade union in the passenger transport enterprise which is the basis of Volodya's first paper. As Volodya shows, in all these cases the militancy of the unions, however much it might harness the aspirations of the workers, and however much it might express the authentic radicalism of their leaders, links up with conflicts within the managerial apparatus, and serves objectively to further the interests of one or another faction within that apparatus.

As Volodya notes, militant trade union activity is only really to be found in those branches which remain part of the state-dominated sectors of the economy, in particular coal mining and various forms of passenger transport, where the strategic significance of the branch has both protected it from subjection to the full rigour of the market economy, and also given both workers and management some leverage in pressing their demands against local or central government. In this respect it might be argued that his analysis is somewhat one-sided in focusing on those branches which remain within the state sector, so that his conclusion that the external contradictions continue to be dominant, and that trade union activity is therefore constrained by objective conditions to be collaborative, is overstated. However, the next paper, by Irina Tartakovskaya, provides striking confirmation of Volodya's analysis in a case study of an independent trade union in a now privatised enterprise.

3 For a detailed study of the new workers' movement, focusing on the Kuzbass miners, Sotsprof and the air traffic controllers, see Simon Clarke, Peter Fairbrother and Vadim Borisov, *The Workers' Movement in Russia*, Edward Elgar, Cheltenham, 1995.

Irina Tartakovskaya's paper complements Volodya Ilyin's analysis by presenting a case study of the development of a small independent trade union in Samara, 'Solidarity'. On the one hand, the case study presents a clear picture of the typical day-to-day problems faced by independent workers' organisations in making progress against the opposition of both management and the official trade union. On the other hand, Solidarity is not typical in that it is one of the few such trade unions which has managed to survive. Irina is undoubtedly right in attributing considerable importance to the personality of the Solidarity leader, Aleksandr Belenko, and the transparency and informality of the organisation in this respect. However, other factors were also important in explaining the appeal of Solidarity to the workers, and its relative immunity from management persecution.

Solidarity was attractive to workers for its commitment to the defence of workers' rights, and particularly for its refusal to sanction dismissals in an enterprise facing growing economic difficulties. The close connections of the Solidarity leaders with local leaders of the democratic movement, including both people's deputies and press and television journalists, were very important in giving Solidarity a degree of protection from victimisation in the initial period of its existence. Subsequently, although it was something of a thorn in the flesh of management, its commitment to pursuing disputes through legal channels, and its growing opposition to strikes on both political and pragmatic grounds, showed management that Solidarity could play an important role in defusing increasingly frequent shop-floor conflicts. Thus, at the end of 1992 Solidarity secured official recognition, with the check-off of union dues and participation in the negotiations for the 1993 collective agreement, which accorded Solidarity full recognition, while the more militant deputy leader of Solidarity, who had threatened to split the union, failed to secure support and moved to another job.

In its subsequent development Solidarity confirms the analysis offered by Volodya Ilyin in the previous paper. The continued control of the social and welfare system and of the distribution of benefits by the official trade union meant that Solidarity members were at a symbolic and a material disadvantage, making it very difficult for the union to expand, and forcing Belenko into an accommodation with the official trade union and management at shop level, while joining the other independent trade unions in lobbying the government, without success, to withdraw the privileges of the official unions. In the meantime

Belenko was confined to largely symbolic opposition, for example to the form of privatisation of the company, and attempting to extend his network of alliances.

Despite internal divisions, and differences with other independent unions, Solidarity has managed to survive, and to provide its leadership with a platform from which to criticise the official unions. Although it seems doubtful that independent trade unions, such as Solidarity, can develop effective trade union activity of their own in present circumstances, their existence is nevertheless important in providing a potential nucleus of opposition to management and the established trade union and so providing some counteracting force to the tendency for the established union to act as a branch of management, without regard to the interests of its members. In this respect Solidarity plays a similar role to that played by the Party organisation in the past in encouraging the established trade union to represent workers' grievances to management, if not to act as a representative body.

Irina concludes her paper by arguing that Solidarity is unique, and not typical of workers' organisations in Russia. However, this by no means implies that we cannot draw general lessons from a unique case study because, as noted above, the unique case study describes the limits of the possible. Solidarity's uniqueness lies not in its existence as an independent trade union, since there are hundreds of similar tiny trade unions scattered across Russia, comprising a handful of individuals grouped around a charismatic and energetic leader, based in one plant, or one shop of one plant.[4] Solidarity's uniqueness lies in the fact that it has been able to hold onto its membership and to survive as a trade union, even expanding beyond its home base. However,

4 Most Sotsprof primary groups have precisely this character. The Sotsprof groups in Novosibirsk appear to be the most comparable to Solidarity, with Vladimir Kovalev, Viktor Popov and Pavel Taletskii playing the role of Sasha Belenko, the leader of Solidarity. However, most Sotsprof groups emerge at a moment of conflict and then dissolve. This is partly because most of the leaders of Sotsprof are outsiders looking for a political base, and are not so committed to the routine organisational work of trade union activity as is Sasha Belenko, relying more on legal proceedings and exemplary actions than on collective organisation to defend their members' interests. Similarly they are less willing to make the kinds of compromises necessary to protect their members and to enable their organisation to survive, so that the history of most Sotsprof groups is one of victimisation and failure. See Clarke, Fairbrother and Borisov, *The Workers' Movement in Russia*, for an overview of Sotsprof activity. The periodical publications of the Russian-American Fund, *Soobshcheniya korrespondentov fonda*, and *Iz pisem v fond* include reports on their struggles to survive from the leaders of liberal-democratic micro-unions, most of which are connected with Sotsprof.

Solidarity has had to make a whole series of compromises in order to defend its members' interests and to protect them from dismissal, to such an extent that its former deputy leader can charge it with being completely inactive. At the same time, the fact that the destruction of the union was the only alternative to such compromises is best indicated not only by the fate of comparable micro-unions which adopted a more confrontational position, but also by the fact that the members of the ultra-militant Party of the Dictatorship of the Proletariat, which is also based in Samara, and which condemns trade unionism in principle as reformist, nevertheless established a cell of Solidarity as the basis of their own self-protection.

The example of Solidarity confirms the barriers faced by attempts to establish an independent trade unionism identified by Volodya Ilyin. Leaders of the liberal democratic 'alternative' unions had hailed privatisation as the key to the development of an independent trade unionism, because only with privatisation would the interests of workers and employers be clearly distinguished from one another. However, the naïvety of this position has become only too clear as privatisation has progressed and economic crisis and growing unemployment has progressively strengthened the hand of employers. The story of Solidarity is in many respects a pitiful one, yet Solidarity is one of the very few independent trade unions to have managed to survive in a privatised enterprise, albeit a privatised enterprise which is in the military-industrial sector and can therefore continue to hope for state support. The analysis is only further confirmed by the fact that it has proved virtually impossible to establish any kind of effective trade unionism in 'new' private enterprises.[5]

The prospects for independent trade unionism in Russia were bleak through 1994, but became even bleaker through 1995 as the State Duma considered successive drafts of the new labour code, all of which threatened considerably to reduce the legal rights of workers, which had hitherto provided the basis for such effective trade union

5 The argument is also confirmed by the attempts of Sotsprof to establish a presence in the textile town of Ivanovo in 1994–5. Ivanovo had been hit harder than any other place in Russia by the crisis, with very low wages, long shut-downs and mass unemployment. However, despite the anti-management rhetoric of Sotsprof, it was only when the Ivanovo employers began to campaign for financial support from Moscow that Sotsprof was able to find an opening in the textile plants.
Independent 'trade unions' flourished in the new co-operative and private sectors from 1989. However, these were usually established by the owners of these enterprises to provide social and health insurance for their workers outside the state system, the trade union form being adopted because of the tax privileges it provided.

activity as was possible, and to remove the legal basis for trade union pluralism, which would enable the official unions to enforce their monopoly of representation of the labour force. At the same time, the relation between the 'internal' and 'external' contradictions, described by Volodya Ilyin, was changing, as is discussed in the remaining papers in this volume.

While employers in such industries as coal mining and public transport continued to rely on the support of the workforce in their attempt to maintain state support, and in the military-industrial complex and hard-hit textile industry in their attempt to lobby for such support, in other branches of production employers were looking more and more to their own devices to survive in the environment of the market economy. Economic and financial instability meant that even in these branches of production opportunities for profit derived more from the parallel financial and commercial speculations of management than from the productive activity of their enterprises. Nevertheless, they were increasingly constrained to live within the resources at their disposal, and so to reduce their production costs by holding down wages, delaying the payment of wages, putting workers on short-time and sending them on 'administrative vacation', and laying-off workers in increasingly large numbers. The twin processes of bankruptcy and post-voucher privatisation were driving an increasing wedge between management and the workforce, as enterprise managers established close connections with the local administration and with new commercial and financial structures increasingly with a view not to 'preserving the labour collective', but to intensifying its exploitation. However, far from encouraging the growth of independent trade unionism, as the leaders of the liberal-democratic 'alternative' trade unions had hoped, the polarisation between workers and employers was linked to an even more direct absorption of the trade union apparatus into management, leaving the workers with no organised defence of their own interests.

If we focus on the traditional institutions of working class organisation, [6] trade unions and associated workers' political organisations,

6 Left and 'socialist' political organisations are in an even more pitiful condition than are the trade unions, with very little contact with such workers' organisations as do exist. Despite the ideological affinity of their leaders, even the various re-formed communist parties have been unable to establish effective institutional links with the official trade unions. The leaders of the 'alternative' unions have largely lost faith with the 'democrats', but have shown no inclination to turn to the self-proclaimed left for political leadership.

the picture in Russia appears to be very bleak. However, it would be a mistake to identify social forces solely with their institutional expression. Within the Soviet system the fact that the trade unions and Communist Party were instruments of state power rather than organisations expressing the interests of the workers did not mean that workers were an atomised, alienated and defenceless mass. While the contradiction between the workers and the system that exploited them was not directly articulated organisationally and institutionally, it nevertheless existed and pervaded everyday existence, underpinning a distinctive working class ideology which turned the rhetoric of the system against itself, and underlying social conflicts within and beyond the workplace which thereby, as Volodya argues, expressed the fundamental contradictions, albeit in fragmented, displaced, and often mystified forms.

The underlying contradiction, and the ideology which articulated it, is going through a process of transformation, but it is by no means dissolving. The objective basis of conflict therefore remains, even where the underlying contradictions do not manifest themselves in direct and overt forms of organised and self-conscious class conflict. Moreover, the development of this underlying contradiction is by no means a spontaneous or an automatic process. The conflicts to which it gives rise, however fragmented and displaced they might be, are nevertheless at the most fundamental level conflicts around the development of this contradiction, whose outcome determines the development of the system as a whole. In this sense every act of resistance, however unsuccessful and however futile it might appear to be if viewed in isolation, has an impact on the development of the whole. Social change is necessarily and inevitably the outcome of conflict over the form and direction of that change, and every conflict impresses itself on the form and direction of change. However, it is only through a theoretical analysis of the relation between contradiction and conflict that we can make any sense of the relationship between conflict and change, and so understand the sense and significance of the changes which are taking place in Russia today.

Volodya Ilyin's theoretical papers stress the complexity of the contradictions which arise at different levels, and which can be manifested in quite different lines of cleavage and conflict, depending on both subjective and objective factors. The opening up of the contradictions internal to the enterprise by no means implies that the primary line of division will necessarily be that between management and the workers, since there are already well-established lines of division within the workforce, which any reasonably astute manager is able to exploit, just as the government is well able to exploit traditional divisions between branches of production. The primary lines of division within the traditional Soviet enterprise were those between workers, on the one hand, and management and technical workers, on the other; between 'productive' and 'unproductive' workers; and between 'main' and 'auxiliary' workers. Differences based on skill, grading and age and experience were also recognised. All these differences and divisions were institutionalised within the Soviet enterprise, and were reflected in pay, status and working conditions. It is clear that these differences could be, and still are, exploited by management to divide the workforce in the face of the intensification of the exploitation of the workforce as a whole.

In the next paper, Irina Kozina and Vadim Borisov discuss the very important changes which have taken place in the status hierarchies within the labour force in industrial enterprises, concentrating particular on the status of workers, to ask what are the emerging lines of division and conflict within the enterprise. They argue that these changes have been very profound. Within the enterprise as a whole, production work, which was formerly elevated above all other forms of employment, has been downgraded in comparison with commercial and financial activity, with a corresponding impact on those engaged in such work. Alongside this, the power and status of production workers has considerably declined in relation to that of management, primarily as a result of the removal of the whip of the plan, the decline in production and, above all, the pervasive fear of unemployment. This growing differentiation between workers and managers has been considerably reinforced by the process of privatisation, through which senior managers have been able to transform themselves into property owners, while workers are transformed into hired labour, fearful of losing their jobs in enterprises which were once theirs, but over which they have lost all control.

There have also been considerable changes in the status hierarchy within the industrial working class itself. Most of these changes involving a growing homogenisation of the labour force, as the ending of the plan, the collapse of highly skilled military production, and labour shortage removes the most highly skilled workers from their former pivotal position; as the collapse of the Party removes the privileges and high status positions of the *kadrovye* workers; as main production loses its former priority over auxiliary production, the important thing being to have a job, rather than to be too fussy about what one does; and, at the other end of the scale, as the former reserve army of unskilled surplus labour is dismissed. Similarly, the dismissal of working pensioners and the failure to recruit young workers means that the age profile of the labour force is becoming more compressed.

There is also some tendency to homogenisation in the changes in the relative status of different kinds of production and different occupations. While military production and heavy industry, which had formerly been the most privileged branches of production, have been hardest hit by economic decline, so that their employees have seen a corresponding erosion of their status position, other branches of industry and other occupations have seen a relative increase in their status as they are able to guarantee higher earnings and greater security of employment. Similarly, while skilled basic production workers were the best paid and most privileged workers in the Soviet period, primarily for ideological reasons, with the transition to a market economy it turns out to be the skilled auxiliary workers, such as electricians and toolmakers, who are in the shortest supply and so able to secure wages equal to, or higher than, those of direct production workers.

The main exception to this tendency to homogenisation of the labour force is the restructuring of the gender division of labour. Here there is a gender homogenisation of the labour force in particular enterprises and occupations, associated with a strengthening of gender segregation and a deterioration in the status position of women workers, as men take over the better paid jobs, leaving women with the lower paid and less desirable work.

These changes in status are influenced by, and are reflected in, changes in the dominant ideology. While the stereotypes and symbols of the Soviet period, eulogising the working class, have gone, the new ideologies of private ownership and the market still have little relation to the reality of working class life. Shareownership gives little power and few privileges, while there is no satisfaction in producing a useful product, rather than achieving the plan, if nobody can afford to buy it. All these aspects of the decline in the status of industrial work lead to growing demoralisation and insecurity within the working class.

The twin processes of differentiation and polarisation of owners, managers and workers, on the one hand, and the homogenisation of the working class, on the other, raises the central question of class formation, class consciousness and class conflict. It is clear that a process of class formation is under way, even if it has not proceeded very far and is not yet irreversible. It is also clear that, while many managers and politicians espouse the new rhetoric of property and the market, this has no meaning for the mass of the working class, who remain attached to many of the values of the old order, and in particular to the egalitarian conception of social justice. Nevertheless, Irina and Vadim argue that conflict over wages is often not motivated primarily by economic considerations, nor by considerations of social justice, but in fact represents a displacement of workers' anger and frustration at the erosion of their status position and at the growing insecurity of that position, workers seeking to restore their position and to secure its recognition through monetary gains. Thus they tend to demand pay increases by referring to real or mythical differentials between themselves and management, or themselves and workers in other enterprises, but not to put forward demands that concern the more fundamental issues of ownership and control that really underlie the decline in the workers' status. Thus Irina and Vadim are not especially optimistic about the prospect of workers developing a class perspective from which to contest their position in the foreseeable future. Nevertheless, Vadim and Irina do see signs of the emergence of a class consciousness among workers in their willingness to address demands to management, rather than to be deflected into seeking redress from above. Similarly, they see the emergence of unemployment as shutting off the traditional individualistic response of job mobility, so that the existing small scale developments may anticipate the politicisation of the workers' movement in the future. While one would not want to stifle such optimism, one might wonder to what extent Vadim and Irina underestimate the possibility of new divisions emerging, particularly on the grounds of skill, age and gender, and being exploited to further divide and disorganise the working class.

Vadim and Irina raise the question of gender differentiation, arguing that this is the principal exception to the tendency which they identify to the homogenisation of the working class. One of the most striking features of Russian society for an observer from the West is the fact that there is virtually no ideological or institutional recognition of what would appear objectively to be one the starkest bases of differentiation of the Soviet labour force, that of the gender of workers. Statistically, women workers appear disadvantaged in relation to men in almost every respect, and to approximately the same degree as in the capitalist world. Moreover, it appears that women workers are disproportionately bearing the initial brunt of the economic crisis, both at home and at work. Yet most Russians, men and women, including social scientists, will insist that there is little or no discrimination against women in Russia, that women have equal opportunities with men, and that women's disadvantage has nothing to do with their gender. The fact that women work in lower paid professions and branches of production, and happen to have lower levels of skill and education, reflects their own aptitudes and priorities. If there is a problem, the problem is that of the aspirations and motivation of women.

It is very easy to dismiss such arguments as nothing more than an expression of the power of a neolithic patriarchal ideology, decisive evidence of the totalitarian character of a patriarchal power which not only induces women to submit voluntarily to their own subordination, but even persuades them to deny that it exists. This leads to the common perception in the West of Russian women as passive victims of their fate, who need to be helped to understand their position of subordination before they can begin to change it. However, this is by no means the perception which Russian women have of their situation: they certainly do not see themselves as passive victims, nor do they act as passive victims. Although these issues have already been fairly extensively discussed, at least among feminists, the dominant Western perception of the passivity of Russian women has limited the attention which has been paid to the issue of how Russian women themselves perceive their situation and what they are doing about it. This is an issue taken up by the next two papers in this volume.

Galya Monousova's paper takes up an issue which is likely to become increasingly important with the restructuring of the labour force consequent on the transition to a market economy, that of the differential responses of male and female workers to structural change. There is growing evidence that the gender recomposition of the labour force, both at management and shop-floor level, is one of the most significant aspects of labour force restructuring in Russia, with clear tendencies to increasing gender segregation, to the further marginalisation of women in lower-paid and lower-skilled occupations, and to the growing use of women as a flexible and disposable component of the labour force, an issue which is discussed by Irina Kozina and Vadim Borisov in their paper.

Women workers in Russia have been stereotypically considered to be passive and compliant, with narrowly instrumental work orientations, because their first commitment has been considered to be to their homes and their families. The specific interests of women workers have nominally been protected by legislation, rather than by their trade union organisation, legislation which is systematically breached, with women working illegally long hours in illegally harmful conditions. Neither their trade union organisations, which have tended to treat women as beneficiaries of social and welfare policy more than as workers, nor the women themselves, for whom longer hours and harmful conditions provide the opportunity to make up for their low pay, have been active in defending the rights of women workers.

Galya's paper challenges this stereotypical characterisation of women workers by comparing patterns of conflict in four industrial enterprises with mixed or predominantly female labour forces. On the one hand, her paper clearly shows that women workers are systematically disadvantaged, working at lower grades, receiving lower pay, and having less power and independence than their male colleagues. On the other hand, she shows that women workers are by no means necessarily passive, with women in three of the four enterprises being more militant than the men in the face of what they consider to be violations of their rights, while it is the men who continue to pursue traditionally individualistic solutions (although Galya still thinks that individualism is a typically female response). At the same time, it is striking that in none of these cases did the women workers express their grievances *as women*, and Galya insists that in only one of the cases did the women base their demands on a comparison of their position with that of their male colleagues. She also insists that the women did not feel any sense of injustice or discrimination in comparison with the men, despite the fact that the women were clearly systematically disadvantaged in comparison with the men. In her paper Galya raises the question of the extent to which the differences in patterns of behaviour in conflict situations are to be attributed to the specific factor of gender, or whether they are to be explained by other technical and social features of the positions occupied by women in the labour force.

The extent of gender segregation in industrial enterprises makes it difficult to distinguish these factors from one another. Women tend to occupy quite specific positions in the labour process. In the structure of management women tended to dominate in routine office and administrative work, predominantly involving the collecting, recording and reporting of statistics, and routine calculations of wages, benefits and norms, while they were largely excluded from the chain of managerial authority, which passes from the director through the chief engineer to shop and section chiefs who, even in 'women's' enterprises, would often be exclusively male. On the shop floor, women predominate in the lowest skilled auxiliary occupations, and within the production labour force women predominate in work which is considered to be monotonous and routine, often in harmful conditions, with relatively low levels of mechanisation with medium to low skill grading and, correspondingly, low rates of pay.

The fact that women are concentrated in relatively low-paid, low-skilled, routine occupations, with little independence or authority, is not a matter of chance. On the one hand, it is underpinned and reinforced by traditional stereotypes of women's character and psychology. Thus women are considered to be better-suited to monotonous work, and are considered not to be career-oriented or to be psychologically prepared to wield authority. On the other hand, it is underpinned and reinforced by the material situation of women, which is one in which women take responsibility not only for themselves, but also for their families, relatives and close friends, which both make demands on their time and energy, and make them more vulnerable to the loss of income and employment, so that it is relatively easier for management to divide and control women than men workers. This means that it is questionable whether one really can or should distinguish between gender and other social and technical aspects of the work that is done by women, looking instead at the labour force hierarchy as one which is inherently gendered. This certainly corresponds to everyday consciousness, for which there is a very clear gender stereotyping of jobs and occupations, regardless of whether the particular job happens to be filled at the time by a man or a woman, which is the theme of Elain Bowers's paper.

Looking at the labour force hierarchy as inherently gendered in this way also helps to explain what appears at first sight to be Galya's paradoxical assertion that she did not find any evidence of discrimination against women in any of the enterprises that she studied, nor did women complain of any such discrimination, despite their pervasive and transparent disadvantages as compared to men. On the one hand, both men and women regarded women's disadvantages as being attached to the particular occupational roles that they filled, so that low pay and harmful conditions were attached to the supposedly undemanding work that women did, work which is done predominantly by women because women are supposedly naturally more suited to such work. On the other hand, both men and women regarded the lower pay of women as being justified in terms of the supposedly different social roles of men and women in society as a whole. In this sense the systematic disadvantages of women that are inherent in the job hierarchy are regarded as corresponding to inherent social and psychological characteristics of women themselves, and not as representing any kind of discrimination. It is in this context that Galya argues that she found no evidence of discrimination, in the sense that it was in principle open to individual women to prove themselves capable of carrying out 'men's' work, in which case they would be treated equally with men.

Against this one could argue, on the basis of the evidence in Galya's paper, that women can never prove themselves capable of carrying out 'men's' work, because the characteristics of the job are redefined as soon as a woman does it — another respect in which one cannot abstract job characteristics from gender, but has to see the employment structure as inherently gendered. For example, even where men and women apparently do exactly the same job, working on the same machines, as on the new line in Pizza, the men's work will be higher graded and higher paid than that of the women, and this discrimination will normally be justified on the grounds of supposed differences in the content and responsibility of the job (for example, in relation to setting-up or maintaining and repairing the machinery).

The role of gender in the social organisation of production is very striking in Galya's analysis of forms and patterns of management. The general pattern of management in the labour-intensive enterprises that tend to be dominated by women workers is strongly authoritarian and paternalist, to the extent that it can literally be referred to as 'patriarchal', the authoritarian directors in two of the four enterprises studied being universally referred to as 'Papa'. Such authoritarianism has even been reinforced by economic change, as management seeks to reduce costs by intensifying labour, improving discipline and disposing of 'surplus' workers. Galya argues that women prefer such a management style. On the one hand, women want a strong management which can guarantee their earnings and employment. On the other hand, women need and appreciate the range of paternalistic benefits that tend to accompany such a patriarchal management style. However, it appears from Galya's examples, and from other observations, that it is most specifically the women workers who are subject to authoritarian management. In Pizza, Device and Mikron the skilled male workers had sufficient autonomy and sufficient confidence in their indispensability that they felt that they could simply by-pass or ignore authoritarian decrees from above, while in Lenkon it appeared that the female shop chief had insufficient authority to control the male workers in her shop. (We have observed a similar situation with regard to male maintenance and repair workers in female shops in a number of different enterprises.) The women, on the other hand, could not simply ignore the authority of management but had to find other ways to challenge or subvert it.

In Pizza the women expressed no hope of being able to act collectively to resist the intensification of labour, but expected to be able to subvert the director's attempt to change the vacation schedule simply by taking sick leave when they had to care for their children. Thus Pizza is still characterised by the typically Soviet individualistic response to intensified exploitation of taking time off for sickness, or leaving to find work elsewhere, with the only collective representations being channelled through foremen and shop chiefs. Management's response to such individualistic resistance was equally traditional, to focus on increased incentives, in the form of improved pay and benefits, as implicit compensation for the intensification of labour. In Device, on the other hand, no such individualistic response was available to the women workers, and they responded by forming a branch of the alternative trade union, Sotsprof, and calling a strike, which ultimately led to the replacement of the director of the enterprise.[7] There was a range of factors involved in this dispute, but the specific characteristics of the workers in question were, on the one hand, that they were among the lowest paid production workers, who were the hardest hit by the new management system in which pay was tied directly to revenue from sales of the product and, on the other hand, the massive increase in pay differentials between workers and foremen had completely undermined the traditional informal management structure by eroding the workers' trust in the foremen, and so removing the traditional channels through which workers could air

7 The case of the strike in Device provides another vindication of Volodya Ilyin's analysis: the contradictory position in which women find themselves, with low pay, insecurity and bad working conditions, is almost universal, but this is usually bridged by personal, informal, individualised relations with the line manager, so is not expressed in conflict and collective action. In this case the new pay system, with wide pay differentials, broke the link between worker and foreman, so the contradiction was now expressed in a strike, and ultimately the removal of the director. Once the pay differentials are reduced and the link is reestablished, conflict ceases, although the contradiction is not removed.

their grievances. In Mikron the response of two groups of women workers within the same shop to the blatantly discriminatory wages policy of the shop chief differed quite fundamentally, the more vulnerable unskilled and older women complaining verbally, but taking no action, while the more highly skilled women machine-operators, without the support of the shop chief, threatened the director with a strike which secured a factory-wide pay rise. The comparison of these three cases appears to bring out clearly the argument that the passivity or militancy of women workers is not a matter of women's 'psychology', inherent or otherwise, but of their social situation within the enterprise.

In her paper Galya argues that a decisive factor in explaining the development of conflict is the gendering of the management structure in the enterprise. In Pizza the shop headed by a woman has a completely different management structure from those headed by men, with the woman shop chief being much more authoritarian than the men, devolving no significant power to the (female) foremen, but relating directly to the individual workers on an informal basis, establishing their direct dependence on the chief herself. In the shops with male management, by contrast, the shop chief is happy to devolve responsibility to his (male) foremen, and it is at this level that informal relations of dependence are established. In Lenkon the woman section chief was distinguished by her insecurity, which was hardly surprising since she had to manage a predominantly male shop, and felt that her job was under threat from a male subordinate. As in Pizza, this section chief tried to keep all the power in her hands, but with a predominantly male labour force had little scope to employ informal relations, so that relations remained on a formal basis.

Galya argues that conflict broke out here primarily because of the inability of the shop chief to juggle the various interests within the shop, and in particular to balance the demands of male and female workers. In this shop the men are paid at significantly higher rates for work which is not obviously any more skilled than that of the women, and seem to be less subject to pressure from shop management than are the women workers (so that, for example, the women workers' complaints about the poor quality of the men's work are without effect). It would seem that this relative freedom of the men derived not so much from the scarcity or value of their skills, as from the weakness of the shop chief, which was in large part a result of the gender structure of the shop. This would in turn seem to be an explanation for the lack of collective action on the part of the male workers, faced with what they saw as an erosion of their privileges when the women workers received additional bonuses to compensate for their losses of pay under a factory-wide re-grading. The collective action of the women workers can also be plausibly related to the gender composition of the shop, since the shop chief did not have the ability to satisfy their grievances on her own authority, in the face of an antagonistic male labour force and male superiors.

Galya's paper raises as many interesting and important questions as it answers, not least by cutting the ground from under the conventional characterisation of women workers as inherently passive. Russian women workers have proved very active in defending their interests, not only historically, but also in the contemporary period, as can be seen in the example of Solidarity, whose membership is predominantly female. However, such women workers have not tended to formulate their grievances or to organise *as women workers*, and have proved singularly unresponsive to the appeal of any kind of Western feminism. If women do present their demands as women, it is not as *workers* but as *mothers*, protesting not on their own behalf but on behalf of their children, or, more abstractly, the future generation. This raises very important questions, not only for our understanding of Russia, but also for our conceptualisation of the relation between gender and work more generally.

In the next paper, Elain Bowers takes up these issues within a comparative perspective on the basis of her doctoral research on women and work in Russia, which she has been carrying out within the framework of our collaborative research programme.[8] One of the most difficult tasks for the Western sociologist approaching Russian society is that of identifying some basis of comparison. Many features of Russian society appear, at first sight, very familiar. But then one will suddenly hear or observe something which throws all that familiarity into doubt, so that one has the sense of being in a completely different world. In the same way, features which appear at first sight very strange, may later, in a different light, seem very familiar. This paradoxical character of Russian society, from a Western point of view, appears very starkly when we consider the question of gender relations and the position of women in Russia. It is

8 Elain has played the primary role within our project in developing an analysis that is adequate to the paradoxical position of Russian women, and in working with our Russian collaborators to persuade them to take gender issues seriously.

possible to paint two very different, and equally plausible, pictures of the position of women in Russia. One picture focuses on the 'achievements of the Revolution', on women's access to education and to the professions, on the legal rights and social and welfare benefits accorded to women as workers and as mothers, on positive discrimination and affirmative action to encourage women's social and political participation. The other picture focuses on the persistent inequality to which women are subjected in all spheres, their lower levels of pay, skill and training, their inferior working conditions, their exclusion from positions of authority, their double burden as men avoid any domestic responsibility, and the pervasiveness and institutionalisation of deeply embedded chauvinistic attitudes to women.

These two pictures can be reconciled in various ways: on the one hand, the negative aspects of women's position can be attributed to the persistence of elements of the patriarchal culture of a peasant society, or even as expressions of the uniquely Russian soul, which even seventy years of state-socialism had not been able to eradicate. From this point of view the 'transition to the market economy' is freeing those chauvinistic forces, marking the revenge of the *muzhik*, and the priority for women is to defend 'the achievements of the Revolution'. On the other hand, the patriarchal culture of Russian society can be seen as being deeply embedded in the Revolution, which systematically exploited women to the full both as workers and as mothers, so that women have even more to gain than men from the overthrow of the old order, even if this is only the prelude to a struggle for their own liberation from their dual subordination to men and to the state. This latter perspective leaves open the question of the site of their struggle. For some commentators the family remained a haven for women, their own private realm which can provide the basis for the emergence of a new 'civil society' based on voluntary association. For others, including Elain, the family was no less penetrated by the dual power of men and the state than any other sphere and, far from providing a space from which women can struggle for their liberation, is the space of their isolation and confinement. From this point of view the only basis on which women can struggle for their liberation is their position in the workplace, struggling for the equality of their rights as productive members of society, building on rather than abdicating the role that women had achieved through their participation in social production. As Galya's paper shows, it is in this sphere that the transition to the market economy is threatening the basis of women's social existence in Russia, and it is in this sphere that, in appropriate circumstances, women have already shown themselves ready to struggle for what they see as their rights. Nevertheless, again as Galya shows, the more usual response of women (as also of men) to violations of their rights remains the typically individualistic forms of behaviour to which workers were confined under state-socialism.

Elain takes up these issues by focusing on the stereotypes which define the gender characteristics of particular occupations in Russia. The immediate comparative problem is that the gender division of labour appears at first sight to be very different in Russia from that in the capitalist world, with women dominating both professional and heavy manual occupations which in the capitalist world are thought to be archetypically male. From the Western point of view, and that of Soviet propaganda, this gives the impression that women in Russia have gained access to male occupations, even if at the cost of relatively lower pay and status and inferior working conditions. Nevertheless, Elain argues on the basis of her own research, the differences lie not in the stereotypical characteristics of men and women, which are remarkably similar in Russia and in the capitalist world, but in the characterisation of particular occupations. This implies that the characterisation of a particular occupation is by no means independent of who it is who works in that occupation. Thus, an occupation which is dominated by men in the capitalist world but by women in Russia will be characterised quite differently in the former and the latter.[9]

In order to develop this analysis Elain discusses the results of her research in two printing enterprises in which what was universally considered to be 'men's' work was in fact carried out by women. In this case it was perfectly clear that women could do what were defined as men's jobs, and when they talked about their jobs it was obvious that they got a great deal of satisfaction from their work. Nevertheless, even though women had been doing this work, in many cases for more than twenty years, the women themselves continued to consider this to be men's work, and asserted that men should be doing this work, exemplifying the transition from the argument that this was work which women *could* not do, to the moral argument that this is work which women *should* not do.

9 The redefinition of the essential characteristics of an occupation in the course of its feminisation can be observed historically in the capitalist world. The transition from the nineteenth century clerk to the twentieth century secretary is the classic example.

Elain indicates the implication of this analysis in her conclusion, when she argues that the language of stereotypes in which women talk about their work is completely contradicted by the reality of their experience. This becomes extremely significant in a period of change, in which labour shortage is giving way to the threat of unemployment, and in which new technology is being introduced to reduce costs, because women find themselves without a common language to articulate and generalise their individual experience, within which to struggle to defend what is important to them in their working lives: the right to work in jobs at which they are skilled, for which they are qualified, and from which they derive satisfaction. Instead, as Elain argues, they still see themselves as intruders in a men's world in which they have no rightful place. This leaves women in a vicious circle, for the alien language in which they articulate their experience prevents them from organising collectively as women, yet it is only by organising collectively as women that they can develop a common language which does articulate their own experience and aspirations. This conclusion then leads us back to the problem of Galya's paper: under what conditions do women workers in Russia organise collectively as women?

The last two papers move beyond the enterprise, to look at conflict and change in the context of the relationship between economic and political power, particularly at regional level. This relationship was seriously disrupted by the disintegration of the Communist Party, which had been the body which had maintained co-ordination between various bodies at regional level, and which, at least in principle, had mediated between regional and 'national' interests. Although there has been considerable continuity in personnel at regional level, with the new elite very much comprising the people who would in all likelihood have emerged as the next generation of the old elite, there has been no such institutional continuity, with economic and political power being fragmented and distributed between local and regional legislative and executive bodies, new financial and commercial structures, and former state enterprises and organisations, all of which have their own economic, social and political roots and their own lines of communication to Moscow. Conflict and change within the enterprise cannot be properly understood without consideration of this wider environment within which the enterprise is embedded, and in particular at the jockeying for power between all these various institutions.

If the period from 1989 to 1992 was a period of fragmentation of power, since 1992 there appears to have been a steady move towards its consolidation, with the resurrection of old alliances and the formation of new ones, leading first to the formation of contending blocs, but then to the coalescence of forces at regional level. The regional power structures are still in the process of formation, and are not usually as monolithic and hierarchical as was the apparatus of the regional Party committee in the past, but nevertheless it would seem that powerful coalitions have formed at regional level, which take a considerable interest in what happens in the principal enterprises in the region.

The paper by Pavel Romanov looks at this question from the perspective of the implementation of bankruptcy legislation, which has always been supposed to be a pivotal component of the process ofliberal economic reform. Although bankruptcy legislation was introduced at an early stage of reform, the systematic implementation of this legislation did not even begin to get under way until the second half of 1994. Although the law lays down criteria and procedures for declaring enterprises bankrupt, in practice the authorities enjoy a great deal of discretion in the implementation of the law. Although it is in principle the regional branch of the Federal Bankruptcy Administration which is responsible for implementing bankruptcy procedures, in practice the bankruptcy administration can only work with the close co-operation of the regional political authorities and the dominant financial and industrial leaders of the region. Thus, as in so many other areas of reform, the attempt to impose Moscow's writ is subverted by the reality of power at the regional level.

Pasha's paper focuses on the first stages of the implementation of the bankruptcy procedures in the Samara region, with some evidence drawn from elsewhere. Although based on only one region, there is no reason to believe that Samara is atypical in the methods or motives according to which the intentions of Moscow are subverted in the implementation of this legislation, and in which bankruptcy is used to further the monopolisation of the economy and the consolidation of regional power structures, particularly since Samara, under the regional chief of administration, Titov, is one of the regions most 'loyal' to Moscow and to the process of reform, and the enterprise on which he focuses his case study was put under the administration of a dynamic young 'new Russian' who had made his name in commerce and finance. Thus we would expect the 'subversion' of the legislation to be even more radical and more blatant in other regions.

Pasha's paper raises very important issues of the development of economic and political structures at the regional level, and particularly the relation between economic and political power, between state and market, between the government, the financial system and industry. Much is spoken about the shadow structures of economic and political power at national and regional level in Russia, but little is published about them, and they are barely researched, often for very good reason! However, Pasha's paper also raises the question of the social foundation of the 'subversion' of reformist legislation. Samara provides an ideal case for study not because it is a typical region, but because it is atypical, the regional leadership being one of the most committed to reform, the new management of the aircraft factory being new Russians, oriented to the market and with the appropriate entrepreneurial skills and motivation. If reform is subverted in the aircraft factory, it cannot be because of the conservative opposition of traditional communist politicians and red directors. It must be because such 'conservatism' has a rational foundation, as the expression of deep-rooted social interests.

In the case of the aircraft factory, Pasha identifies these interests as the common interest of the local administration and the local population in sustaining the enterprise as the source of employment, the provider of housing and a wide range of social and welfare services, and a major contributor to the regional and municipal budget. In short, the importance of the enterprise not merely as a profit and loss account, but as a social institution which is the life-blood of the local community. The fact that the market for aircraft had collapsed meant that the new management of the aircraft factory soon found itself in close alliance with the local authorities in turning to the government for support. But this call for support was by no means merely the selfish appeal of one enterprise to be treated as a special case. The appeal of the aircraft factory for support was an appeal not only on its own behalf, not only on behalf of the region, but also on behalf of the aviation industry, whose collapse had removed the market for new aircraft and even for the servicing of existing fleet. In short, economic, social and geographical interdependencies, dismissed and ignored by neoliberal economists as 'externalities', make planned state investment in the aircraft industry eminently rational from the perspective of the Samara aircraft factory and its employees, of the Samara region, of the aviation industry, and for all those who use the services of that industry, including those Western economic advisers who still do not fly by private jet. It is hardly surprising, and it is certainly entirely desirable, that the hare-brained schemes of the Moscow reformers are so often subverted by broad coalitions of forces.

The final paper, by Veronika Kabalina, addresses some of these same issues by studying in detail two very similar enterprises, one of which remained under the firm control of its management, the other of which fell into the hands of a leading Moscow bank, not through bankruptcy but through an investment auction. The first enterprise had decided to privatise under the variant according to which the labour collective obtained a majority shareholding on privileged terms, while the second enterprise decided to privatise under the variant which gave the labour collective a minority of non-voting shares free of charge, but the majority holding was sold at auction. This was the basis on which the management of the first enterprise was able to retain control, while the majority holding in the second was bought by a large Moscow bank. The different patterns of control were soon reflected in differences of management structure, with the first enterprise having a homogeneous management structure, a single instrument of the power of the General Director, while the second enterprise had a Directors' Council, dominated by the external owners, and a subordinate Board as the executive body.

Despite their very similar circumstances, the two enterprises developed in very different ways. The differences cannot simply be attributed to differences in the form of ownership, since the latter reflected another fundamental difference between the two enterprises. The first enterprise had a relatively new and dynamic management team, headed by a strong authoritarian director, while the second had an ageing management team and a weak director, with no clear perspectives. This difference in the character of management underlay the close links between enterprise management and local authorities in the first case and the weak links in the second, the retention of control over financial and commercial activity in the first case and growing informal links with the shadow economy in the second; and finally it was this difference that was the primary reason for the retention of managerial control in the first enterprise and the loss of control in the second.

Once the process of privatisation was complete, the two enterprises began to develop in divergent directions. Both enterprises were, on the one hand, typical Soviet enterprises in having widely diversified economic activities and in being economically, socially and politically embedded in their local communities. On the other hand, both enterprises also had potentially very favourable economic prospects as iron ore extracting enterprises which could sell their product on world markets, although export possibilities were limited by high transport costs, following the substantial increase in rail tariffs in the middle of 1993, and the relatively low quality of ore. The second enterprise, coming under the control of the Moscow bank, adopted a development strategy which accorded with the capitalist demand for realisable short-term profits and the prescriptions of Western management consultants, in severing its financially burdensome links with the local community, curtailing and abandoning subsidiary economic activities which were not directly related to its core activity, and seeking to expand its export contracts, although the realisation of this strategy was impeded by opposition from a significant part of management within the enterprise. Although the bank had committed funds for investment in the enterprise as part of its bid for shares in the investment auction, it was cautious about undertaking any serious investment in the face of continuing economic instability.

The development of the first enterprise retained a high degree of continuity with its past, in marked contrast with that of the second. Management sought to consolidate its links with the local power structures, expanding its contribution to the social and welfare apparatuses in the region, it further diversified the economic activity of the enterprise, bringing various agricultural production and processing activities under its wing and investing in new facilities. Despite the general economic uncertainty management prepared an extremely ambitious investment programme designed to reduce the costs of production and improve the quality of the product in order to strengthen its position in the domestic market and improve its access to world markets. While the second enterprise had used its export earnings to buy consumer goods for its workers (before it came under the control of the bank), the first enterprise used its funds for investment.

The first enterprise was able to pursue a more dynamic and far-sighted policy in part because it was protected from the influence of outside shareholders demanding short-term profits, but also because its management retained very considerable political influence, both locally and nationally, which enabled it to obtain various fiscal concessions and which also helped it to retain its large share of the export market, which was a vital cushion when domestic demand fell sharply in 1993–4. Ironically, it is the first enterprise, which remains archetypically Soviet, which has been successful in raising foreign and domestic bank finance for its ambitious investment programme, while the much more modest investment plans of the second enterprise, financed by the funds committed by its majority shareholder, have yet to get off the ground.

In the sphere of labour relations and social policy, the management of the first enterprise has also retained its commitment to Soviet values and practices in maintaining wages, employment and social and welfare services. Although there have been two waves of redundancy, these have been based on the voluntary severance of working pensioners with special compensation, with retraining and redeployment of other workers, as part of a programme to rejuvenate the labour force, while overall employment in the *kombinat* has increased through diversification. Such a paternalistic strategy is not entirely beneficent: on the one hand, it is part of the General Director's concern to retain control of the enterprise by retaining the support of the labour force while, on the other hand, it is a part of the strategy of reducing labour turnover and upgrading the labour force. While the General Director's concern for the labour force appears not to be entirely instrumental, it does not extend to any commitment to democracy or participation in management, the trade union having been reduced to a branch of the administration of the enterprise, which has taken to imposing its collective agreement unilaterally on the union.

The second enterprise, before it came under bank control, had pursued a much more passive employment policy than the first, carrying through a similar scale of redundancies, and redeploying rather than dismissing workers, but without developing new spheres of employment or attempting positively to restructure the labour force. Wages are much lower than in the first enterprise, and are more frequently delayed, while dividend payments are also lower, and there has not yet been any attempt on the part of management to increase pay differentials in favour of managers and specialists, unlike the case of the first enterprise. Similarly, the enterprise has been cutting back on its support for social and welfare facilities, under pressure from the bank. One result of these developments is that, in sharp contrast to the first enterprise, the trade union has seen a decline in its role as a welfare organisation, has been largely excluded from management, and its leaders have begun to show increasing independence, although they pursue their position on the basis of external political activity and an alliance with the opposition faction within management, without seriously seeking or obtaining significant support from the labour force, which nevertheless is increasingly alienated from management. However, it is not unlikely that in future these forces will coalesce into a significant oppositional force within the enterprise.

The implications of Veronika's study are very similar to those emerging from Pasha's paper: in both cases external financial control has not been associated with any significant internal restructuring of the enterprise, but only an orientation to short-term profit through commercial and financial activity, with more radical changes blocked by the unprofitability of investment in conditions of economic crisis, by the embeddedness of the enterprise in local economic, social and political structures, and by potential opposition within management and the labour force. On the other hand, Veronika's study shows that insider control is by no means a barrier to the development of the enterprise, and certainly cannot be seen as a conservative response to the threat of change. Her first enterprise, in which management retained control, has seen radical and far-reaching changes, with an ambitious programme of diversification and investment in production and in the social sphere, combining a 'Soviet' commitment to the wages, welfare and employment of its workers, with an orientation to strictly centralised authoritarian management, the curtailing of the individual rights of workers, and a marked widening of pay differentials, despite which worker discontent is relatively low in this enterprise, while in her second enterprise the potential is building up for explosive conflict. Perhaps the most important implication of Veronika's paper is that one can understand nothing of the changes taking place in Russia, nor can one provide any useful prescriptions for the future economic and industrial development of the country, unless one considers the industrial enterprise not as the 'black box' of the economists, but as a social institution which is embedded in wider social and economic structures. And, of course, many sociologists would argue that the same is no less true of the capitalist West.

Although we hope that each paper in this and our other volumes stands alone as a contribution in its own right, we also hope that the papers as a whole amount to more than the sum of the parts. A society is indeed comparable to a living organism, in all its complexity, but one in which each of the parts has its own independent dynamic, so that there is never a close functional integration of the parts into the whole. This means that the reproduction of the whole is always the outcome of conflicts which are themselves the manifestation of underlying contradictions. At certain historical periods, in certain parts of the system, institutions exist through which conflict resolution is consistent with the stable reproduction of the system as a whole, and in such circumstances of systemic stability it is legitimate to isolate the part analytically from the whole, although it is always essential to recognise that such an analytical isolation is only ever provisional. However, in periods of systemic transformation there is no such stable institutional environment, so that even small changes in a remote part of the system can have repercussions which reverberate through the system as a whole. In such revolutionary periods it is impossible fully to understand one thing without understanding everything else. But at the same time, it is impossible to understand 'everything else' without understanding the small changes which make up that everything else. This leads to two conclusions. First, each of our papers aims to provide an insight into a small part of a total process, which cannot be totally comprehended, but which has to be theorised as a whole, a task which remains to be accomplished. Second, the new Russian society will not be created by the 'clever dicks' and 'fluffy cheeks' of the World Bank and its partners, but will be the outcome of pervasive conflicts. Even though there may be no organised or mass opposition to the devastating programmes proposed by the neo-liberals, they are nevertheless opposed every day in myriad acts of subversion and resistance in which even individual actions can have an effect, not as heroic acts but as part of a matrix of social action structured by the contradictions that it expresses and in which the possibilities of collective and self-conscious action are inscribed.

2. Social Contradictions and Conflicts in State Enterprises in the Transition Period

Vladimir Ilyin

The subject of this article is the social contradictions and conflicts in Russian state enterprises in the period of transition from a state-socialist to a capitalist market economy. The object of the article is the analysis of a passenger transport enterprise in a northern Russian provincial city in which research into the dynamics of labour relations has been conducted since 1989.

The passenger transport enterprise (hereafter PTE) is the only enterprise in the city providing passenger transport services. The organisational structure of PTE is determined by the functions it serves and the equipment used: one column works on the busiest routes in the city and is equipped with large Hungarian Ikarus buses, another serves less busy routes and is equipped with Soviet buses of medium capacity, there is a column specialising in inter-city transport, and until the beginning of 1993 there was a column of taxis. Alongside these is a repair-mechanical workshop (RMW) which services all the columns.

In recent years about 1,500 people worked in the enterprise, but there has been a steady reduction in employment. However, so far this process has proceeded relatively painlessly since no workers have been laid off, but jobs have been eliminated for various reasons.

SOCIAL CONTRADICTIONS

Before beginning the empirical analysis it is necessary to define some key categories used in it, without which the research would be confused and contradictory.

The obvious analogue of any social organisation is a honeycomb: a unit consisting of a set of interconnected cells. A social organisation is a system whose elements include status positions — a set of rights, responsibilities, social expectations and material attributes without which organisation is impossible (instruments of labour, premises, means of communication and so on). The status positions making up the organisation are multi-layered, one is a component of another which is part of a third and so on. So an individual status position (a job) is an element of the status position of a group (shop, department or professional group), which in turn is a sub-system of the status position of a higher level — the enterprise (firm).

The status position gives rise to a social interest, which represents the optimal way of satisfying the needs of the subject or, to put it another way, the shortest route in social space to the satisfaction of those needs. Interest is always tied to the place occupied by a given status position within social space. As a social organisation consists by definition of status positions distinguished by their place in social space (above all by the quantity of power, rights, responsibilities, functions and so on), the heterogeneity of interests presents itself as an attribute of the organisation. The multi-layered character of statuses gives rise to the multi-layered character of interests: the individual holding a particular job has one interest, as a member of a brigade she also appears as bearer of a group interest, as a worker in a particular shop she is bearer of the shop interest, as worker of her enterprise she is a bearer of its interests, as a member of society she is a bearer of nation-wide interests.

Social contradictions are an expression of the objectively existing multi-directionality of interests. Thus differences in the vector of interests can vary from a few degrees to a complete contrast, that is, up to 180 degrees. They arise most clearly in relation to any distribution of limited resources (power, money, equipment, raw materials and so on). In relation to external resources every member of the organisation has, as a rule, a common interest, since the personal well-being of each depends, more or less directly, on the stability of the position of his or her organisation in the market or the system of administrative relations. The collapse of the organisation leads to a loss of jobs, income and so on. When it comes to the internal distribution of resources, interests begin to diverge more or less strongly, since when the pie is divided an increase in the share of one subject inevitably implies a reduction in the share of another. Hence the director, accountant, driver, mechanic, cleaner inevitably have different interests, that is to say they have different objectively optimal ways for them to satisfy their needs for food, housing, accommodation, comfortable working conditions, recognition of the environment and so on. So the interests of various subdivisions of the enterprise are diverse and contradictory.

The multi-layered character of social interests allows us to reconcile the functionalist and conflict paradigms of sociology. The unity of external interest is interwoven with contradictions between the internal interests of elements of the social system. The social organisation is unitary and contradictory at one and the same time.

Interests arising from status positions, and accordingly the contradictions arising between them, have a status character, and are consequently anonymous and impersonal. In other words, the person occupying this or that office, working in the cab of a lorry, or at a particular machine might change, but the status contradictions remain. They arise not from the personal features of the people occupying these social cells, but from differences in the places occupied by these cells in social space.

FROM SOCIAL CONTRADICTION TO CONFLICT

A social contradiction is an objectively existing divergence in the optimum routes to an aim in social space. The people occupying a status position may correctly perceive their interests, may have incomplete information about them or not be generally aware of them at all, or may present them in a completely illusory way. But the direct cause of social action is not objective interest, but the subject's representation of it (conscious interest).

If a social contradiction arises from a divergence of objective interests, then conflict represents a condition of the relations between people occupying particular status positions. Contradiction is a feature of social space, while conflict characterises the behaviour of people who have perceived their contradictory interests and have entered into conflict with one another in the assertion of their interests. Conflict is the open form of existence of a contradiction, which is its essential form under certain conditions. Thus the immediate reason for conflictual behaviour may be correct, or it may be an illusory representation of a contradiction. Therefore certain conflicts are inevitable, natural, and reflect the objective discrepancy of interests, while others are the results of people's delusions about their interests.

The transition from contradiction to conflict is a possibility which is only realised under a whole series of conditions:

1. The contradiction must be perceived by people holding contradictory status positions as a discrepancy or even mutual exclusiveness of interests. This in turn assumes a number of further conditions:
   a) the contradiction must be accessible to direct observation, even if only partially, having revealed itself, for example, through highly visible signs of social differentiation.
   b) thc possibility of thc subject reading the whole text of social relations from the observable signs (level and character of education, propaganda and agitation as factors predisposing to reflection, availability of analytical ability and so on).
2. Social inequality caused by the contradiction should be considered illegitimate by at least one party. The most important manifestation of such a situation is a recognition of existing social relations as unjust. This evaluation arises as a result of the interaction of the analysis of the social situation by the subject and the models of social justice which are dominant in society and shared by the subject.
3. The availability of an opportunity to resolve the contradiction to the benefit of one of the parties initiating the conflict. If there is no chance of success, even if the first two conditions are present, the subject will not enter into a conflict, unless the situation is one in which the subject departs from the framework of ends-rational behaviour and begins to behave under the influence of irrational factors, such as emotion, social-psychological suggestion or contagion and so on.

THE LEADING ROLE OF EXTERNAL CONTRADICTIONS

In state-socialist society the social status of an enterprise depended on its relations with the external administrative environment, above all with the bodies which distributed resources. These bodies determined the plan, allocated monetary resources, equipment, raw materials, fuel, defined the wage level of each category of worker and so on. Therefore the social well-being of every worker in the enterprise depended almost wholly on this external factor. This was where the basic social contradiction for the enterprise arose.

In the transition period the market position of many enterprises still depends strongly on relations with the external political-administrative environment. However, there have been fundamental changes in these relations:

1. Enterprises have become independent in their administrative relations. In the resolution of the bulk of small problems they no longer depend on higher management bodies. They are free to dispose of their own resources. They bear a significant responsibility for the results of their own economic activity.

While PTE remains within the structure of the territorial association, the latter hardly interferes in its activity and appears primarily in the role of intermediary, providing the enterprises with services in the purchase of equipment, fuel and so on. Thus in this sense the social contradictions of administrative relations, which formerly played the leading role, have been reduced to a minimum. The Russian Ministry, which previously played the decisive role in the external administrative environment of the enterprise, has been liquidated.

Present relations with the association are accordingly marked by a significant degree of indeterminacy in the absence of a clear normative basis for their relations. In the course of an interview the chiefs of the PTE could only define in the most general terms the boundaries between the responsibilities of the enterprise and the association. Their relationship is full of contradictions which should not in general be permitted within a management system. Thus, for example, the enterprise is completely independent in its economic activity, its relations with the association are based on commercial payment for services, but at the same time such matters as the dismissal and the appointment of a new director are for some reason within the competence of the association. By virtue of this the director is independent of the association, but at the same time in taking decisions he has always to look over his shoulder, to take his own position into account.

2. Enterprises have passed to market economic conditions. Therefore the key role among the external factors is played by the market situation of the enterprise. It determines not only the dynamics of the revenue of the enterprise and the incomes of its workers, but

also the level of sharpness of internal social relations as well as relations with organs of power and management.

PTE has found itself in a very adverse situation with the transition to market relations. Unlike many other enterprises, it cannot inflate its prices without forcing its customers up against the wall. As soon as prices of tickets are increased, the number of those travelling without tickets increases sharply. Buses begin to work for nothing. Strengthening of ticket inspection leads to a substantial increase in salary costs, which only leads to a new increase in prices. It is a vicious circle.

3. External bodies of power and management still play a significant role in the life of virtually every enterprise. However, among the levers of power which they use a crucial role has come to be their manipulation of the market situation both as a whole (through the tax system) and selectively (by the granting of tax privileges, issue of export licenses and so on). The degree of dependence of enterprises on external authorities varies: the higher the rate of profit, the less the degree of dependence. Trading enterprises are in the most favourable situation of all.

Unprofitable enterprises, of which PTE is one, are only able to keep afloat thanks to substantial state support. PTE depends to a decisive degree on help from the municipal administration, which provides it with large grants covering the difference between its modest revenues and its enormous costs. In this situation the form of the principal contradiction has been displaced from the line enterprise–association–ministry to the line enterprise–organ of state power (for the miners this is the Russian government, for PTE this is the municipal administration). Administratively the enterprise is independent of the city administration, but economically it is completely dependent on it. Therefore all the key economic questions are decided only with the approval of the municipal authorities (for example, increases in fares, purchase of new equipment).

This situation predetermined the content of the basic social conflicts in Russia at the end of the 1980s and into the first half of the 1990s: all major conflicts have included state bodies as their principal actors. The miners, teachers, medical workers, air traffic controllers all addressed their demands to the Russian government. Transport workers all address their demands to the municipal administration. These are essentially not market but political-administrative conflicts.

4. The fundamental liberalisation of the political regime has expanded the arsenal of methods by which collectives can defend their interests: in the past they could only make requests, supported by the diplomatic skills of the enterprise director, bribe the people responsible, or establish informal and semi-formal relations with them. Open conflict, which under the old regime was absolutely inconceivable, a recipe for suicide, has become possible in the new conditions.

In 1989 the miners demonstrated to the whole country the powerful opportunities provided by a method of struggle new to Russia, the strike. This experience was made accessible to everybody through the influence of the mass media. It became obvious that the organisation of a strike no longer leads to the deprivation of freedom which had earlier been its inevitable consequence, but even has a good chance of immediately resolving the problems of a single enterprise or a whole branch of production, of the organisers acquiring the image of defenders of the people, while opening up prospects of an administrative or political career for the workers' leaders. (The leaders of the Independent Miners' Union have provided a shining example of this for all other trade union activists.)

The PTE drivers have been among the most active followers of the miners. As soon as it became necessary to obtain a substantial pay increase a spontaneous strike would immediately break out. As a rule the workers did not specify to whom their demands were addressed, but it was obvious to everybody that it was only the municipal administration that could provide the resources to increase their pay. Under the conditions of a liberal political regime it was necessary to enter into negotiations and to grant more or less significant concessions. As a result the strike became a standard element in the procedure for increasing wages in line with the rate of inflation.

THE LABOUR COLLECTIVE AS THE SUBJECT OF CONFLICT

The concept of the labour collective played an important role in the ideology of Marxism-Leninism in the 1970s and 1980s. In the 1990s it has begun to disappear from the vocabulary of the Russian social sciences, mass media and daily speech. However, the labour collective was not simply an ideological construction, beneath this concept lay a very real social phenomenon.

The decisive role of external factors in determining the development of the enterprise created a configuration of interests in which the generality of interests of all workers blocked the expression of the internal contradictions, and this formed the basis of a 'social contract' inside the enterprise. The social basis of the formation of the labour collective was the generality of the status of hired labourer which united everyone from cleaner to director. This makes it possible to speak about the labour collective as a specific social community, including all the employees of the enterprise.

The reality of the labour collectives was expressed in the fact that in negotiations with external management bodies not only the director but also the president of the trade union committee and the secretary of the Party committee took part. Thus all workers of the enterprise had an interest in the successful outcome of the process of negotiation. There are numerous visible indicators which support the theoretical hypothesis of the importance of the labour collective as a real social community.

In new conditions the labour collective is no longer a universal phenomenon. In private enterprises management already has a set of interests which are significantly different from the interests of the rest of the workers. During the process of privatisation the labour collective usually appears as the subject of the process and almost all of the workers acquire shares. However, privatisation, even in this form, marks the beginning of the decomposition of the labour collective, since the bulk of the shares are concentrated in the hands of a narrow circle of people, and the mass of the workers are only formally owners. As a result the internal contradictions come more and more to outweigh the external contradictions. However, in the majority of unprivatised enterprises, to which PTE belongs, the labour collective remains as a social community.

As a result of this, in conflicts with the external environment it continues to be the labour collective which appears as the subject of conflict. It is true that the management of the enterprise tries to distance itself from the organisers of strikes, but they have an obvious interest in the success of such strikes, during which demands to increase the resources granted to the enterprise are put forward. Thus the common character of the self-conscious interests of workers and managers is quite distinctly manifested in many activities. This is very clear in all the material on the miners' movement, where the enterprise directors participate in the strikers' negotiations with the government, helping to work out their package of demands. The collective of PTE equally acts as the subject of conflicts.

In the spring of 1992 a spontaneous strike flared up. The trade union committee decided to direct the conflict into legal channels. A strike committee was elected in the enterprise and the workers elected the deputy director for operations as its chair. After some prevarication he agreed to serve as chair and the strike committee, under his leadership, drew up a package of demands to the city and regional authorities. With this the activity of the strike committee came to an end, although it was not dissolved. However, the participation of the administration in strike activity did not stop there. The new director of PTE, who arrived in May 1993, acknowledged in an interview that the deputy director for operations and one of the department chiefs had directly incited the workers to strike. He explained their motives very simply: the strike was used as a means of resolving their managerial problems (forcing money out of the local administration to pay for the development of production) and of raising their authority among the workers.

The previous director had not been involved in urging on strikes, but this was primarily because of his bad relationship with the collective (see below). However, he still had a basic interest in the use of the strike lever to resolve the problems of the enterprise. So in one interview he complained about the lack of united action with the trade union committee, which did not turn to the enterprise administration for help with the competent preparation and substantiation of its demands, and which did not negotiate directly with the city administration, where it could play a considerable role, backing its demands with the threat of a strike. (The director did not want to reveal his own interest in the use of such a weapon in front of representatives of the city administration.)

THE MAIN INTERNAL SOCIAL CONTRADICTION

In state-socialist society the main social watershed passes between the managers and the managed. Administrative power is the principal basis of stratification. It defines the contours of social stratification of the enterprise, where the most fundamental contradiction is that between administration and workers.

This is a status contradiction which exists independently of personal characteristics and relations, independently of whether people are conscious of it or not. The status of an administrative employee includes rights and responsibilities related to the management of workers, control over their labour, so the major criterion of evaluation of the activity of the manager is his or her ability to impose strict control and to intensify the labour of the workers. The latter in their turn are alienated from ownership and management. In many cases the interests of workers and managers are directly opposed to one another. For example, in all enterprises the accounts department is paid a bonus for saving money from the wages fund, which defines their interest in an antagonistic relation to the interest of the workers: the less the worker receives, the more the accountant saves. A driver who observed all the rules laid down in the regulations would find his job impossibly complex and exhausting. Therefore he naturally disregards those which are inconvenient. Nevertheless, the workers in the administration monitor his work, punishing him by depriving him of his bonus. One could draw up a long list of manifestations of the contradiction between workers and managers.

Social action is not the consequence of objective interests, but of the subject's consciousness of his or her interests. In turn, conflict follows from the consciousness of opposing interests. The basis of such conflict existed in Soviet enterprises almost everywhere and at all times.

Empirical research in PTE in 1989 unequivocally showed the existence of a conscious opposition of interests of workers and managers. During numerous interviews the workers expressed not merely a negative attitude to those working on the 'fourth floor' (the part of the administration building in which the senior managers worked), but also a belief in the incompatibility of their and the managers' interests. Research over the past five years has not shown any changes in this situation.

One of the main factors promoting the workers' consciousness of the antagonism between themselves and the administration is the fundamental difference in the content and conditions of their work. The work of the bus driver is obviously difficult and socially useful. Even the most superficial observation convinces one of the pressure of driving a bus on snow-covered streets with heavy traffic and that without their work the life of the city would be paralysed. This is the objective basis of the high self-evaluation of the drivers.

At the same time the labour of the manager is not amenable to such a simple and unequivocal evaluation. The driver or mechanic, coming into the office, sees the manager working in a clean warm room. The manager's work hardly corresponds to the workers' stereotype of labour. Many describe the work of the administration as 'shuffling papers'. With only elementary observation even an expert cannot tell the difference between effective administrative work and the mere imitation of work. It is even more difficult for a worker to do this, having no experience of administrative work. Many workers remarked in the course of interviews, describing the labour of managers, that they drink tea all day. For drivers and mechanics this is a completely unfamiliar form of taking a break from work, serving as an argument in support of the thesis that managers do nothing.

A typical and universal feature of any management apparatus is the aspiration and ability to increase its own numbers. In conditions of state-socialism this feature assumed a special significance in view of the fact that the managers' pay level was controlled and limited from above. Therefore the administration was strictly limited in the extent to which it could assert itself socially by increasing its income, which was linked to the wage-level of the workers. But while it had little chance of increasing its income, there was the possibility of reducing its work load by increasing the number of managers. As a result it was typical to find that a particular function that was originally carried out by one worker is later carried out by two, three or four. This growth of the apparatus did not escape the attention of the workers, who loved to recall that 'earlier' there were fewer people on the fourth floor, even though the volume of work of the enterprise was the same. Many remarked that the introduction of computers into the office had not led to any reduction in the number of employees.

The good working conditions, doubts about the usefulness of the managers' work, the inflated staff, numerous examples of 'slacking', tea-drinking, complaints about the quality of administrative labour, taken together all provide an objective basis for the perception of the administration as a group of parasites living and prospering at the expense of the workers.

Thus, the contradiction of status position of the workers and administration is supplemented by the workers' consciousness of this contradiction. It is fertile ground for the occurrence of conflict.

MIDDLE AND LOWER LEVELS OF THE ADMINISTRATION

The administration is not internally uniform. It consists of levels comprising significantly different status positions. Correspondingly it is necessary to provide a more detailed analysis of the social contradictions that follow from the main social contradiction in the enterprise.

The middle level of management comprises heads of subdivisions, and the lowest level ordinary employees of the administration. These two levels occupy a specific position in the social relations of the enterprise: on the one hand, they are part of the administration, on the other, they are in direct interaction with the workers. These managers are involved in two different social fields, with different interests, norms and values. Both of the fields press on them, each trying to subject them to its own logic. The management of the enterprise demands that the heads of columns, dispatchers and so on precisely fulfil their duties and strictly control the labour of the workers, achieve its intensification, increase its quality, and so on. The workers in turn exert pressure with the aim of making their immediate chief more loyal to them, more sensitive to their problems. Thus the interests of managers of the middle and lower levels tie them to both social fields: the fulfilment of the demands of management is a condition of the preservation and enhancement of their administrative status, taking account of the pressure of the workers allows them to find a common language with them and to achieve the diligent fulfilment of their orders. The chief of the enterprise can issue an order, without giving any thought to how the order will be carried out. The chief of a column always comes up against the problem of the workers' understanding of his order and their readiness to execute it. Therefore, as often as not, he has to amend the order sent down from above to make it more conducive to the workers and so to increase the chance of its fulfilment. The duality of the status position of the chief of a column is reinforced by his social origin: as a rule this post is filled by former drivers who have furthered their education (usually up to middle special level).

As the chief of column has opportunities to 'amend' orders and choose among variants for their fulfilment, the workers are obviously not indifferent to who fills this status position. Therefore the appointment of somebody to this post is an object of struggle between the management of the enterprise and the workers. The former's interest is in having a 'strong' chief who will keep the workers under strict control. The latter's interest is that it should be one of the lads, who understands and takes account of the interests of the workers.

On this basis in PTE there was always open and latent struggle. According to both workers and senior managers, the drivers of the first bus column, who were the most militant group of workers, regularly managed to replace chiefs who did not suit them. The last one, a former driver, suited the workers and had been in the post for quite a long time. However, although he suited the drivers, he did not suit the management of the enterprise, who considered him too soft, and asserted that he took the side of the workers. In 1993 the management of the enterprise found a way of resolving this problem. As the number of buses had been reduced it was decided to combine two columns into one, and the chief of the smaller column, which was combined with the first column, who was much stricter, was appointed chief of the united column. This gave rise to indignation on the part of the workers of the first column, who saw this reorganisation as a disguised attempt to violate their rights since, in their view, the new chief tries to please the director rather than to protect the interests of the workers. A spontaneous strike broke out. The drivers demanded the return of their former chief. The director carried out a flanking move, having worked on the former chief of the column: he was offered the job of chief of the garage. The former chief of the column, having become a subject of the conflict, realised that a return to his former job as a result of a strike would imply an open challenge to the administration, with all the consequences which would follow from it. As a result he rejected the demands that he return to his former job. The workers had to back down.

The lowest level of the administration of PTE is represented first of all by the dispatchers who regulate the movement of the buses and taxis. Their status is extremely inconsistent. In terms of their wage level, their status is much lower than that of the workers. On the whole they are women, who do not have any special training. Their basic function is to monitor the observation of the timetable, which gives them a certain authority over the drivers. So, the dispatcher can report an infringement and the driver will lose part of his (or her — there is now one woman bus driver in Syktyvkar) bonus. In an emergency the dispatcher has the right to decide to transfer a driver temporarily to another route (for example, in the event of a breakdown). As different routes have different working conditions, such a transfer is seen by the drivers as an unpleasant surprise. Many try to avoid carrying out such an instruction, which leads to micro-conflicts. With unrestrained emotion the drivers can very rudely refuse to carry out the instruction, considering it humiliating that 'any slut [*devchonka*]' has used her own discretion to select precisely him for this unpleasant procedure, and immediately suspecting prejudice against him.

However, in this area of social relations there is an objective mutual interest in compromise based on status: the driver understands that if he (or she) has bad relations with the dispatcher, in the end the dispatcher has many opportunities to do the driver a bad turn within the framework of the duty instructions (for example, by reporting all his little infringements, transferring him to awkward routes, and so on). At the same time the dispatcher understands that she does not have enough authority to get the drivers to fulfil all her instructions. In this situation a zone of informal relations arises, ensuring that there is a compromise: the driver will carry out the instructions of the dispatcher without argument, and she in turn will 'not notice' minor infringements, and if she needs to find someone for a bad route will transfer an obstinate driver.

MAIN AND AUXILIARY PRODUCTION

The enterprise consists of a lot of divisions, performing various technological functions, playing different roles within the internal division of labour. These distinctions of status position necessarily underlie differences of interest. This already provides the potential threat of conflict.

In PTE the main production is that of the bus drivers, auxiliary production is that of the mechanical repair workshops. These two groups are distinguished not only by their place in the industrial division of labour, but also by their social status: the repair workers have below-average wages, harmful working conditions, lower prestige, and always wear dirty working clothes, while the drivers frequently go to work in a white shirt. Therefore in the enterprise there is always a problem of the relationship between the wages of these two categories of worker. Interviews show that there is discontent at the existing inequality, but it is seldom manifested as observable conflict: it is more usual for the manifestation of the contradiction to be limited to expressions of discontent in a narrow circle. Thus the repair workers are aggrieved at what they regard as the unjustifiably large gap in wages, while the drivers in their turn are no less aggrieved at any steps which bring the wages of the repair workers closer to those of the drivers.

Significant friction arose in 1992 when it turned out that the wages of drivers of the repair shop who moved buses around within the bus park were almost equal to those of drivers on the line. On this occasion long negotiations were conducted, during which this contradiction was transformed under the influence of the principal internal social contradiction, so that the problem of the differential between the two categories of workers was transformed into the problem of an increase in the wages of the line drivers. The administration, in response to the demand of the line drivers for a pay increase, wanted to 'make a knight's move', proposing to reduce the pay of the repair workers. Such a resolution of the problem threatened to divide the workers and give rise to open conflict between the two groups. The line drivers could not go down that path and managed to resolve the problem through an increase in their pay.

Apart from the spheres of production and distribution there are other contradictions which arise between the main and auxiliary workers deriving from status contradictions. The wage of the drivers largely depends on the amount of time they spend out on the routes. Therefore breakdowns and delays in repairs have a large impact on their material interests. Moreover a poorly repaired bus makes their work more difficult and stressful. But the repair workers have a different point of view. They cannot see any point in exerting themselves for a very low wage and usually work at a leisurely pace, with plenty of breaks. Various attempts to reconcile the interests of the two groups by reforming the payment system have produced no results, since it is very difficult to distinguish objective (absence of spare parts) from subjective (absence of a desire to work, slipshod work) factors. In order to complete the repair more quickly the driver helps out, taking over a part of the work of the mechanic, who at the same time does not see any reason to hurry. Therefore one can sometimes see the driver working on the repair of his bus while the mechanic has gone off for a smoke. If there is a special urgency about completing the repair the driver of the bus may even treat the mechanic. However, this obvious and sometimes acute contradiction is expressed in discontent only in a narrow circle: the drivers restrain themselves from openly expressing their complaints against the repair workers, rightly being afraid that it will only aggravate the situation, creating a negative informal relation the consequence of which will become apparent later.

A column of taxis was a part of the structure of PTE from the beginning of the 1970s to 1993, which always occupied a very specific position in the enterprise. Taxi drivers were always the freest and most freedom-loving group of workers; they worked in a fairly free way, and in recent years, in connection with the leasing of the automobiles, had become completely free. In addition to their wages they earned a substantial income on the side, and, in recent years, again, have lived on the proceeds from which they paid the rent of the automobiles. Their very particular status put them in a special position in the collective. They always kept aloof, and other workers looked askance at them, with envy. However, between the bus drivers and taxi drivers (the two groups of main production workers) there was simply an indifferent alienation, caused by the absence of any common interest. The status positions of the taxi drivers and repair workers often gave rise to opposed interests.

The incomes of the taxi drivers (salary plus 'tips') always depended to a considerable degree on the serviceability of their automobile and on the number of hours spent on duty. Therefore any repair hits the taxi driver hard in his pocket. As we have seen, this did not concern the mechanic to anything like the same extent, since he had a fairly stable wage and had no interest in working quickly or well. Since the taxi drivers have always acted in the role of illegal petty producers they (by contrast to the bus drivers) had a direct interest in using part of their incomes on the side to resolve this social contradiction: the taxi driver paid the mechanic from his own pocket to ensure a speedy and high quality repair.

In the last year the taxi drivers have leased their taxis, transforming themselves into legal petty producers. They no longer received a wage and did not hand over their fares, but paid only rent and taxes, bought their own spare parts themselves and so on, and nobody paid them for any stoppages. Formally the enterprise undertook to provide them with spare parts at moderate prices, but in practice this undertaking was implemented very poorly. The relation between the taxi drivers and the repair workers has therefore acquired a purely market character. Accordingly their contradictions have lost their administrative nuance and have become purely market-based. As there was not really any competition and spare parts remained scarce the repair workers tried to force the taxi drivers to pay high prices. Thus they sold them parts which they had bought on the side, as well as parts belonging to the enterprise, inflating the prices often to a staggering degree.

This monopoly position arose out of the objectively existing market contradiction. In conversations in the office of the taxi column it was frequently possible to hear stories about the literally extortionate actions of the mechanics. The taxi drivers complained that they had to pay mad prices for trivial parts, that the mechanics were drunk and repaired the car badly, that they literally extort vodka, and so on. However, this sharp contradiction is not transformed into conflict because the taxi drivers have no interest in aggravating the contradiction, assuming that the formation of negative informal relationships would put them in an even worse position. Therefore they only spoke about their relations with the mechanics in a whisper after going out into the corridor, or more generally took the position that it was impermissible to wash one's dirty linen in public and denied the existence of any contradiction between the drivers and the mechanics. Here we find the phenomenon of a conscious smoothing of a perceived objective social contradiction.

SEPERATISM OF A PROFITABLE SUBDIVISION

The subdivisions of any enterprise are distinguished by their contribution to the income of the whole. The reasons for this can be both subjective and objective. But in either case it gives rise to a contradiction between the interests of these subdivisions and their workers, connected with the distribution of the wages fund, investment in production, and so on. This was characteristic of enterprises within the administrative system of management and remains so in the present system of the wild market.

In PTE traditionally the most profitable, and sometimes the only profitable, subdivision was the taxi column. The urban buses were planned to be unprofitable, the inter-city buses made ends meet. Wages and investment in production were determined independently of this factor. During our research in 1989 we found serious dissatisfaction among the taxi drivers over this situation. The thesis 'we feed everyone' expressed the main basis of their demands to the management of the enterprise. Interviewees complained about the fact that in the 1970s the independent taxi enterprises were liquidated for no reason and attached to PTE. The taxi drivers were indignant, insisting that they did not need the huge administrative apparatus of PTE for their work, all they needed was one accountant and one dispatcher. Here also the main social contradiction of the enterprise transformed the organisational-structural contradiction in which stress was put on the claim that 'we have to feed a huge apparatus'.

In the 1990s, with the transition of the taxi drivers to leasehold, the contradiction 'column-enterprise' and 'taxi drivers-enterprise administration' became transparent and very obvious. In the course of interviews taxi drivers regularly showed how much they paid to the enterprise for administrative services and argued that these services were not necessary for their work. In this context the relationship between the taxi drivers and PTE was perceived as being very exploitative. Their consciousness of their material interest pushed them towards the separation of the column from PTE as the most simple and effective way of resolving this contradiction.

On this basis a sharp conflict arose between the taxi drivers, led by the chief of the column and chairman of its trade union committee, on the one hand, and the chiefs of the PTE on the other. The taxi drivers were interested in separating from PTE as rapidly as possible, while the chiefs of PTE sought to prevent this. The conflict was referred for resolution to the republican bodies of power and management, but there it got bogged down.

Eventually the decision to establish the taxi column as an independent enterprise and to privatise it through auction was accepted. Tenders were issued at the beginning of 1993 in which two firms and the taxi drivers submitted bids. Eventually the taxi drivers' collective was given the right to purchase the enterprise. The column was therefore established as an independent enterprise in which all the drivers held equal shares.

A similar situation arose after the creation at the enterprise of a section for the repair of the bodies of buses and private automobiles, although it did not lead to so much conflict. This section turned out to be a very profitable subdivision. Soon it separated out into an independent enterprise, renting its facilities from PTE.

The history of other enterprises in transition in Russia shows that the tendency to isolation and then separation of the most profitable subdivisions is universal. On this basis the interests of the enterprise and the subdivision always collide. In some cases the separation of profitable subdivisions, which are included in a single technological cycle, has resulted in serious failures in basic production.

In PTE no such problems have arisen because of the technological isolation of the taxi column. However, serious contradictions appeared in the resolution of the problem of the distribution of property. The taxi drivers, having privatised their automobiles, hoped to receive a part of the garage and workshops. The management, after a long struggle against the separation of the column, eventually agreed only to the privatisation of the automobiles, and this was accepted by the State Property Fund as the basis of the auction. The taxi drivers were only given the opportunity of leasing part of the garage and workshops for a number of years. However, the new director of PTE imposed the condition that the taxi drivers should fence off their part of the premises at their own expense. However, in their new enterprise the taxi drivers did not have the money to do this, and they thought that the advantages were rather doubtful, considering they only had a short-term lease so, after half a year's struggle, the taxi drivers had to concede and decided to try to move to some other premises. Thus an internal structural conflict was transformed into a conflict between independent enterprises.

INFLUENCE OF SOCIAL-PSYCHOLOGICAL FEATURES OF DRIVERS ON CONFLICTS

One of the important factors influencing the process of transformation of objective contradictions into conscious conflict are the social-psychological characteristics of passenger transport drivers as a professional group. The character of their labour itself creates individualistic personalities, used to relying on their own resources. The driver works alone, his (or her) only regular contact is by radio with the dispatcher, and only seeing his colleagues and other workers in the enterprise now and then. Isolation at work also contributes to an individualistic model of perception of social reality, where there are two parties 'I' and 'they' (the bosses, passengers, and so on.)

Thus both the bosses and the passengers appear as opposed social forces, imposing on the interests of the driver. The bosses constantly try to pay less and impose more. The passengers constantly irritate the driver with their uncivilised behaviour: they climb onto overcrowded buses, break the doors, engage in arguments over trifles, venting their irritation at having got up early or at breakdowns. Moreover, from time to time passengers make written complaints about drivers, alleging infringements of the regulations that lead to a loss of bonus. Therefore the relations between the driver and passengers are no less inconsistent than those between the driver and his bosses. The driver and his passengers have inconsistent status positions, so their interests do not objectively coincide. A natural consequence of this is social-psychological tension in their relationship.

These attitudes, which are not directly visible, appear in various forms of behaviour. Above all in the daily dialogue between the drivers and passengers, in which the driver is not always able to conceal his irritation. A typical scene: the passenger asks to buy some tickets from the driver; the driver clearly pretends not to hear; this goes on for quite a long time until eventually the driver answers with irritation, 'can't you see that I do not have any tickets'.

The behaviour of drivers during strikes is only another manifestation of all these negative attitudes to the passengers. All the strikes at PTE were spontaneous. In the context of this social relation this means that crowds of people gather at the bus stops in foul weather, expecting the arrival of the bus in ignorance of the real situation. After a long wait standing in the freezing wind they are late getting their children to their kindergartens or getting to work. All this can only generate a correspondingly negative reaction on the part of the passengers to the bus drivers' strike.

In their discussions with striking drivers the director of the enterprise, the city authorities and journalists all put forward the same argument, 'you are punishing innocent people — the passengers'. However, the drivers do not usually take this argument seriously, since they do not consider the passengers to be in any way friendly. Therefore the drivers' actions both in everyday and in extreme (strike) situations are undertaken under the influence of this factor. This is one of the reasons for the determination of the drivers, who have repeatedly displayed their ability to stop work as soon as they feel aggrieved. In doing so, they take no account of the effect of their action on others — a typical display of individualism.

The autonomy of the drivers' labour creates serious obstacles to the organisation of concerted trade union actions. The leaders of the trade union in PTE, analysing the situation, regularly complained that it is difficult to get the drivers together to discuss their problems, that it is in general difficult to get them to organise. Therefore it is not by chance that there has not been a single strike in PTE that has been organised according to the law, and all those which have taken place have been spontaneous.

The most common form of strike occurs as follows: having received his wages, one of the drivers expresses his indignation. He then exchanges information with others who find themselves in the same situation. If their emotions coincide, they take their buses to the administration building and tell the chief of their column that they are not going to work for that kind of money. Gradually other drivers come to collect their wages, find out what is going on, collect their wages, and join the protest. Meanwhile, the drivers who have not been collecting their wages at the moment at which the burst of indignation has flared up, quietly continue their work, without suspecting that their enterprise is on strike.

A high level of self-valuation is typical of bus drivers. Their everyday labour process supports their argument that without them the life of the city and of other enterprises would be paralysed so that, if not the main force, they are one of the main forces in the city. Thus their perception of their importance to others is focused through the prism of an individualistic personality which, in contrast to an altruistic personality, does not take pleasure from its importance to other people, but seeks to use this dependence of others as the basis for its own social self-assertion.

This aspect of the personality of the driver is not directly accessible to observation or to empirical confirmation, but it is displayed in various kinds of behaviour which can be interpreted precisely on this basis. The work of the bus driver is highly stressful and tiring; however, it cannot compare, either in its physical demands nor in its skill, to the other highly paid categories of labour in the city. The main argument in support of their demands for higher pay is not the content of their job, but its importance for the city. As soon as the city authorities forget this, and the increase in bus drivers' pay lags behind inflation and the pay of other categories of worker, they remind the city authorities by going on strike. Forcing the city authorities up against the wall, the city administration has to dig into its reserves and increase the drivers' pay so as not to paralyse the life of the whole city.

At first sight the trade union committee gave the impression of strong and well-organised trade union work. However, on more detailed analysis it became clear that the individualism of the drivers has impressed itself on trade union activity. The main participant in conflicts with the director was not the whole trade union organisation, or even the trade union committee, but its president. In the trade union committee itself the initial basis of decision-making in all serious questions appeared to be fragmentation and individualism. For example, a member of the trade union committee might change an agreed position at a decisive moment, if he or she felt that new circumstances had arisen. Thus a campaign to collect signatures in support of a vote of no confidence in the director collapsed, the workers' representatives unexpectedly deviated from the position of the trade union committee in the negotiations for the collective agreement and so on.

The relative independence of character of the drivers, having a significant impact on relations with the administration, is conditioned by the status position of drivers in state enterprises: their opportunities for both upward and downward social mobility are quite limited. This limits the dependence of the fate of the driver on the will of the boss. As against a factory, where a worker can be given profitable or unprofitable work to create or to limit the possibility of achieving high earnings, in PTE the administration has no such levers of authority. Any obstacle to the work of the driver leads the administration of the enterprise into conflict with the municipal authorities. The driver knows that it is rather difficult for the administration to find fault and to affect his earnings.

It is true that the column working on the Ikarus buses is considered the elite among the drivers (their earnings, prestige and the comfort of their working conditions are all higher). The drivers of the other columns have lower status. Thus the Ikarus drivers are the most militant and obstinate in their relations with management, and one can sometimes hear them making scornful remarks about the docility and compliance of the drivers of the other columns. They cannot explain the differences beyond saying that the other drivers are afraid of the bosses. Although it seems strange at first sight that there should be such distinctions of behaviour between drivers within the same enterprise, the reason appears to me to be that the drivers of the less prestigious columns have the possibility of social mobility: if the managers look favourably on them then they have the chance of being transferred to the Ikarus buses if a vacancy arises, while those already working on the Ikarus buses have few chances of making further progress. At the same time they are afraid of nothing, since under the existing labour legislation and the relatively slight reduction in passenger transport, they can be dismissed only for the grossest violations of discipline. Thus there is little prospect of either upward or downward mobility for the Ikarus drivers. On the one hand, this removes a basis for satisfaction with their social status and, on the other hand, allows them to be independent in their relations with the administration.

INSTITUTIONALISATION OF SOCIAL INTERESTS

Organisations are the most widespread and effective form of institutionalisation of the articulation, expression and defence of interests. Until 1991 various organisations were active in Soviet enterprises: the enterprise itself as an administrative organisation, Party, trade union and Komsomol organisations. Under the conditions of the political regime at that time they all primarily represented general state interests, and this was laid down in their constitutions.

However, in their real activity each of these organisations also expressed and protected the interests of its members. So, the administration of the enterprise as a sub-system of the organisation watched over the interests of its members by means of the bureaucratisation of activity: the inflation of staff and the division of the work of one person among several executors, protection against pressure from workers and higher bodies and so on. The trade union organisation was not so much involved in the mobilisation of labour potential (socialist competition), as protecting the interests of its members through the distribution of apartments, goods, the right to work and so on. The Party organisation, while being strictly oriented above all to the resolution of production problems, could not at the same time evade responsibility for the protection of the social interests of its members. Thus the real social activity of organisations in the enterprise was structurally very different from that laid down in their constitutions.

This left its impression on the role of organisations in the resolution of conflicts and in the regulation of social contradictions. The interest of the state is constantly pushed aside by the real personal interests of the members of the organisation. One of the most obvious manifestations of this was the question of the dismissal of those who infringed labour discipline, where the trade union committee would, as a rule, refuse to give its consent, without which the decision of the administration to sack somebody was invalid. And this was despite the fact that at that time the trade union committee almost always followed in the footsteps of the administration's policy on all the important issues. However, precisely because they were an appendage of the administration, they were often able to check technocratic tendencies in its activity.

The Party organisation was one of the most important mechanisms for regulating social contradictions and resolving conflicts. As a whole it was under the strong influence of the administration, and the secretary of the Party committee, as a rule, acted as one with the director. However, since it had the right to monitor the economic activity of the administration, the Party organisation could, and often did, correct the actions of the administration, eliminating errors which were fraught with the complications of the social conditions in the enterprise.

In 1991 primary Party organisations at enterprises were liquidated, although they had already been pushed aside from any monitoring of the activity of the administration. In the majority of cases this has not led to any democratisation of the management of the business, but to the establishment of an authoritarian regime much stricter than in the period of Party rule. The trade union organisation has remained as the single counter-weight to the administration. However, its legally established rights are by no means comparable to the rights which used to be enjoyed by the Party organisation. Moreover, the trade union has not traditionally enjoyed any authority among either the workers or among management. As a result, in the majority of cases the trade union has become even more dependent on the administration than it was in the past. The result is that directors in the first half of the 1990s enjoyed an unlimited right of one-man management such as had never existed in Russian or USSR enterprises since 1917.

In a very small number of enterprises the trade union organisation was dragged away from the control of the administration and turned into an independent body for the expression and protection of members' interests. As the workers are numerically predominant, such organisations began above all to express the interests of workers. In some cases the change in the social essence of the trade union took place as a result of the creation of a new trade union (for example NPG, FPAD); in others it came about as a result of the transformation of the traditional trade union organisation. This was the case in PTE at the end of 1989 and beginning of 1990, when the informal workers' leaders, who were in a bellicose mood, with the support of the secretary of the Party committee, changed the composition of the former pocket trade union committee and created a new one, which was composed of people well-known in the collective for their activism against the administration. This inaugurated a new period in relations between the administration and the trade union committee, characterised by incessant struggle, which only came to an end in 1993 with a vote of no confidence of the labour collective meeting in the director, who was thereby forced to resign.

THE STRUGGLE BETWEEN THE TRADE UNION COMMITTEE AND THE DIRECTOR

The situation which arose in PTE in the relations between the director and the trade union committee is not typical, but at the same time one cannot call it unique. A similar model of conflict has been observed by us in many of the enterprises looked at in the course of our research. In particular, I know of very similar examples in two passenger transport enterprises and in one large coal mine, all in 1993.

In PTE the change in the trade union committee was followed soon after by a change of director. The new director came from a similar post in a motor transport enterprise in an industrial town. He had an authoritarian style of management, typical of the majority of Soviet economic chiefs in the period before perestroika. In his new job he took no account of the qualitatively different power relations and a trade union committee of a type to which he was unaccustomed. He tried to operate PTE just as he had operated his previous enterprise. And he was immediately faced with the powerful reaction of the trade union committee, and especially its chairman, Novikov.

The essence of all the deepening conflict was the struggle for spheres of influence. In the old Soviet system, where the trade union committee was merely an appendage of the administration, there was no particular need to make a strict demarcation of these spheres. The director could influence decisions made about any issue which came within the sphere of authority of the trade union committee; but at the same time the chairman of the trade union committee was involved in the discussion and resolution of industrial questions, although they were not formally included among those issues subject to agreement with the union.

In conditions in which the trade union committee has become independent of the administration and conflict has begun to deepen, the problem of the differentiation of spheres of competence assumes a fundamental significance. Both parties appealed to different documents, but this solved nothing since a further series of questions then arose: which of these documents were still valid, since almost all of them dated from the Soviet period; where does a normative act end and where does the commentary relating to its application begin; what is the normative context of these acts, and so on. They regularly had to resort to lawyers for help, but with the intricacies of the normative base of the transition period their inconsistent explanations did not carry much conviction. Analysis of similar situations in other enterprises shows that this problem is universal, and is resolved on the basis of the balance of forces, the management strategy of the administration, informal relations and so on.

Both parties very quickly realised the incompatibility of their interests. Objectively the inevitable contradiction had developed into open conflict, in which both parties conducted a total struggle to remove their opponent. The conflict appeared to be all-embracing, so in this short discussion we will confine ourselves to the basic directions of the struggle.

STRUGGLE AROUND THE COLLECTIVE AGREEMENT

In the traditional Soviet system of labour relations, where individual conflict was the only overt form of conflict allowed, the collective agreement played a purely formal role. The administration and trade union committee were two parts of one triangle (the Party committee forming the third part), so the agreement was established by their common effort on the basis of a standard model handed down from above. Formally all members of the collective could take part in the discussion and revision of the collective agreement. However, in practice this hardly ever happened because everybody understood that the collective agreement was 'empty paper' which was not going to affect the resolution of the social problems of the collective in any way. Therefore the majority voted in support of the collective agreement at meetings and conferences without having read it. After its signing, the agreement went into the bottom drawer of the desks of the director and president of the trade union committee.

In the contemporary transition situation this former circuit remains intact in many enterprises. Where the trade union committee remains an appendage of management, the role and functions of the collective agreement have not changed. However, in some enterprises trade union committees with some independence from the administration exist, for which the collective agreement has become the legal basis for a struggle for the social rights of the labour collective. As a result, in such enterprises a struggle has developed around the preparation and monitoring of the collective agreement. PTE is an example of such an enterprise.

After the changes at the beginning of 1990 the trade union committee and director of PTE took the first early steps towards changing the contents of the collective agreement. The trade union committee insisted on including a number of items, officially securing already existing social rights and extending them slightly. The administration raised no particular objections, since it had never taken this document seriously. But when conflict between the director and trade union committee flared up the collective agreement became an important instrument of struggle. Both parties became aware of this in 1992.

In the 1992 collective agreement the trade union introduced a number of clauses extending the social rights of the collective and the obligations of the administration. The administration representatives on the commission preparing the agreement did not pay any attention to this. At the conference which approved the agreement the obligations of the administration were further extended: proposals were put forward from the floor, voted on and adopted. The director then understood that in the context of a hostile relationship with the trade union committee such a development contained serious dangers. After the conference he retrospectively drew up a 'memorandum of disagreements', in which he itemised points in the agreement which he considered impossible to implement, and sent it to the trade union committee, considering this to be a sufficient basis on which to implement the collective agreement in a cut-down form. The president of the trade union characterised this 'protocol' as 'a piece of paper with no legal force'.

In the autumn the trade union president went on to the offensive and, having collected information on breaches of the agreement by the administration, took the director to court. The court dragged this unusual case out for a long time, on the one hand not knowing how to resolve it and, on the other, hoping that the parties would resolve the issue without the intervention of the court. However, the trade union president was persistent. Having heard both sides of the case the court tried to reach a compromise decision, not wanting to provide any basis on which the court could be accused of violating the laws in a very difficult case. The decision of the court was that it recognised that the collective agreement had been violated, as the trade union claimed, but that the administration was not able to fulfil all its responsibilities. The court issued a warning to the administration that in the event of the subsequent recurrence of these infringements appropriate measures would be taken against the administration.

During the negotiations over the fulfilment of the 1992 collective agreement and the preparation of the agreement for 1993 the administration became more cautious and the process dragged on into the spring of 1993. The main struggle took place around the areas of activity subject to monitoring by the trade union committee. In the end the director, who felt that his days at PTE were numbered, had to make a series of concessions. The agreement was accepted and at the beginning of May 1993 the director was dismissed, having passed the rights and responsibilities of implementing this collective agreement to a new director.

BARTER OR PRIKHVATISATSIA?

Commercial activity becomes an important source of conflict in the transitional period, in which it is not always easy to identify in whose interest particular commercial transactions are undertaken. The same facts can be interpreted in a number of different ways, depending on the context of the social relations in the enterprise. Corresponding to the differences in interpretation one can propose various different models of behaviour.

The most obvious facts in this respect at PTE, which are not subject to doubt, are the following. Over a short period during 1991–2 the director sold a significant number of Volga automobiles on the side from the taxi park to various organisations, mainly co-operatives, at nominal state prices which, at that time, co-existed with the much higher market prices. Simultaneously a bus and a pigsty, which had been re-equipped as a cafe, were sold at nominal prices, similarly symbolic in comparison with the market prices.

The director, Petrov, explained that this action was to the economic advantage of the enterprise. Most of the automobiles were sold in the period in which the rouble was virtually useless. The director presented the sale as a pure barter transaction: a building co-operative was sold the automobiles for a nominal state price, and in return the building co-operative carried out work for PTE using its own materials at equally nominal state prices.

The trade union committee, taxi drivers and a significant part of the rest of the labour collective interpreted the same facts very differently: the director could not have sold the automobiles at such a ridiculous price without making some personal profit. There was one additional fact that supported this version of events: the director's wife just happened to be the accountant in one of the private enterprises which acquired some of the equipment on barter terms. Such an interpretation of events was supported by the general context of social relations in the collective, the atmosphere of distrust of the director, and the knowledge of similar activions of directors of other enterprises involving the covert grabbing [*prikhvatisatsia*] of state assets.

All these facts were collected and handed over to the police. The investigation found no evidence of any violations of the law and the case was closed. The investigator established that under the law the director had the right to sell the assets of the enterprise.

The trade union committee was not able to bring forward any further evidence which would prove that the case involved violations of the law, rather than the expedient use of enterprise resources. The real situation with regard to the activities of the director remained unknown. However, in general his opponents would not recognise the legality of his actions. The conclusions of the investigation could be easily dismissed, on the basis of the general context and the existence of plenty of cases of bribery of the police. Moreover, within the collective there were unconfirmed stories that the chief of the city police had been seen in one of the Volgasin question.

This interpretation of the facts became the basis of the campaign to remove the director for 'selling off the property of the enterprise'. Such a campaign brought together the interests of various participants in the struggle. The interest of the chairman of the trade union committee, Novikov, was in the removal of the director, who had tried to remove Novikov and turn the trade union back into a pocket body of the administration. Novikov used the allegations described above as the basis of a campaign to mobilise forces for the removal of the director, in the name of the 'protection of public property' and the 'defence of the interests of the collective'.

The taxi drivers could not care less who was the director of the enterprise or what happened to the trade union committee. The motivation for their battle with the director was the fact that he had sold off Volgas which they had hoped to privatise themselves. The actions of the director had touched very painfully on the most powerful motive for social action, private material interest. Thus the struggle of the taxi drivers on the basis of the facts described above developed in two directions: 1) support for the struggle of the trade union committee for the removal of the director, 2) their independent struggle to leave the structure of PTE.

For the bus drivers these facts had a fairly neutral significance. They had little interest in the fate of the Volgas or the cafe, as none of them had suffered personally from their sale, and they were not particularly concerned about the interests of the trade union committee and the taxi drivers. At the same time the style of behaviour of the director did not arouse their sympathy. The main arguments against him came down to his rudeness, his ignoring the people, and so on. Nevertheless the bus drivers had every reason to interpret the director's behaviour as dishonest. Their actions were based on foundations of moral rationality. The first time a vote of no confidence in the director was taken it was not passed. At the conference a year later the scales had tipped in favour of the trade union committee, and the director lost.

A NEW DIRECTOR— A NEW SOCIAL STRATEGY

The new director, Magomedov, arrived at PTE in May 1993 from a similar enterprise in another city in the region. His arrival signified in many respects an attempt to try out a different model of social relations.

The selection of Magomedov was made by the regional motor-transport association and the city administration, with consultation with the chairman of the trade union committee. Magomedov's candidacy suited everybody in every respect. The information collected about him made him appear both a leader well able to organise the work of the enterprise, which suited the administration of the city and the association, and also able to stabilise the living standards of the labour collective, which suited the trade union committee.

Magomedov, having agreed to become the director of PTE, knew the unfortunate history of his predecessor. However, in his view this had happened because of obvious failures in economic and social policy. On this basis he hoped, with the help of a different management strategy, to change both the economic and the social situation.

The new model of social relations was laid out by Magomedov on his arrival at PTE, when he said to the most active leaders of the trade union committee, 'You have been fooling around here. Now let us get out of this difficult situation together … It is easy to criticise, but I am proposing that we work together'. This approach was made very concrete: the president of the trade union, who had not long before completed his higher engineering training by correspondence (he had previously been a driver), was offered the post of first deputy director for production (a post which had not previously existed). The president accepted the offer. One of the leaders of the trade union committee was offered the post of chief of one column, and he accepted the offer, although another offer of a job was refused on the grounds of age. As a result the most militant trade union leaders were absorbed into the administration. Then the administration together with the trade union committee considered the question of suitable replacements for those who had left. The director offered the post of union president to the deputy director for social questions, who had been responsible for the social and welfare activity of the administration. The trade union committee supported this nomination. At the trade union conference one of the most militant members of the trade union committee, who had been actively fighting the administration for many years, was unexpectedly nominated. However, to many people's surprise, he attracted only two votes, including his own. This was a clear expression of the willingness of the collective to support the strategy of the new director, based on a strong social contract.

The new director also decided to make considerable changes in the social and welfare policy of the enterprise. He secured the help of the city administration and was able to resume the construction of housing, as well as taking various other steps in a similar direction.

The arrival of the new director and his choice of a fundamentally new strategy of social management had removed the situation of open internal conflict. However, it had not in any way removed either the external or the internal contradictions in the PTE collective. Thus the potential for new conflicts within the collective remained. Would the existing objective contradictions give rise to new conflicts? This depends on the confluence of many circumstances: errors in the strategy and tactics of the enterprise administration, the development of the self-consciousness of the workers, the position of the workers' elite, the ability of the new trade union committee to express the interests of the collective and to remain independent of the administration, the strictness of the administrative regime, and so on.

The arrival of the new director had changed nothing in the objective relations of the enterprise with the external environment; it had simply imposed another imprint on the subjective forms of manifestation of the external contradictions. The former director had had a dubious reputation in the local power bodies and had not been well received in the corridors of republican and urban administrative bodies because he was morally prepared to use strikes as an instrument of pressure on the mayor of the city in order to obtain financial support. The new director arrived at the enterprise with the support of the principal leaders of the urban and regional administrations, with some of whom he had been well-acquainted in his former job. Moreover, the new director (at least in word) was categorically opposed to the provocation of workers' protest as a means of putting pressure on the local administration (differences over this question was one of the main reasons for the forcible removal of the deputy director from the enterprise).

It was not long before the objective contradictions in the relations between PTE and the external environment began to assert themselves. The director started off trying to use his good connections with the local administration to resolve the contradictions by diplomatic methods, but already in the summer of 1993 a short spontaneous strike took place, which the director neither condoned nor condemned. Over the following year his relations with the local administration deteriorated sharply, so that he was forced to revert to the old methods of his predecessor. The issue over which relations broke down was the attempt of the director to persuade the local administration to take PTE back into the regional association, so that it would once more have the status of a municipal enterprise. However, Magomedov misled the city's mayor in the attempt to secure the latter's approval for the change of status, as became clear when the higher authorities ruled that the mayor had exceeded his authority, so that the mayor lost face in the eyes of his superiors as a result of Magomedov's scheming.

The same issue undermined Magomedov's good relations with the trade union committee within the enterprise in January 1995, as the trade union president refused to back Magomedov, both on the grounds that the latter's strategy was risky, and on the basis of the supposed falsification by Magomedov of the minutes of a meeting of the labour collective, including a resolution critical of the local administration, which the trade union president refused to sign. In retaliation Magomedov sought to revoke the agreement reached between the trade union and the previous director, according to which the enterprise paid the wage of the trade union president, so that the union could use the money saved for cultural purposes. Nevertheless, the objective basis of these conflicts is best evidenced by the fact that the former militant president of the trade union committee now backs the director in his conflict with the trade union.

CONCLUSION

The enterprise is an atom of the socio-economic system of society, in whose structure and social relations appear all the main features of society as a whole. Moreover, in essence all state enterprises are alike. Therefore it is possible to use a case-study of PTE to say something about the essence of social relations, contradictions and conflicts in state enterprises throughout Russia. However, as we know from Hegel's dialectic, the appearance is important, but it is the essence that appears. Essence and appearance as forms cannot coincide, as different phenomena of one essence appear at different points in social space and time. Therefore the situation at PTE expresses essential characteristics inherent in other state enterprises in the countries of the former Soviet Union, while in the form of their appearance they are unique. However, this uniqueness is expressed basically at the level of forms of existence as conscious open conflicts. From the point of view of the study of contradictions and conflicts the choice of PTE turns out to be very fortunate since facts here appear in open form which at other enterprises only appear in a hidden form, not amenable to observation. But this is a difference at the level of phenomena: in PTE conflicts were displayed in open form which, in the majority of enterprises, exist only in the form of potentiality, in the form of an objective contradiction, which is amenable to open observation only with difficulty.

3. Russian Trade Unions and the Management Apparatus in the Transition Period

Vladimir Ilyin

The aim of this article is to analyse the social principles and mechanisms of interaction of different types of trade union with the administration of the enterprise. The work is based principally on my own empirical research into these processes involving the Russian Independent Trade Union of Employees of the Coal Industry (NPRUP, otherwise known as Rosugleprof), the Independent Miners' Union (NPG), the Trade Union of Managers, Specialists and White-Collar Employees in the Vorkuta Coal Industry (PRSSUPV), the Federation of Trade Unions of Air Traffic Controllers (FPAD), the Trade Union of Flying Personnel (PLS), and the primary organisation of the Trade Union of Oil and Gas Industry Employees (PRNP) in the Sosnogorsk gas-processing plant. However, the analysis also draws on extensive research into the development of post-Soviet trade unions and workers' organisations conducted collaboratively within the framework of our common research programme.[1]

SOVIET TRADE UNIONS AND THEIR PERCEPTION AS A PART OF MANAGEMENT

Principal features of Soviet trade unions

Western trade unions arose from below as a form of institutionalisation of the social interests of hired employees, and above all of those with the fewest rights, the workers. Their principal function was to improve the market conditions under which the members of the trade

[1] An earlier version of this paper was presented to the conference of the British Association of Slavonic and East European Studies, Fitzwilliam College, Cambridge, 26 March, 1995.

union sold their labour power. Soviet trade unions had a completely different origin: they were created from above as an organic part of the system of management of society and its industrial cells, as 'transmission belts' from the ruling Communist Party to the masses. At the national level the management system included state bodies (of branch and general character), Party and trade union bodies. At the level of the enterprise the basic elements of the system of management were the administration and the primary Party and trade union organisations. This fundamental feature of our trade unions has been preserved in a somewhat transformed form (the Party bodies having disappeared) into the post-Communist period.

The basis, the precondition, of any system of management is power. Its first root is real or potential force: the ability of the managing subject to execute an administrative decision irrespective of the wishes of the managed. In the Communist period a rigid authoritarian regime at the level of the country as a whole, as in the enterprise, served as the guarantee of the implementation of decisions taken. In the post-Communist period this fundamental feature of power has been preserved. However, power has been significantly weakened at all levels.

The second root of authority is its legitimacy. The managed, recognising managerial authority as legal, take on themselves the responsibility of carrying out its decisions. The legitimacy of authority is expressed in various forms. One of the most important forms of legitimacy is based on the recognition of the managed that the management body, to a greater or lesser degree, expresses their own interests, so that submission to it is in their interests. The power of the CPSU or the administration of the enterprise was not founded only on force or fear. People also obeyed because they saw that, to a greater or lesser extent, its actions were directed at the protection of the interests of the managed. This applies fully to the trade unions as well. They were not only a transmission belt of the will of the ruling subject, but also realised the reverse relationship, informing the Party-state of the needs of the masses. The trade unions performed their protective function, in this way reducing social tension and strengthening the existing political regime at the level of the country and the authority of the administration at the level of the enterprise. At the level of the enterprise, trade union organisations, being above all a part of the system of management, at the same time carried out the important social function of counteracting excessively technocratic tendencies in the activity of the administration. Many social interests of the workers were realised through the trade union organisations, down to the prevention of their sacking without good cause. In essence, the trade union and Party committees carried out functions which in a capitalist enterprise are normally carried out by management through its personnel department.

In the post-Communist period the monolithic character of the trade unions and the universality of both the forms of their organisation and the content of their activity have disappeared. However, the majority of trade union organisations are still part of the system of management, performing vitally important social functions for the workers. This gives them legitimacy and explains why the vast majority of workers in Russian enterprises, even though they understand that the trade unions are still just as much an appendage of the administration as they were in the past, and that their independence is often more than doubtful, nevertheless remain members and pay their dues. One must bear in mind that nowadays membership of the trade union is radically different from what it was in the Communist system. Then workers were under various forms of compulsion, including from the administration, to be members of the trade unions. In the 1990s membership became really free, while the administration often either covertly or overtly encouraged workers to leave the trade union.

The workers' awareness of the fact that their trade union is in practice an appendage of the administration only occasionally leads to an aspiration to break with the management union. The reason consists in the nature of the labour collective, which was such a fundamental feature of the enterprise in state-monopoly-socialist society. The essence of this phenomenon consists in the fact that everybody who works in the enterprise has the same status as a hired labourer. Thus contradictions between the interests of workers and those of the administration, while they are very significant, nevertheless take second place to the contradiction between the labour collective of the enterprise and the external administrative, and now even market, environment. In other words, the common interests of the workers and the director in the face of the government and the market extinguishes their contradictoriness. In such conditions even a clear consciousness of the subordination of the trade union to the administration does not exclude the simultaneous recognition that the trade union also expresses the interests of the workers to the extent that the latter do not contradict the interests of the administration.

However, it is impossible to underestimate the importance of the changes which occurred after the destruction of the political system of the CPSU. In those conditions there was a unified Party-state management apparatus, working as one, if rather battered, mechanism. From the end of the 1980s the process of decentralisation of management began. The management of enterprises began to acquire a great deal of independence in relation to central bodies, and eventually became almost independent subjects of economic activity. This had a significant impact on the place of trade unions in the system of management. In the Communist system the VTsSPS (All-Union Central Council of Trade Unions) was in practice a department of the Central Committee of the CPSU, and the trade union committee of the enterprise was the department for social affairs of the administration of the enterprise, obliged strictly to follow the directions of the central organs — the leadership of the Central Committee of the CPSU.

In the present conditions of decentralisation the Federation of Independent Trade Unions of Russia (FNPR) has also lost its rigidly centralist character. It is a genuine federation of trade unions. Moreover, it is a federation of primary organisations, which in the event of disagreement are free to leave the branch trade union and FNPR, and stop paying their dues. Therefore, the authority of FNPR, as against Soviet trade unions, derives from its primary groups (which does not exclude the intensive bureaucratisation of its leading bodies). Below, at the level of the enterprises, the primary organisations remain a part of the system of management, an instrument of social management in the hands of the directors. Correspondingly, FNPR as a whole is the representative above all of labour collectives as economic subjects, uniting all hired workers — from cleaner up to director. However, despite their formal equality as members of the trade union, the influence of the cleaner and the director is certainly not identical. Thus FNPR represents the common interests of labour collectives, uniting the administration and the workers. Their conflicting interests are put into the background or generally ignored.

In contemporary conditions the interests of the enterprises as producers, and the interests of the state as the collector of taxes and regulator of economic activity, not only are distinct, but are directly opposed. True, even in the past they were far from being harmonious. However, in current conditions the political regime allows struggle between opposing interests, which was unthinkable within the administrative system of the CPSU. In such a situation the traditional trade unions which belong to FNPR often serve as an instrument of the struggle of labour collectives, headed by the directors, against the destructive economic policies of the post-Communist government, which has, whether deliberately or not, led to the collapse of production, the de-industrialisation of the country, unemployment and bankruptcy. Thus contradictions between FNPR and the government to a significant extent reflect contradictions between various echelons of the management apparatus.

The distributive functions of traditional trade unions

The traditional trade union organisations, which now belong to FNPR, being part of the management of the enterprise, always carried out important functions in the distribution of social goods and benefits. In conditions of a non-market economy these functions were especially large. A significant proportion of goods and services were not sold, but were distributed in enterprises, where the distribution among workers was carried out by the trade union committees. In contemporary conditions of the transition to the market this function has lost some of its significance. The social and welfare apparatus belonging to enterprises has been heavily cut back. However, this process is far from being complete. Moreover, in a situation in which the living standards of wide layers of the population have fallen sharply, the loss of the social support for workers provided by the enterprise risks a still larger fall in living standards and the growth of social tension. Thus the trade union organisations, with the support of the administration, continue to carry out this function of social support for the workers, distributing goods and services. This is the main reason for the survivability of the traditional trade unions.

Case: Gas Processing Plant (GPZ)

One of the workers at GPZ assessed the trade union committee of his enterprise, which belongs to FNPR, thus: 'Everywhere the trade unions have already become nothing, but they still take notice of our trade union committee'. The workers and the administration both take notice of it. On the behavioural level this is indicated by the fact that only one person has voluntarily left the trade union (the deputy head of the Department of Labour and Wages at the factory), but after some time even he reconsidered and submitted an application to re-join the union. The administration also takes notice of it, bringing various papers to the trade union committee to sign, for example the rules for bonus payments, which are reviewed annually.

There is only one basis for the authority of the trade union committee in the collective: the right to distribute barter goods and *putevki* (vouchers for vacation trips). At the beginning of the 1990s barter was the most effective form of trade, and barter goods the most attractive form of payment for labour. The management of GPZ tried to secure payment for the goods sold by the factory in goods which were in short supply (at that time almost all goods were in short supply). The factory received automobiles at state prices. Since the market price was much higher (by a factor of at least two) than the state price, and since it was absolutely impossible to buy an automobile outside the factory, the factory workers valued their privileged position highly. GPZ traded quite actively on the international market. In payment for these sales, which were made through the association, an abundance of imported consumer goods arrived, which the workers could also buy at prices far below those of the market. The distribution of all barter goods, including automobiles, was conducted through the trade union committee, although under the unobtrusive supervision of the management. When the supply of goods turned out to be smaller than the demand (at the 'ridiculous' prices at which the goods were offered), the job of allocating rights to buy them became extremely stressful. Quarrels arose around barter, there were suspicions of injustice and so on. The administration did not want to get involved, and transferred these functions to the trade union committee. The goods, which arrived in large quantities, were distributed by the trade union committee between the shops and subdivisions, where the shop committees drew up waiting lists or conducted lotteries. In the case of the most scarce commodities, such as automobiles, the trade union committee drew up a waiting list covering the whole factory, taking account of the length of service of workers at the enterprise.

After 1992 the rouble once more began to acquire an appeal as a means of payment. Simultaneously the consumer market was saturated with goods which were now expensive in relation to the incomes of the population. However, at the same time the problem of non-payment arose. It became more advantageous to the enterprise and to the labour collective to receive payment for goods in money, but many customers were not able to pay. Rather than find themselves in the position of creditors, waiting for ever for payment in depreciating money, the management of the enterprise agreed to accept payment in various goods. However, these goods were no longer in short supply and indeed their sale had now become a serious problem. Its resolution was handed to the trade union committee in the traditional way.

While I was present at the trade union committee people kept rushing in and the telephone kept ringing. All discussions, without exception, concerned barter goods and *putevki.* This is the basis of the real power of the trade union committee over the collective. However, this power actually derives not from the collective but from the administration: because it has other things to do, and does not want to get involved in conflict-generating activity, it has transferred the right to distribute the goods that it receives to the trade union committee. Since it has transferred this right, it can take it back at any time, and entrust it to some department of the administration. Thus the real basis of the authority of the trade union committee is its good relations with the administration, which gives it control over consumer resources.

Case: Coal Association

During the first half of the 1990s (to some extent even in 1994), enterprises which belonged to the coal association received some of the proceeds from the sale of coal in the form of barter goods. When there was a substantial difference in the price of coal between domestic and world markets, combined with the unreal rate of exchange between the rouble and the dollar, barter trade with foreign countries was very favourable. Workers in the mines received a significant proportion of their wages in the form of barter goods. The distribution of barter goods was carried out by the STK (Labour Collective Council) and the trade union committees. Thus the trade union committees carried out a part of the function of the Department of Labour and Wages.

All barter belongs to the mines, that is to the administration, and transferring its distribution to social organisations was a form of payment for their loyalty. If the trade union committee withdrew from the role of unestablished department of the administration, the channel of barter would risk being cut-off, which would inevitably undermine its authority in the collective.

The trade union committees of the new NPG (Independent Miners' Union) originally declared their refusal to engage in distributive activities. The main emphasis was put on the organisation of strikes. However, when strikes lost their former effectiveness and came to hit the miners hardest of all, the reasonable question arose, 'Now what are we going to do? How can we keep our members from transferring to the competing Independent Trade Union of Coal Industry Employees (NPRUP)?' In these conditions the NPG trade union committees had to become involved in distribution of barter goods, which in turn demanded that they normalise their relations with the administration, since such distribution is in essence an honorary assignment to carry out administrative functions.

In the conditions of a polar miners' city, where this association is located, the possibility for the workers and their families to go to the southern parts of the country for their holidays in the summer is extremely important. The distribution of *putevki* for holiday centres and sanatoria, the provision of financial assistance to buy tickets, the organisation of pioneer camps and the organised and orderly transport of hundreds of children in special trains, were all carried out by NPRUP at the regional as well as at the primary group level. However, all the money that they need to carry out these activities they receive from the administration.

NPG at first did not pay much attention to this work, but then it became clear that their members had as much interest in *putevki* as did the members of NPRUP. Gradually NPG began to get involved in this work, which also required the normalisation of their relations with the administration. However, the main levers of management of this process remained in the hands of NPRUP, and NPG found itself dependent on its competitor, which pushed it into constructive co-operation.

Once, when I was in the NPG trade union committee offices in one of the mines, the question of the purchase of *putevki* to a holiday centre in Krasnodar Krai arose. As the president explained, the previous year a man had dropped in to the trade union committee who was a 'messenger' from a southern collective farm, which had its own holiday centre not far from the sea. He offered a barter arrangement: the collective farm would provide *putevki*, and the mine would provide coal. It seemed like a good idea to the president of the NPG. He went with the representative of the collective farm to the director, and there and then they struck a deal. But the distribution of the *putevki* was entrusted to NPRUP.

Management functions in the social and welfare sphere

In state-monopoly-socialist society the function of social protection consisted in the organisation of a system of collective provision of material and social goods which, in conditions of strictly limited resources and low wages, prevented absolute pauperisation and the formation of a pauper layer dangerous to the state. The trade union network of holiday centres, sanatoria, profilaktories, cultural centres, pioneer camps, the distribution of scarce goods at subsidised prices and so on, was the concrete embodiment of this function. In many enterprises a diversified network of social establishments (factory holiday bases, kindergartens, cultural centres, sports complexes and so on) was created. These objects were always under the dual management of the enterprise and the trade union, which jointly financed them. It was almost impossible to distinguish the administrative activity of management and the trade unions in this sphere. In a political respect this activity stabilised the rule of the CPSU, weakening the social roots of opposition, but at the same time this function fully corresponded to the immediate interests of the mass of ordinary workers in Soviet enterprises and organisations. They had an interest in the trade unions, which opened up the attractive channel of distribution of goods which were otherwise inaccessible to them.

In post-Communist society the social and welfare apparatus has not automatically disappeared. There has only been a tendency to its curtailment, following from the new economic conditions. At the same time new market conditions have made the network of sanatoria, resorts and tourist bases absolutely inaccessible to wide layers of the population: the prices of *putevki* have risen out of all proportion to the average level of wages. This has strengthened the interest of collectives in the enterprises in the preservation of social and welfare facilities even when they have become economically unviable. Accordingly trade union organisations, which traditionally managed this sphere, have preserved their former role and appeal.

Case: Gas Processing Plant (GPZ)

The rich raw material extracting and processing enterprises of the north always aspired to the creation of a rich social and welfare apparatus. This tendency was underpinned to a significant extent by the policy of local Party bodies, which used the strength of Party discipline to press the chiefs of the rich enterprises to create departmental social and welfare facilities, which, however, served the whole population of settlements which were usually monocultural. These included the town of Sosnogorsk, where two enterprises dominate the life of the town: the railway depot and station and the gas processing plant. Thus the town falls into two monocultural parts, the 'railway' part, which is the main part of the town, and Sosnovka, which is separated from the main part of the town by waste ground, centred on GPZ.

In Sosnovka GPZ has constructed and maintained a network of children's pre-school establishments, a large cultural centre and sports complex. In the days of the administrative economy all of this network was no burden on the enterprise, since nobody took any notice of income and expenditure, the most important indicator of the work of the enterprise being its fulfilment of the plan. Expenditure on social and welfare facilities enabled the enterprise to increase the real standard of living of the workers, despite the officially limited wages. It was much easier for the director to spend millions of roubles on building a cultural centre than to increase the wages of his workers by 50 roubles.

During the 1990s the situation began to change. The factory began to be involved in market relations. It became necessary to establish a relationship between income and expenditure. At the same time the President and government of Russia began to press enterprises to divest themselves of their social and welfare facilities. In these conditions the GPZ management had to reassess the requirements of the factory and concluded that it was necessary to abandon that part of its social and welfare provision that met the needs of the town and not those of the members of the collective. They discovered that only 30 per cent of the children in their pre-school establishments were the children of their own workers. However, attempts to force the other parents and their enterprises to pay for the support of their children in the kindergartens were unsuccessful. Nor was it possible to throw these children out. Then, in 1993, two kindergartens were transferred to municipal ownership. The cultural centre was also used more by the citizens of the town than the factory's own employees, so that its support was a very expensive matter for the enterprise. Therefore the cultural centre was also handed over to the municipality. In many cases enterprises hold on to their social and welfare facilities, but rent out the premises to commercial structures. GPZ has not gone down this road. It is difficult to say what are the real reasons for this decision, but the deputy director for finance explained that the management of the factory did not want to follow such a self-seeking course of action and considered that the kindergartens and cultural centre should be maintained to serve the needs of the city.

The factory kept in its own hands a sanatorium-profilaktory and three kindergartens. At the same time there was a regrouping of the children: their own children were concentrated in their own kindergartens. The management insisted that they would have liked to have preserved the remaining facilities, but it was impossible to realise this wish. At the beginning of 1994 about 30 per cent of the factory's profits were devoted to the support of the social and welfare apparatus, although there were economic reasons for this as well since this expenditure was exempt from taxation. In the event of a deterioration in the economic position of the enterprise this would no longer be sufficient reason to preserve the social and welfare apparatus. Everyone understands this, so that the possibility of the complete closure of the social and welfare apparatus of GPZ hangs in the balance, seriously frightening all those working there.

The sanatorium serves both the factory's workers and the general population. During the years of perestroika an energetic and forceful chief doctor persuaded the rich factory to create ideal and expensive material facilities: a large building with more than one hundred beds, so that patients do not have to go home after treatment, an excellent restaurant, consulting rooms all with the best equipment, some of which is unique in the region. Thanks to the prosperity of the factory, the sanatorium was able to acquire imported equipment and medicines. Nobody knows precisely how much all this cost, but at the beginning of 1994 the factory workers paid only 30,000 roubles for a course of treatment whose full cost was 400,000. The main users of the sanatorium are the pensioners of the factory. Outside organisations were users of the sanatorium from the beginning, but as the price to them has increased they have found it increasingly difficult to afford its services. In an attempt to increase revenue the quota of places allocated to the factory's workers and pensioners was halved in 1993, but still nothing is said about the profitability of the sanatorium, or about bringing income and expenditure into balance.

All the indications are that nobody has yet given any thought to the economic aspect of the problem. At present the administration is trying to keep it operating as in the past, since trips to southern sanatoria have become inaccessible for the majority of citizens, because of the cost of travel and *putevki*, so that a local sanatorium-profilaktory has some chance of commercial survival, although certainly in a reduced form. The deputy director for finance does not consider that there is even the remotest chance of closing the sanatorium completely; in the extreme case he will only acknowledge the possibility of transferring it to the prosperous gas company, Komi gazprom. However, the head of the sanatorium does not exclude the possibility of its transfer to the social insurance fund, which is in principle ready to take it over. Following the revaluation of assets, the sanatorium was worth one billion roubles ($625,000), but even this is an undervaluation. It is a prime candidate for privatisation. The building could very easily be adapted for commercial purposes.

The management of the social and welfare facilities was and still is carried out by the administration and the trade union committee. The facilities were constructed using the resources of the factory, but the trade union pays the basic salaries of those who work there. However, it was usual for the factory to pay them from its own wage fund, so that their salary levels were much higher than those of municipal employees. All questions of the current management are also decided jointly by the administration and the trade union committee, which continues to act as the branch of the administration concerned with social matters.

The authority of the trade union organisation, its ability to keep its members, is largely determined by its ability to provide additional services for the workers of the enterprise. At the same time this ability depends wholly on the trade union committee's constructive relationship with the enterprise administration. In the case of possible conflict the administration can speed up the transfer of social and welfare facilities to municipal ownership or can take them into its own direct management (although it is true that it has no interest in doing so). Thus both the trade union committee and the administration are interested in close co-operation over questions of the social management of the collective.

Participation in personnel management

In Soviet enterprises the president of the trade union committee was a member of the so-called triangle (director, Party secretary and trade union committee president) which actively participated in the selection and assignment of the leading personnel in the enterprise, judged those who violated regulations, and so on. This was done either by the triangle, or by the Party committee, which brought all the parts of the triangle together, or by a joint meeting of the Party committee and the trade union committee. In addition to this, the trade union committee had wide legal powers to control the dismissal of employees by the administration. Not one employee or worker could be sacked without the agreement of the trade union committee. They created comrades' courts, which struggled against disciplinary violations, carried out raids to check up on labour discipline, and so on. Most of the work had a rather formal character, but the monitoring of dismissals was handled quite carefully, so that the administration agreed them not only with the president (its own man), but also with the whole trade union committee, which usually defended the person dismissed.

In the post-Communist period the Party committee was liquidated. At the level of legislation and managerial practice the rights of the trade union committee in the sphere of personnel policy have been encroached upon. They have been considerably restricted, although not entirely removed. Where the trade unions have a significant influence, as in the coal mining industry, the administration has to take account of the trade union committee in the sphere of personnel policy to a much greater extent than is stipulated in law. The traditional trade unions have themselves refused to continue to carry out the function of enforcing labour discipline. Thus, Soviet trade union committees actively carried out all the functions of personnel management jointly with the administration, but in the post-Communist period this function remains only in relation to that part which concerns the defence of members of the trade union against unjustified dismissal or punishment. Alongside this, the administration has fairly wide discretion for the independent determination of ways of involving the trade union committee in the discussion of personnel matters. If the trade union committee proves to be obstinate, its role in personnel management can be reduced to a minimum. Thus the role of the trade union committee in this sphere is also largely the result of the attitude the administration takes to it.

Mass-cultural work

Soviet trade unions played a large role in the management of cultural centres, pioneer camps and in the organisation of amateur artistic performances and exhibitions. At the level of the enterprise the trade union committee supervised amateur artistic performances and groups, sports sessions and organised special evening events for holidays and anniversaries and so on.

In the post-Communist period there has been an appreciable reduction in such activity. This is in part connected with the decline in non-professional cultural activity in the country as a whole, but also with the tendency to cut back on the social and welfare apparatus, which was everywhere being transferred during the 1990s to municipal authorities, handed over on a leasehold basis or sold to commercial organisations. Nevertheless, at the level of primary organisations such activity continued, even though on a much reduced scale. The trade union committees still organise evening events, celebrate anniversaries and so on. Such activities rally the collective, create a good psychological atmosphere, improve relations with the administration, and so the latter welcomes it. Very often the trade union committee appeals to the administration for financial support for such events, which it usually receives.

In Zapolyarnaya mine in Vorkuta the president of the trade union committee of the independent ITR trade union (a very energetic woman) explained the mechanism of interaction with the administration. She prepares a programme and goes to the director for financial support. The director is himself a member of this trade union and is usually willing to meet her. Sometimes he calls her himself and asks her to prepare something for the traditional macho holidays — Army and Fleet Day. She reported that he laid out his proposal, provided financial support and himself took an active part in the evening. The leader of the primary group is not a 'free worker' (not being paid) and so relies on her official position as the head of the personnel department. It is often difficult to tell where her official duties end and trade union duties begin.

Mass-industrial work

Soviet trade unions revealed themselves most fully as a part of the system of management in their participation in so-called mass-industrial work. They organised socialist competition, supervised its conduct, announced its results, distributed bonuses together with the administration, monitored the observation of safety measures, struggled for economy in the use of energy and materials. In essence this was purely managerial work. However, from the period of industrialisation in the 1920s it had been the basic activity of the trade unions.

With the beginning of the workers' movement the trade unions began to show their independence of the authorities, including the enterprise administration. One of the main steps in this direction was their refusal to carry out mass-industrial work. The administration was not happy with this, but usually understood that the trade union's participation in management betrayed too clearly its role as a non-established branch of the administration.

Part of the functions of the trade union in this sphere has been taken over by management at various levels; part hangs in mid-air. Among the latter are safety precautions. The decline in the observance of safety precautions has been especially marked in the coal mining industry. Here there were two processes in play: first, a weakening of management control of the observance of safety precautions (the repeal of the disciplinary regulations); second, the removal of the trade unions from this work. The result has been an abnormal increase in the incidence of industrial injuries. This has touched on the interests both of production and of the workers themselves. First the administration and then the workers themselves became gradually aware of this, although nobody wanted to return to the previous situation. But at a meeting in the coal association the general director complained explicitly that the trade unions had been removed from this important work.

However, this does not exclude the administration from drawing the trade union leaders into the performance of various administrative functions.

Case: The taxi column of a passenger transport enterprise

In the taxi column some years ago the director put his own man in place as chief and together they began to conduct the mutually advantageous policy of selling automobiles to individuals and organisations. The taxi drivers, who wanted to buy these automobiles, organised a strike and expressed a lack of confidence in their chief. In the end the director was forced to transfer the chief of the taxi column to another section. Under pressure from the collective he was forced to nominate a new head of the taxi column, who had special middle technical education, elected by the drivers.

The new chief of the column and the president of the shop committee of the trade union had a very close business relationship. I was often there when the chief was absent, at which time his functions were carried out by the chairman of the shop trade union committee. For a long time the column struggled to be converted into an independent enterprise. In essence the problem was one of a change of management strategy. The leaders and organisers of this struggle were the chief of the column and the president of its trade union committee. In the end the drivers decided to buy their enterprise at auction. Fierce bidding developed at the auction between the taxi collective and two outside firms. The taxi drivers' bidding was conducted by the president of the trade union committee.

Rotation of staff

The president of the trade union committee was always selected from the employees of the enterprise, with very rare exceptions being someone drawn from the ranks of the ITR or departmental management, often someone who was not able to cope with the duties of his or her post. For many it marked a significant increase in their social status. However, formally the post of president was temporary. Whether it turned out to be temporary or permanent, and whether the individual could return to his or her professional work in the same or a higher post, all depended on his or her relations with the director. In the majority of branches of the economy, with the exception of the coal mining industry, this situation has not changed. The personal career of the president of the trade union committee depends entirely on the director.

The chiefs of enterprises in which there is a pocket trade union committee understand that it carries out some of the functions of the administration and this determines their relationship to it. In a clothing factory, which has a strict authoritarian regime, the director decided not to play the trade union game and directly nominated the trade union president as his deputy director for social matters. This was not a bad career move: a young woman had been promoted from foreman to trade union president and then to deputy director.

However, the process of knitting together the trade union committee and the administration does not always proceed so smoothly.

Case: the passenger transport enterprise

In the bus enterprise in 1989 the tame trade union president, who could not control growing discontent within the collective, left his post to return to his former job as an ordinary engineer, with the support of the Party committee. In his place a bus driver was elected on the basis of his authority within the collective. Conflict with the administration began when the trade union committee refused to turn a blind eye to the director's selling automobiles and equipment cheaply to his own people to whom he had also rented a part of the property of the enterprise. A fierce struggle between the director and the trade union president continued for several years. The director tried to buy the president off, offering him a job as his deputy. However, the president refused knowing full well that they were personally incompatible and that, once he had lost the protection given by his post as trade union president, he would soon be legally dismissed from the new post. In the end the collective voted its lack of confidence in the director and his association and the local authority removed him (although formally he resigned of his own accord).

The trade union president participated in the search for a new director. They found him in a similar enterprise in another town. The new director immediately offered the trade union president a job as his deputy which he accepted (he had just completed a correspondence course at an engineering institute). For the vacant post the director and the former president, now deputy director, recommended the man who had until 1991 been secretary of the Party committee, for whom the post of deputy director for social matters had then been created. The trade union conference elected him, and the director liquidated his post. Another active member of the trade union committee was appointed as chief of the bus column. The end result was that the trade union committee had lost its leaders and had become the social department of the administration. The new director, relying on the support of the tamed former trade union leaders, has established a rigidly authoritarian regime and, for the smallest infringement of the rules or display of disloyalty, sacks or forces the resignation of the offender. Workers in an interview said frankly that under the new director the trade union committee has effectively disappeared.

In enterprises which have completed the process of privatisation the tendency to subordinate the trade union to the discipline of the administration is particularly strong. The passivity of the collective means that the president stands alone with the director. It is obvious that their power is unequal and the president is obediently subject to the director, expecting as his reward a decent place in the administration.

Case: A private construction organisation

In the construction organisation T, which works in the oil extraction industry, the atmosphere of a capitalist firm was established almost from the very beginning. This enterprise appeared at the end of the 1980s as a co-operative, and was transformed into a joint stock company at the beginning of the 1990s. In an interview, the president of the trade union committee claimed that the issue of conflict with the administration was patently absurd: ‘What conflicts? The trade union committee was created to help the administration’. A couple of years later, when the transformation to a private enterprise had been completed, in the course of a regular interview the director answered a question about his relations with the trade union. His position was simple: the trade union committee does not interfere, because it simply does its job. ‘And if it did interfere?’, I naïvely asked. ‘Then I would dissolve it’, the director confidently replied.

NEW INDEPENDENT TRADE UNIONS AND MANAGEMENT

Apart from the interests which are common to the whole collective of hired employees, there are also the interests of particular occupational groups. These interests often do not coincide with the interests of the main part of the collective, and may be completely opposed to them. At the end of perestroika such occupational interests found their expression in workers’ committees, and then in new trade unions. Their main feature was their refusal to attempt to express the interests of the whole collective, behind which most often lie the interests of the management of the enterprise, often sharply distinguishing their interests from those of the bulk of the employees. The other feature of the new trade unions was their striving for independence from the director, ceasing to carry out managerial functions. A logical consequence of this strategy was the refusal to participate in the management of the social and welfare apparatus, mass-cultural work, the functions of distribution of goods, travel warrants and so on.

However, in the few years of their history the independent trade unions have drifted significantly in the direction of a *rapprochement* with the traditional trade unions. The reason for this is not the opportunism or irresoluteness of their leaders, but the logic of the development of social interests, among which the common interests of labour collectives and branches have dominated over the interests of narrow occupational groups, and the external contradictions have played a leading role in comparison with the contradictions between the workers and management of the enterprise.

Independent Miners' Union (NPG)

Social aspect of NPG

The underground workers in the development and extraction sections constitute the traditional labour aristocracy in the coal mining industry. They always had the highest prestige, the highest pay, and an increased sense of their own importance. Every occupational group has the illusion that it 'feeds' others. In the consciousness of the labour aristocracy this illusion was reinforced by their pseudo-proletarian ideology, a key element of which was the idea of the exclusive role of the working class in public production, in the life of the country. At the level of the ordinary consciousness of the workers this idea was transformed into the evaluation of everyone who does not extract coal as a parasite, living at the expense of the exploitation of the labour of the workers in the core occupations.

The workers of the underground groups were not in a position to separate from the collective as a whole. Therefore, the aspiration to protect themselves from egalitarianism appeared in the form of isolationism: the attempt to put themselves in a privileged position in the distribution of the income of the enterprise and of state subsidies. The Independent Miners' Union was created as an instrument of this struggle.

The strongest argument in favour of the separation of NPG as a trade union uniting the key groups of workers was the leading role of these groups in the work of the mine. A strike by these groups paralysed the mine. Therefore, this relatively small group could enter into negotiations with the employers backed up by the threat of imposing large potential losses, which gave their demands considerable weight. Thus, a huge destructive potential was in the hands of a relatively small group, making it easy for the authorities to meet their demands. It is more advantageous for workers in such leading occupations to have their own separate trade unions, because it is then possible to achieve concessions for themselves alone, rather than for the collective as a whole. However, the organisation of the workers of the development and extractive sections alone rested on a logical weakness, for the extraction of coal does not finish under the ground. In the end NPG opened its doors to all the workers involved in the technological cycle. The same logic of the production process also required them to admit mine foremen into their trade union.

The taming of NPG

NPG arose in contrast to NPRUP as a trade union directed against the administration, which emerged in the strikes of 1989 as the main and immediate enemy. However, the mine directors and heads of the associations had no difficulty in persuading the workers that the issues that were exciting them could only be resolved at the level of the ministry and the government of the country. Thus, dextrously parrying a powerful attack, management moved the focus of the attack to the leadership of the CPSU and the USSR government. More than this — with a minimum of words, the workers' movement was transformed into an instrument of lobbying to beat out additional appropriations for the development of the industry. Since the generality of the interests of all the employees of the mines and the industry was more than obvious, it was not difficult to persuade the workers that it was necessary to act together. The regional coal associations played an active part in working out the particular demands to be presented by the striking workers. In their turn the heads of the associations at first included the leaders of the workers' movement in their negotiations to 'beat out' help in Moscow.

At the same time, at the level of the mine, unity soon emerged between the directors and the leaders of the workers' movement in the matter of management strategy. At the first stage of the workers' movement there were very insistent demands to abolish the association as a parasitic structure and demands were put forward to transfer the mines to full economic independence. This left aside the representation by the workers and the directors of their own interests — the demand for economic independence united them. Indeed, their unity was so complete that numerous interviews with senior managers and NPG leaders have failed to uncover who was the originator of this idea.

However, a few years of experience of the reality of the idea of mine independence has shown that the coincidence of representations of the interests of the parties is by no means the same thing as the coincidence of their interests themselves, as the objectively optimal form of social self-realisation. The directors of many mines have in practice used the liquidation of administrative control on the part of the association to implement deliberate policies directed at their own enrichment. Of course, nobody can prove the existence of such egotistical motives. But actions are judged not by the interpretations of their subjects, but by their real results. Up to 1994 there were many obvious facts which showed that some of the directors were disposing of the mines as though they were their own enterprises, which they were soon going to have to give up. Alongside this, things were handed out to the workers in the form of unfounded increases in wages, barter at ridiculous prices and so on. When some mines found themselves in a desperate economic position as a result of their indebtedness, their directors left, either willingly or under pressure from the labour collective, leaving the latter with disrupted production, while the former directors made off with their savings. Since they had been acting independently, it is almost impossible to find fault with them and to prove that their behaviour was driven by mercenary motives. Certainly a number of investigations carried out at Vorkuta mines have been unable to prove anything.

Case: Severnaya mine in the Vorkutaugol' association

The director of this mine was elected by the labour collective with the active support of NPG in the mine. In effect he arrived as the workers' own director. True, he retained the whole management team as an inheritance from the previous director. NPG advised him to clean out the administration, but either he decided not to, or he did not want to. For some time the workers had no particular reason to regret their choice: the wages at the mine were constantly above the average for Vorkuta. However, by 1994 the NPG trade union committee in the mine, under the influence of the management of the association, began to reconsider its relations with the administration. It turned out that the mine was in a catastrophic economic situation, with a volume of debts significantly greater than that of other mines in the association. At the same time both the association and the trade union leaders had their suspicions that everything was not above board. However, it was impossible to prove the presence of criminal intentions behind the actions of the clever and highly skilled managers who had brought the mine to the brink of ruin, although a series of questions was raised to which it was difficult to find sensible answers. For example, why did they buy a coal extracting machine complex in Germany at a price significantly higher than the list price?

In the end doubts developed into certainty that it would be sufficient to change the management of the mine to achieve satisfactory economic results. The leader of the trade union and the management of the association made a joint statement to this effect. When the mine trade union leaders met the general director to express their complaints first about the unsatisfactory and, at times, downright suspicious work of the mine leadership, the general director (who was usually referred to behind his back simply as 'the general') replied laconically: 'No problem. Write a statement and the question will be resolved!'

At the beginning of 1994 the leaders of NPG and PRUP changed their strategy in relation to the association in Vorkuta. On the one hand, the experience of economic independence had clearly proved unsatisfactory for the majority of the mines. This was understood by everybody who had any knowledge of the state of affairs in the city's enterprises. The directors of many of the mines, who had no intention of abandoning their enterprises, and trade union leaders had come to the same conclusion. On the other hand, the management of the association, Vorkutaugol', had also changed course in the spring of 1994, actively moving in the direction of centralisation. Yu.R. Lobes, who had been director of the fairly stable though not prosperous Vorkutinskaya mine, became the new general director of the association. He only agreed to take up the post on condition that the mines supported his policy of reconstituting the association as a unified industrial complex with a unified system of accounts and a unified technical and economic policy. He received this support from both the directors and the trade union leaders.

At the same time, at a number of mines in which the director had for one reason or another not been able to carry out his managerial functions, a coincidence of interests had developed between the labour collective and the association, the mine's trade union leaders and the general director, concerning the unsustainable direction of the management of these mines. In this context it was not uncommon for the management of the association to make direct contact with trade union leaders, both at a group level and, in particular circumstances, on an individual basis. The management of Vorkutaugol' began to hold a monthly meeting with the leaders of all trade union primary groups. It was common at these meetings for both the general director of the association and the trade union leaders sharply to criticise the unsuccessful mine directors. The leadership of the association wanted to involve the trade union leaders in the execution of their strategy of restructuring management and overcoming the difficult situation in the enterprises. The leaders of NPG Vorkuta, as well as of the primary organisations, were clearly inclined to support this strategy.

NPG Vorkuta and wider politics

The miners' movement arose in 1989 as the only powerful and well-organised social movement in the Soviet Union. On the one hand, it obviously frightened the apparatus of the CPSU and the USSR government who could not hide this fear. This in turn gave the miners a huge, and greatly exaggerated, confidence in their ability to influence wider political events. Kuzbass and Vorkuta began to be visited by the top leaders of the USSR. Local trade union leaders became participants in negotiations at the highest levels. The Soviet Prime Minister Ryzhkov visited Vorkuta in the winter. They decided to show him the unadorned reality of polar life. (This was a completely new strategy of dialogue with the top leaders: to show them not the facade which had been painted over in advance, as was the case in the past but, conversely, to lay it on thick, so as to prove more easily the need for a special relationship). And in this they were over-zealous. The Prime Minister's convoy of automobiles was caught in a snow storm and could not move so that rescue parties had to be sent out. The premier got off with a fright, but some of those protecting him died. However, the diligence of the leadership of the CPSU and of the USSR government in trying to domesticate the workers' movement turned out to be in vain. The movement was transformed by the efforts of its leaders into a clearly oppositional social-political force. Alongside its economic demands, anti-Communist political slogans became increasingly common.

Leaders of a large number of Moscow political parties and organisations poured into Vorkuta and Kuzbass in the hope of securing the support of the miners. But only disappointment awaited them: the miners' leaders, who were able to kick open the doors of the top leaders of the government, greeted the leaders of the pygmy parties, who could not even dream of sneaking into the waiting room of a single minister, with some arrogance. The miners' elite claimed for itself an independent political role and did not require any teachers. It was a cold shower for the democrats' attempt to go to the people.

However, Boris Yeltsin, having become President of the Supreme Soviet of Russia in 1990, *could* tame the miners' movement and use it in his struggle with the Union centre. His unrestrained populism struck a chord with the miners, coinciding with their anti-bureaucratic ideals of social justice. Yeltsin understood the significance of the miners' movement as the single organised social force on which he could lean. And so in 1990 he also flew to Vorkuta. Here, following the by-now established tradition, they showed him life in all its beauty. They took him down Yuzhnaya mine, one of the oldest mines, with difficult geological conditions, and they kept him there for quite a long time. Although Yeltsin had made great play of his sporting activities in his memoirs and on television, the miners were surprised by Yeltsin's lack of physical fitness: on the short walk underground to the face he kept asking them to stop so that he could get his breath back. When he got back to the surface, by now completely exhausted, and was asked about his impressions, he replied laconically: 'I don't envy you lads'.

Having understood the power of the miners' movement, Yeltsin counted on the NPG as his political ally. He gave more than 40 million roubles for the establishment of the new trade union in Vorkuta — an enormous amount of money in those days. As a result he achieved his aim. NPG began to play the role of his political ally, where necessary resorting to the weapon of the political strike.

In the summer of 1991 Yeltsin was elected President of Russia, which was then still a part of the Soviet Union. After the August 1991 *putsch*, when the USSR was disintegrating, Yeltsin and his team were faced with the need to pay their debts to the miners, who considered that they had now got their President. Not everyone in Vorkuta shared in the euphoria that prevailed in NPG. However, in response to any expression of doubt as to his merits, the reply was: 'We put him there, and if necessary we will remove him'. Without any economic justification, the leaders of the by now independent Russia gave the miners a massive pay increase, the politically determined inequality of which gave rise to large-scale dissatisfaction among broad strata of the population. The threat arose of many occupational groups, some of which were vital to the life of the country, being drawn into strike movements, so that they too had to be given large pay rises. The country found itself in a vicious circle as what had begun as modest inflation rapidly escalated.

It eventually became clear that the Russian government did not have the economic resources to buy the political loyalty of the miners, particularly as this only led to the general destabilisation of social relations. Gaidar's monetarist policies in particular required a change of direction in relations with the miners. Nobody spoke about this openly, but little by little the flow of subsidies to the coal mining industry was cut back, and it became increasingly difficult for the NPG leaders to gain access to the Russian leadership.

All of this began to give rise to growing disappointment and discontent among the ordinary miners. 'Their' President was more and more obviously ignoring his allies. It is true that in periods of acute political crisis, as in March and October 1993, NPG came out in support of Yeltsin. But there was already no confidence that the ordinary miners were ready to subscribe to this support.

At the end of 1993 the patience of the Vorkuta miners was obviously reaching its limits. Under pressure from below the leadership of NPG, after a long period of loyal silence, started to talk once more about the possibility of striking with demands against the Russian government. The political alliance of NPG and Yeltsin's team was obviously beginning to fall apart, which was particularly dangerous on the eve of the elections to the Russian parliament to be held on 12 December 1993. And indeed it was not by chance that it was at precisely this moment that NPG made its loudest voice heard.

In the depth of the polar winter and the midst of the election campaign the then vice-premier Yegor Gaidar was forced to fly urgently to Vorkuta. Here a small event took place, which was nevertheless important for understanding the situation. Gaidar flew to Vorkuta, but nobody invited any of the leaders of NPG to meet him. The latter discovered that the vice-premier had gone directly to a meeting with the leaders of the city and the association, and was planning to fly back to Moscow immediately after dinner. Upset at such blatant disregard for them, the leaders of Vorkuta NPG organised a small demonstration from the building of the association Vorkutaugol', where their office was located, to the city administration building. Hearing the noise, Gaidar came out with his guard. In the lobby they asked him: 'Whom have you come to see?' 'The miners.' 'But with whom are you negotiating at the moment.' 'With them.' 'No, you are meeting the *nomenklatura*.'

They demanded that Gaidar meet with the leaders of NPG at once. He proposed to do so immediately following the meeting that was already in progress. However, the NPG delegation did not agree, insisting on meeting in the building of the association. In the end the meeting was held. The outcome of Gaidar's visit was a bundle of documents which were put together jointly by the administration of the coal enterprises and the union leaders. On the eve of the election Gaidar was surprisingly compliant. However, immediately after the election he left the government. Following the already established Russian political tradition, nobody was willing to carry out the obligations into which he had entered. If the leaders of NPG still had political illusions about Gaidar and Yeltsin at the end of 1993, the ordinary inhabitants of Vorkuta, the miners, had clearly already got rid of them. Vorkuta, not long before one of the most politically active cities in Russia, responded with mass abstention to the call to back with their votes the democracy which had been won in October by force of arms: in some polling districts fewer than a quarter of registered voters turned out. Among the small number who went to the polls Russia's Choice turned out to be the most popular Party, but the Liberal Democratic Party came next. The sympathy of the miners was beginning to turn more and more obviously to Zhirinovskii.

In 1994 the process of delimitation of the interests of the miners of Vorkuta and the leadership of Russia advanced rapidly. Under pressure from below the leaders of NPG also began to change their position. They began to address increasingly sharper criticisms to Yeltsin and the government, and calls for an all-Russian strike began to ring out increasingly frequently in labour collectives and in NPG offices. It is remarkable that various statements included the declaration that if the demands were not met they would call for the re-election of the President and the resignation of the government.

For example, in September 1994 a joint resolution was adopted:

> Having repeatedly discussed the social and economic situation that has arisen in the enterprises of the Vorkutaugol' association, understanding that the present economic policy of the Russian government is leading to the breakdown of the Russian coal industry, the trade unions NPG and NPRUP of the city of Vorkuta decided to conduct a one-day warning strike from 7 a.m. on September 19, 1994...

After a number of economic demands addressed to the Russian government, the statement sounded a warning:

> If the demands laid out above are not met within the period indicated, [the trade unions] will stand up for the labour rights of the workers, up to the declaration of an indefinite strike with the advance of political demands.

NPG Vorkuta and NPG Russia

The Russian miners do not have uniform social interests. The main contradictions arise between the miners of Vorkuta and the miners of Kuzbass. The natural consequence of these contradictions are the differences in tactics and strategy between NPG Vorkuta and NPG

Kuzbass and NPG Russia, which is dominated by Kuzbass, and is consequently headed by a former Kuzbass miner, Sergeev.

The government strategy of cutting coal production in Vorkuta to maintain Kuzbass as the main base for the production of coal determines the greater loyalty of NPG Kuzbass to the government, in comparison with Vorkuta which had, from the end of 1993, moved more and more overtly into opposition to the leaders of Russia.

The Russian economy has experienced a decline in production the depth and duration of which is unprecedented in the world in peacetime. The question naturally arises: who is to blame? It is even more natural that everywhere and always the government wants to avoid taking responsibility for this. Thus the President and the government of Russia try to turn enterprise directors who are not able to reconstruct themselves into one of the scapegoats. The law on bankruptcy is directed at this: the bankrupt state expresses its horror at the financial condition of enterprises which have been ruined by its own policies. In his speeches Yeltsin has repeatedly tried to direct the anger of workers against their directors.

NPG Russia in principle holds to the same line, as an ally of the reformist democratic centre: the directors are opponents of reform, responsible for their failure. Referring to the loyalty of Sergeev, the president of NPG Russia, to those in power, one of the leaders of NPG Vorkuta declared, 'I do not understand his position as a member of the trade union, but I can completely understand his position as a member of the Presidential Council'.

In Kuzbass many primary groups supported such a tactic and there some NPG primary groups instigated legal proceedings against their directors over delays in the payment of wages. This was a surprisingly successful manoeuvre, securing payment for small groups of workers, while providing the opportunity for a convincing imitation of militant activity. It was hardly fair to condemn the director, since the usual reasons for non-payment do not depend on him, but the whole collective would see an active struggle, while the attention of the angry workers was diverted from the reformers in the Kremlin.

The leaders of NPG Vorkuta changed their social strategy, having refused to form a bloc with the centre ('the centre is conducting a war against the north', one of the leaders of NPG Vorkuta said angrily) and having chosen to cooperate with the administration of the mines and the association Vorkutaugol'.

On 10 October 1994 the council of representatives of NPG Russia adopted a document in which it was said, in part, that

> taking advantage of legal chaos, the directorate has carried out a practically complete grab for power in enterprises. The directors have appeared as the dictatorial managers of enterprise property. This domination allows them to operate the enterprises irresponsibly and to enrich themselves personally.
>
> The directors skilfully direct the discontent of the workers to beat out resources from the federal budget, then pumping them into their own pockets. The worse the miner lives, the better the bosses live. It is enough for the bureaucrats and directors to beat out money. For the workers it is time to think of themselves.

The president of the Vorkuta NPG tried to introduce an amendment to this document, replacing 'the directors' with 'some directors'. The amendment was a small one, but it represented a fundamentally different approach. However, the majority did not support this amendment. Commenting on this document, the vice-president of NPG Vorkuta said

> You see we have new directors. If you go to them and show them this document they will be offended by it: 'is this what you think of us?'

Strikes and NPG

NPG arose out of the strike movement and at the beginning of its history used strikes widely for both economic and political ends. With the collapse of the political regime of the CPSU, attitudes to strikes changed radically. The argument was put forward that they should try to achieve their programme by peaceful methods.

However, the activity of 'their' people in the government, the Supreme Soviet and the Kremlin provoked more and more disappointment on the part of the miners. In the mines isolated 'wildcat' strikes flared up. The leaders of both trade unions only found out about these when the strike had already begun. Originally the NPG leaders took a negative view of such strikes in the context of 'their' hold on political power, seeing the actions of management as the basic cause of strikes. Their work was reduced to the defence of the interests of the workers by putting pressure on management while they tried to curtail inappropriate strikes. However, the situation gradually cleared. It became obvious that the primary reason was the economic policy of the leadership of the country. In new conditions a new attitude to strikes developed: isolated spontaneous strikes, although just, were ineffective or even harmful; only large-scale all-Russian strikes made any sense. The strike had come to be looked at in terms of its effectiveness as a means of putting pressure on the state. Thus, a joint resolution of NPG and NPRUP adopted in September 1994 contained the appeal: 'the meeting calls on the striking miners temporarily to suspend their strike and to join with all the mines of the association on 19th September 1994'.

Nevertheless, spontaneous strikes continued to occur regularly. They demonstrated that the trade union leaders, and above all those of NPG representing the underground workers among whom most strikes broke out, were unable to control their members. Alienation between NPG and the miners was growing. Increasingly frequently at all levels workers accused the NPG leaders of supporting management.

However, this is only one side of the explanation. The other is that it is often more advantageous for workers in key sections of the mine to carry out spontaneous strikes at the level of one section than to participate in all-Russian strikes. The chances are that the former will yield a rapid and appreciable effect. A spontaneous strike by a development section leads to the instant mobilisation of management's intellectual and financial resources to extinguish the strike with an emergency financial infusion. To satisfy the demands of a few dozen workers by giving them an advance payment is much easier than forcing something out of the government. Therefore spontaneous strikes are still quite effective tactics for workers in key occupations in the mines.

Although it may appear strange at first sight, such strikes, which appear on the one hand as a manifestation of the falling authority of NPG, at the same time serve to strengthen the influence of the NPG primary organisations on management, on their *rapprochement*. Management understands that it is easier to settle the conflict with the mediation of the leader of the primary group of NPG, which in theory shares management's attitude to spontaneous strikes. Thus the administration in such cases always calls the chairman of the NPG, who is in practice beginning to play an important role in supporting order in the mine. The administration is aware of this. Everywhere the representatives of the administration have come to recognise that NPG has a positive role to play in social management. Thus, although it is not clear yet, there appears to be a tendency to include leaders of NPG primary groups in the system of social management of the enterprise (which as a rule was typical of the NPRUP cells).

Rapprochement with NPRUP

The dynamics of the social interests of both the miners and the leaders of NPG has caused a change in the strategy and tactics of the trade union in relation to the political leadership of the country and the management of the industry. One result has been that the distinctions between NPRUP and NPG primary groups in this respect have lost their previous striking contrast.

NPG was created to struggle through strikes and negotiate under the threat of strikes. It was absolutely consistent with this position that NPG should refuse any involvement in the administration of social and welfare functions, distribution of goods and travel warrants and so on. However, it soon became apparent that strikes do not achieve much, that strikes alone do not unify the trade union. At the same time, competition between NPG and NPRUP for members was developing. NPRUP, having imitated NPG's militant populist rhetoric, at the same time maintained its commitment to work to resolve the every-day problems of its members: allocating places in kindergartens, sending children out of the city for vacations, distributing scarce goods and so on. This served as a powerful stimulus to hold on to old members and to attract new ones. Eventually such competition forced NPG to become involved in such activities. However, since NPRUP had the experience, the connections and the staff to manage the social and welfare facilities, NPG had to expand its co-operation with NPRUP.

The change in relations of NPG with the administration described above has resulted in the elimination of any serious distinctions in the style of relations of the two trade unions with enterprise management. Joint work in the preparation of collective agreements resulted in their further *rapprochement*. In their everyday work the two trade unions have come more and more to discuss social questions together and to put common proposals to the administration.

The trade union of managers, specialists and white-collar employees

External contradictions are fundamental for the labour collective. However, this does not mean that one should underestimate or ignore the significance of internal contradictions. The most fundamental internal social contradiction in the labour collective is that between workers and management employees. This fact plays a determining role in the development of trade union organisations. As noted above, representatives of management play the leading role in primary organisations which include almost all of the collective. This in practice transforms the trade union committee into a body of social management, one of the most important parts of the enterprise administration.

However, another strategy is possible: the creation of an independent trade union of managers, ITR (technical workers) and white-collar employees, although one rarely encounters such a strategy. Nevertheless we shall look at one example of such a strategy in some detail. At the first stage of the miners' movement, Vorkuta strike committees and NPG frequently expressed a fairly aggressive attitude to administration employees, considering all office workers to be parasites, with widespread demands for their mass sacking. In these conditions the idea of creating a trade union of ITR arose. The initiators of the idea were the leading mine engineers of Vorkutaugol'. However, the realisation of the idea was not so simple.

Case: Zapolyarnaya mine

On 2–3 December 1991 the workers of the mine organised a strike. One of its central demands was that the number of office workers should be cut by one-third and the wage fund for ITR and office workers reduced accordingly. The director tried to explain to the workers that without such ITR as the mine foremen there would be a serious deterioration in safety, and that a large number of specialists are necessary for the normal functioning of the mine. However, the discussions were without effect. Then the idea arose of responding to the miners with their own methods.

The following is an extract from the minutes of a meeting of managers, ITR and white-collar employees of Zapolyarnaya mine on 27 December 1991, attended by about fifty of 290 employees in these categories. The agenda: 1. Report of the co-ordinating council of ITR concerning the strike. 2. Confirmation of the constitution of the trade union of managers, specialists and white-collar employees. 3. Nomination of candidates for president of the combined trade union of managers, specialists and white-collar employees.

O.E. Zinchenko, deputy director for economics, from the presidium of the meeting, laid out the demands that had been put together: 1. Instigation of criminal proceedings against the three ringleaders of the strike of 2–3 December (Pozdnyakov, Il'yasov and Lakhno). 2. Allocation of 15.6 per cent of the general wage fund to the ITR wage fund.

A mine foreman, F., approved of the proposal to take criminal proceedings against the ringleaders of the strike (members of the council of the enterprise): — 'there are no guarantees that somebody else will not appear as initiator of a new strike. So the case has to go to court'. The mine director tried to soften the counter-attack against the workers. — 'My opinion is that the members of the council of the enterprise should not be prosecuted, and this item of the demands should be removed.' But he was not supported. Thus the mine's chief mechanic said: — 'For how long is the administration going to be trampled on? I think that those guilty must be punished for the strike.' The question was put to the vote, with 22 voting in favour, 13 voting against and 10 abstaining. Then the meeting voted by 42 votes to 7 in favour of the proposal that the director should apply to the court to have the strike declared illegal. The director fulfilled the resolution of the meeting and put the case before the court. A representative of the Republic's supreme court came to the mine. In principle this strike could have been declared illegal, but there was no legal basis on which to punish the guilty parties.

Therefore this matter came to nothing. At the same time they decided to organise their own strike. The idea was supported by the director and other senior managers of the mine. However, by contrast to the workers, the ITR observed every last detail of the law in organising their strike. At the beginning the workers sniggered at such a wonder as a strike of office workers. But then, in the words of one of the ITR, 'they realised that the mine cannot carry on without us'. The NPG leaders came to a compromise. The strike did not take place. However, as a result of the social conflict the trade union of managers, specialists and white-collar employees of Zapolyarnaya mine was established. At the time no other such organisation existed in the city. Lyudmila Dmitrievna, assistant to the director for personnel, was elected as its president. All managers, specialists and white-collar employees of the enterprise were eligible to join the trade union. The union's constitution declared that the category of specialists included workers with higher or middle special education, although few of the latter showed any desire to join this union (a total of five people in 1994). All the senior managers of the enterprise joined the trade union, although the director and the chief engineer (who substituted for the director in his absence) did not have the right to be elected to the trade union committee.

In 1994 the primary trade union organisation of the mine had 185 members (including 56 women) of the 290 ITR and office workers employed. The remaining 105 people were split between NPG and NPRUP, with a few belonging to no trade union. Mine foremen were able to belong to any of the three unions, including NPG. At the end of 1994 there were 102 foremen, of whom around fifty belonged to the trade union of managers, specialists and white-collar employees.

Interaction of the three trade union committees

Two distinct but closely connected processes have developed in the mine: everywhere the anti-apparatus anarchism of the workers and their leaders has weakened, providing a basis on which the NPG and managerial employees could move closer together and mutual understanding could increase. At Zapolyarnaya this process was manifested in the co-operation of NPG, NPRUP and the trade union of managers, specialists and white-collar employees.

'For a year we quarrelled, but now we have found a common language. At first they did not take us seriously', remembered the president of the ITR union, Lyudmila Dmitrievna. 'They asked what we thought we were? Now no important decisions are taken without us. They know that I will have my say.'

The co-operation extends to working out an agreed approach to welfare issues, with mutual assistance. The union president explained:

> Recently a member of our trade union was seriously ill, the deputy director for economics. We sent him to a clinic in Moscow. His treatment demanded a large amount of money: one ampoule costs 45 dollars. I signed an application and took it to the other trade union committees. Everyone signed without hesitation. They came to us with a similar piece of paper from NPG. An alcoholic worker burned down his house when he was drunk. Although he was responsible for it himself, I still signed his application for financial assistance.

All three trade unions collaborated closely in the preparation of the collective agreements for 1992, 1993 and 1994. At first they proposed the old type of agreement to the administration, with a few small amendments. But the following year they attached much more significance to the agreement and, during the period of its preparation, worked on it until ten or eleven at night. On the basic questions all three trade unions took a common position and drew up a single agreed collective agreement.

Features of the interaction of the trade union of managers, specialists and white-collar employees with the administration

If one looks only at trade union activity in the mine, there is little appreciable activity on the part of the ITR union: in contrast to NPG it does not participate in the organisation of strikes or in noisy struggle for the rights of its members. This might give rise to the impression that this union does nothing for its members. However, if one looks at the situation more closely one comes to the conclusion that the militant woman president of the ITR trade union committee at Zapolyarnaya can achieve more than her colleagues.

She acts simultaneously in two capacities, as assistant to the director for personnel matters, as her main occupation, and as trade union president. This means that she does not have to make any special arrangements to see the director on trade union business — she can deal with trade union matters in the course of her normal work. Moreover, it should be remembered that all the senior managers are members of her trade union. They not only work together, but also have common social events organised by the trade union committee, celebrate festivals together and so on. So the director can much more easily sympathise with the position of the members of his own trade union.

According to the leaders of the union they have a number of important social achievements. Since 1991 not one ITR or office worker has been laid off, the prevention of which was the original aim of the trade union. The share of ITR in the wage bill of the mine as a whole has not only been maintained, but has even been somewhat increased, despite the pressure from the workers. In 1994 the trade union committee struggled for two or three months to win additional days of vacation for the senior specialists and department chiefs to compensate for their unlimited normal working day, although this struggle certainly did not require the trade union to enter into confrontation with the administration!

The city trade union

The Association of Engineers and Technicians was established in Vorkuta in 1991. At the end of 1991 the first primary group of the union of managers, specialists and white-collar employees was established at Zapolyarnaya mine. In 1992 in Kuzbass the founding conference of the trade union of ITR, apprentices and office workers of the Russian coal industry was held, with a city organisation being formed in Vorkuta in the same year.

In the words of the president of the city organisation, V.I.Pirozhkov, the purpose of establishing this trade union was to provide a social defence for ITR and white-collar employees.

> In NPRUP this task takes second place, they are not interested in managers and ITR. In the last agreement with the government there was scarcely a word about ITR, although our president in Moscow proposed something to be included. But they work for the mass.

In 1994 the Vorkuta trade union comprised eleven primary groups. They exist in the majority of mines and in UMHO (the service for the installation and maintenance of equipment). The strongest primary groups are those in the mines Zapolyarnaya, Vorgashorskaya, Ayach-Yaga. In a number of mines there are no primary groups (Severnaya, Vorkutinskaya, Oktyabr'skaya, Promyshlennaya). There is no primary group in the apparatus of Vorkutaugol' either, although there have been attempts to establish such a group. At the end of 1994 almost all the employees in the apparatus of the association remained members of NPRUP. Overall by that time the trade union had about one thousand members.

The trade union is not very active in seeking to attract new members. The main direction of expansion is through the formation of primary groups in those mines in which the union does not yet exist. However, there are various obstacles confronting such an expansion, one of the main obstacles being the social-psychological characteristics of ITR and office workers. As V.I.Pirozhkov, president of the city organisation, puts it, 'among workers in the apparatus there is a tendency to wait for orders to come from above. But here everybody has to make up his or her own mind, without any order from the boss. Moreover, the ITR is very dependent on his or her superior. He says "I am not going to work with you", and you are out. Of course the trade union can offer some protection, but you already have no work.' Thus the decisive factor determining the growth of the trade union is the attitude of the director. In Zapolyarnaya in 1991 the director came forward as one of the initiators and inspiration behind the creation of the organisation, which was the main determinant of its success. In other mines the directors have taken a much more sceptical view of the idea. There are many reasons for this. It is easier for the director to work by influencing the bulk of the collective through the NPRUP primary groups. The creation of a trade union of ITR increases their alienation from the workers, which only creates additional problems for management. The rather ambiguous attitude of some of the directors towards the ITR and white-collar employees is also an important factor, together with their continued use of populist tactics of management through which the specific character of the coal industry is still maintained. If the ITR see that the director is unsympathetic to the formation of a new trade union, they do not see any point in taking such a step.

Federation of Air Traffic Controllers' Unions and Trade Union of Flying Personnel

The most effective subdivision of a branch or enterprise, seeing itself as the main source of its income, always aspires as far as possible to restrict the redistribution of resources in favour of the less effective and auxiliary subdivisions. This tendency is manifested in the form of separatism and isolationism. In the civil aviation industry both strategies for the realisation of professional interests have been displayed.

Pilots were traditionally the core workers in air transport. Their elite status position was consolidated by the highest pay in the industry, high prestige, the best prospects of a career in management (as a rule the heads of aviation enterprises and of branch organisations were former pilots), priority in the allocation of housing and so on. The pilots are as interested as any other elite professional group in preserving and enhancing their elite status.

At the end of the 1980s the chance arose to resolve these problems, by putting pressure on the state to redistribute the state budget in favour of their industry. The miners had shown everyone the power of the strike as a means of lobbying the government. However, it became more and more difficult to 'beat out' enough money for the whole branch as the economic crisis deepened. It was much simpler to extract additional money for one key professional group. At the same time, a pilots' strike is the most sensitive of all for the state. In this context the most effective way of advancing their sectional interests was the formation of a trade union of flying personnel, bringing together the elite of the employees of the civil aviation industry.

Here two strategies were possible: separatist or isolationist. Both of these were manifested in the behaviour of this professional group. There were numerous attempts to achieve the separation of the flying crew from airports by forming independent enterprises. Such a strategy promised additional prospects of promotion for the pilot-commanders, who would become chiefs of independent enterprises, instead of merely chiefs of one division. It was precisely this group of pilots, relying to a greater or lesser extent on the support of the trade union, who pursued such a separatist strategy. On the other hand, the ordinary pilots, who dominated the airports, were vitally interested in preserving unitary aviation enterprises. There were very weighty economic reasons for this: the airports were monopolists, and having broken free of the control of the flying staff, had a real possibility of dictating their conditions, pushing up the price of their services and achieving by economic means a levelling of the statuses of pilots and the airport service personnel. Once the airports had been dismembered the ordinary pilots would have lost any levers through which to preserve their elite status. Therefore the strategy of preserving the airports as unitary aviation enterprises with pilots enjoying a privileged status emerged as dominant. It corresponds equally to the interests of the key group of pilot-managers as well as the mass of ordinary flying staff. Although the matrix of interests did not appear as such everywhere. However, the activity of the trade union organisations everywhere appeared intertwined with the internecine conflict between key groups of managers of civil aviation.

The air traffic controllers traditionally occupied a secondary position in the country's airports. In reality, in the early days of civil aviation their role in supporting flights was fairly limited. However, the air traffic controllers' functions expanded in step with technical progress: from the control of take-off and landing to the regulation of all air movements in the region. In practice the air traffic controller has become the second commander of the aircraft.

In parallel with the increased role of the air traffic controllers, their work became more complicated, demanding ever more effort and nervous energy, becoming much closer in this respect to the work of the pilot. A third factor increasing the role of the air traffic controllers is the growth of international air traffic and of the technical possibilities of their being serviced by domestic air traffic controllers, so that Russian air traffic controllers have come to play a full role in managing the over-flights of foreign aircraft. Their services are paid for at international rates in hard currency. This has transformed the air traffic controllers, from the point of view of their economic role, into the complete equals of the pilots. Corresponding to the decline in domestic air traffic and the fall in domestic revenues the role of the air traffic controllers in comparison with the pilots has become much more significant.

Thus the technical revolution has put onto the agenda a kind of social revolution in the relations between the air traffic controllers and the pilots. This concerns both the status of the air traffic controllers as a professional group and the management of air traffic as a subsystem of aviation enterprises. The interests of the air traffic controllers, which were connected with the equalisation of their status with that of the pilots, coincided with the interests of the managers of the air traffic control services, whose interest was in converting themselves into equal partners with the pilot-managers.

At the same time the pilots could not look quietly on at the attempts of the air traffic controllers to deprive them of their exclusive status. When the strike demands of the air traffic controllers were published in 1992, the trade union of flying personnel issued a stern warning: if the air traffic controllers' demands concerning the alignment of pay were met, 'we will turn the whole country upside down'. It is not only the level of income that is an indicator of elite status, but also its exclusivity which creates the basis of prestige. The primary organisations of the trade union of flying personnel played an active part in the anti-strike measures organised by airport management in the 1992 strike. In turn, when the pilots came out on strike in May–June 1994 the air traffic controllers did not display any signs of solidarity.

However, the air traffic controllers were never interested in levelling. Their struggle with the pilots was a struggle between professional elites. Thus the aviation industry trade union, which organised all employees in the industry, could not become the instrument through which either the air traffic controllers or their managers could achieve their aims. Thus, when the political regime allowed social interests to be openly expressed, the professional self-organisation of the air traffic controllers began. In 1989 the All-Union Association of Air Traffic Controllers was established as a kind of synthesis of a department of air traffic control management and a trade union. However, such a synthesis soon showed its limitations. As an organisation which had been created by the ministry, the Association acted within the power framework of departmental bureaucratic relationships. The air traffic control managers, by virtue of their managerial positions, were limited in the extent to which they could express their interests openly. Thus the creation in 1990 of the Federation of Air Traffic Controllers'

Trade Unions (FPAD) was the natural means of tying together the social interests both of the professional group of air traffic controllers and of their managers.

The Association, and then FPAD, directed their efforts to the achievement of two strategic aims: 1. equalising the social status of air traffic controllers and pilots and, 2. transferring the management of air traffic control services to independent enterprises. The main instrument for achieving these aims (one of which was related to a change in the strategy of management of the industry) was to struggle through the use primarily of trade union methods. Between 1991 and 1993 the emphasis was on strikes as a means of putting pressure on the ministry and the government. The main concessions concerning the equalisation of the status of the pilots and the air traffic controllers were achieved by the first strike threat. The air traffic controllers clearly became an elite group in aviation enterprises. Thus, already by 1992 the main aim had become the separation of the management of air traffic control from aviation enterprises and the creation of Rosaeronavigatsia as an organisation which would be independent of the Ministry of Transport.

At first sight FPAD appears to be a completely new type of trade union for Russia, going down the road of militant struggle with management at every level, from individual airports to the government of the country. By contrast to the pilots' trade union, FPAD is striking in the radicalism of its aims and the use of its funds. If the pilots always found a common language with the managers of their enterprises, the air traffic controllers found themselves constantly in latent or in overt conflict with them.

The reason for their greater radicalism is to be found in the specific features of their social-professional status. The air traffic controllers are as much a key professional group as the pilots, they have an equal ability to paralyse air transport in the country. However, the pilots are a traditional elite group, whose status position is fixed both by tradition and by the concentration of managerial power in aviation enterprises in the hands of pilots. Thus the pilots have a large number of levers through which to secure their interests through negotiation, both within aviation enterprises and even within the ministry. Moreover, the pilots are very dependent on management for their own advance: it is always possible to find plenty of 'objective' reasons to block the promotion of a pilot, to reduce the number of hours he flies and so on. Thus the pilot, and the progress of his career, right up to ministerial level, is very strongly dependent on his superiors.

The air traffic controllers are an equally key group, but they cannot lean on tradition, their struggle for elite status is connected rather with the destruction of the traditional professional hierarchy. The ceiling for the managerial career of an air traffic controller is very low, and such a career is open to a very limited circle of people within the framework of unitary aviation enterprises. Correspondingly, the administration has a very limited repertoire of negative sanctions to mobilise against the air traffic controllers. All this compels the air traffic controllers to be radical, and makes it relatively safe for them to act radically. These are the social reasons for the differences in strategy and tactics between FPAD and the pilots' union.

If we look in more detail at the struggles of the air traffic controllers, then one can easily discover the strategy common to all branches of Russian industry of using of trade unions in internal struggles between different sections of the apparatus. The managers of the air traffic control services remained in the shadows, not signing the threatening statements issued by the controllers, and not participating in the organisation of strikes. Their managerial status depended entirely on their being disciplined. However, nowhere and at no time did they ever hinder the most radical actions of their subordinates. This was hardly surprising since, in the event of an FPAD victory, the main victors would be the chiefs of the system of air traffic control management.

One should bear in mind the fact that there is a mutuality of interests in play. The managers of the air traffic control system have a profound interest in supporting FPAD, in using its struggle to achieve their own aims. At the same time FPAD, using its common interests with them, achieved the virtually total loyalty of management to its own activity (the exceptions being connected only with breaches of service discipline). Therefore it is impossible to say who had subordinated whom to their will. At the level of the analysis of behaviour, of course, FPAD was the most important, if not the only subject of the struggle. However, if we look at support for the struggle, at its aims, then, of course, it was the management apparatus of the air traffic control service which had the most profound interest, because success for them would advance their prospects of an administrative career to the level of those of the pilots.

The unsuccessful strikes of 1992–3 led the air traffic controllers to change the style of their relations with the government and to reject further attempts to achieve their strategic aims by means of strikes. Negotiations and compromise came to the fore. Sometimes the chiefs of the service and the trade unions participated in a single team. The first real change came in Siberia, where a separate air traffic control enterprise was created as an experiment. Then, gradually, the government began to make concessions. In the end, air traffic control enterprises were established in many regions of the country, although there was a small amendment to the initial strategy of FPAD: these enterprises included not only the air traffic controllers, but also the workers who maintained their equipment.

However, the separation from airports is not that simple. Although there is a clear separatist interest, shared by the air traffic controllers, their managers, and their trade union leaders, many ties connect them with the enterprises within which they work. Thus, when a real possibility of separation arose, some air traffic controllers began to vacillate. The managers of the airports used economic levers to weaken the separatism. For example, those who separate lose the right to receive the free apartments for which they have been waiting for decades. The management makes new concessions in the sphere of salary. Thus, one of the most militant groups of air traffic controllers, those of Pulkovo airport in Saint Petersburg, along with their FPAD organisation, agreed to remain a part of the aviation enterprise based on the airport.

CONCLUSIONS

The old Soviet trade unions have survived all the radical social and political changes which have occurred in Russia in the 1990s. They have been considerably transformed, but they retain their main feature: they are still effectively departments of the administration for social issues. The reason for this is that the external contradictions (administrative, budget, market) are still dominant. The fate of the workers of an enterprise is decided not in a struggle with the administration, but on external fronts. The preservation of significant features of the old socio-economic system is a factor in the preservation of the old type of trade union. The deep economic crisis threatens the existence of many enterprises, and this gives a further stimulus to the social contract between workers and the administration its logical consequence being the continuation of the fulfilment by trade union committees of the role of department of the administration. Even privatisation does not change this situation, since the market position of these enterprises is no different from that of state enterprises: external factors continue to prevail as before. Thus the common interest of the owners of the enterprise and of its workers, some of whom own a miserly number of shares, prevails over their opposition. The basic contradiction continues to be concentrated along the line between the enterprise and the government, the enterprise and its consumers.

Thus, contemporary Russian trade unions have basically inherited from Soviet trade unions the practice of participating in management on behalf of the administration and in the interests of their members. This interweaving of the interests of the administration, the trade union and ordinary employees has been preserved to a considerable extent in new conditions, thereby creating an objective basis for the continuity between the activity of the old Soviet trade unions and today's FNPR.

The argument that the patterns of trade unionism in Russia express an objective social logic, and are not simply a legacy of the past reproduced by a conservative leadership, is strongly reinforced by the experience of the new trade unions, which arose independently of, and in sharp opposition to, management. Nevertheless, the logic of development of industrial relations wears down the new trade unions, so that they too come to work within the channels of co-operation with the administration which are traditional for Soviet trade unions. These new unions, while they may accelerate the process of change in the traditional unions, do not represent fundamentally new patterns of trade unionism, but express anomalies within the traditional system, providing channels through which sectional conflicts, or conflicts within management, can be expressed which cannot be articulated within the traditionally monolithic structures of management and trade union. Thus, many conflicts which appear at first sight to be between trade union and management, turn out to be conflicts over management strategy and tactics within management itself, conflicts in which the trade union is involved for one reason or another, depending on the particular circumstances.

4. The Trade Union 'Solidarity' — A Case Study

Irina Tartakovskaya

This paper presents a case study of the development of a small but effective trade union, Solidarity (*Solidarnost'*), in the city of Samara in the Middle Volga region of central Russia. The article is not so much an attempt to analyse, as to establish the course of events in one Russian enterprise, where the workers united to defend their rights in a very difficult period of life, for them, for their factory and for the country as a whole. This 'life-drawing' is the result of several years of work of the research group, finding themselves in close contact with the heroes of the article, and is an attempt to understand the sources of their successes and the problems facing the development of a workers' movement in Russia.

We chose the trade union Solidarity as the object of our case study for several reasons. First, this trade union is the single non-political organisation in the city which proclaims as its aim the defence of the interests of the workers, that is to say, it is the only alternative trade union which is not a part of the system of the official FNPR.[1] Second, this is a trade union purely for workers, created by workers themselves, and not the result of the insertion of any kind of ideology into the workers' movement (as is, for example, Sotsprof). And third, and last, Solidarity is purely functional, that is to say it concerns itself with the achievement of precisely those aims which it proclaims in its constitution, and does not serve as a cover for commercial activity or as a trampoline for the political ambitions of its leaders, as so often happens.

The trade union was created in May 1992 in one of the largest enterprises in Samara, the ball-bearing factory of the production association 'Kol'tso'. Before describing the activity of the trade union

1 There are other workers' organisations in the city, but these are all political, rather than trade union, organisations. Apart from Belenko, all names have been changed in this article.

Solidarity in the period of our case study, it is first necessary to provide a short account of the events preceding our research, which began in October 1992.

The roots of the rise of Solidarity lie in the informal social groups of 1988–9, where the founder of the independent trade union, Aleksandr Stepanovich Belenko, and other future activists formed their political views and acquired their experience of practical social activity. These circumstances are very significant, since they determine much of the present day activity of Solidarity. Despite its declared political neutrality (article 3 of the constitution states its 'neutrality between parties and independence from them'), there is a clear orientation to the democratic movement and the leaders of Solidarity maintain personal contacts with representatives of democratic parties and organisations. Thus, the weekly meetings of the co-ordinating committee of Solidarity take place at the premises of the headquarters of the Democratic Russia movement; in preparing for its first (unsuccessful) strike in April 1991 in the ball shop, which was the base for Solidarity, political demands were put forward. Also very typical was the extremely sharp reaction of the leaders of the trade union to the events of 10 December 1992 at the Seventh Congress of Peoples' Deputies of the Russian Federation (Yeltsin's proposal of a referendum, and subsequent discussions). Aleksandr Belenko, for instance, declared that, in the event of a victory for the opposition he would go underground, arguing that it was necessary urgently to organise the collection of signatures in support of the holding of a referendum; another leader, N.F. Lakonov, promised to emigrate.

As a result of such a political position Solidarity has never, in the entire course of its existence, adopted a single resolution criticising the policies of the Yeltsin-Gaidar government, despite the colossal rise in prices and the difficult economic position of Kol'tso.

In 1989 Belenko was the first of the Samara informals to become a people's deputy on the regional soviet (this was still the old soviet, Belenko winning a by-election). Three months later he lost in the elections to the new soviet to the secretary of the Party committee of one of the local factories, a defeat which he willingly acknowledges in his speeches to workers, citing this result as an example which illustrates the reactionary character of the composition of the body of deputies. In general, it is typical for him to draw out definite positive consequences even from his defeats. Several months later he was elected as president of the shop trade union committee of the ball shop and president of the shop STK (Labour Collective Council). Initially his supporters (that is, people who had a negative attitude to the ruling party *nomenklatura* and factory administration) comprised about half the membership of the shop committee. At the next shop trade union conference Belenko insisted that he would only remain in his post if the meeting elected to the shop committee the people whom he proposed. The conference accepted this condition and so a membership of the shop committee was elected which subsequently became the nucleus of the new alternative trade union.

The decisive role in the creation of the new trade union was played by the strike of the workers in the ball shop in December 1991. There had been an attempt to call a strike earlier, with the declaration of a pre-strike situation in the enterprise in April 1991, following the first price increases decreed by Gorbachev's Prime Minister, Pavlov. At that time economic demands for an increase in pay were combined with political demands for the removal of the Party committee from the territory of the enterprise and the resignation of Pavlov and Gorbachev. However, at that stage the trade union committee, led by Belenko, was not able to organise the workers in a mass demonstration. The main reason for this failure was the effective reaction of the administration, which called a factory conference at which the general director promised to increase wages the following month.

By December of that year the situation had finally come to a head: the economic situation of the workers had continued to deteriorate, but the political situation in the country following the *putsch* was such that the workers felt more free, and moreover their leaders had managed to accumulate the necessary experience, including juridical. The strike in the ball shop lasted for two weeks, the demands put forward by the workers at that stage were still purely economic — a doubling of pay — and they made demands only of the factory administration. It is typical that attempts were immediately made to use the strike as an instrument in the struggle between power structures: the president of the regional soviet met with the strikers and tried to persuade them to re-direct their demands towards the regional administration, which had just increased prices. However, this proposal did not attract any support and was seen by the strikers as a provocation. The shop trade union committee, headed by Belenko, played the role of a strike committee. It is important to emphasise one detail: the strike was irreproachably organised from the legal point of view. The demands were put forward in advance, and only when no response was received within the period laid down by the law did the workers stop work. This is another characteristic feature of the activity of Solidarity: the leaders of the trade union try to act strictly in accordance with the existing law, which they have studied thoroughly and follow more closely than the representatives of the administration of the factory. This is related to the enormous role of the personality of its leader, A.S.Belenko, a man of undoubtedly outstanding qualities, whose outlook in many respects defines the practical work of the union.

At the same time as these events in the ball shop in December 1991, a pre-strike situation also arose in the precision bearing shop in the same factory. However, matters did not go as far as a strike because some of the demands of the collective (i.e. sacking of the 'snowdrops' registered in the shop,[2] increase in wages, removal of the shop chief) were satisfied, and it was promised that the remaining demands (a review of the pay system) would be fulfilled.

In October 1992 in the precision bearing shop (TsTP-1) a new pre-strike situation arose. On 9 October the workers in the shop received payslips according to which their pay for the month amounted on average to around three thousand roubles. In September the shop had worked more or less steadily, but the pay that they received turned out to be about equal to the pay of their fellow workers in departments which had been at a standstill and who received only the average pay, having been sent to do agricultural work. An additional motive for the unrest was the steady rise in prices of commodities and food products. A role was also played by the rumours circulating around the factory that the General Director, L.A.Larin, and other representatives of the administration had received an enormous sum in bonuses (figures of 80–130 thousand roubles were quoted).

As a result the workers of the shop (the women, of whom there was an overwhelming majority in section gatherings, set the tone) spontaneously left work; Solidarity did not take part in the preparation of the strike, and a strike committee was not elected. The Solidarity trade union organiser, Lakonov, and his activists (the cell in the shop had around 60 people) then became involved and proposed that the shop should not come out on strike but, for a start, proposed that they should hold a meeting of the workers and meet the administration.

The meeting took place on 14 October 1992 in the 'red corner' of the shop, at which around 150–200 people were present (those for

2 'Snowdrops' are those people who draw their wages from the shop but in fact work elsewhere, for example as personal drivers or building dachas for senior managers.

whom there was not enough room stood in the passages). Lakonov conducted the meeting and, from the administration, the director of the newly-created production complex (combining five shops, including the precision bearing shop), the head of the Department of Economic Planning, and other members attended. Belenko also attended with the president of the Control Committee of the city soviet, A.S.Bakhmetov, who was invited by Solidarity.

The meeting was very stormy. The demands of the workers, apart from the size of their pay, concerned rumours about the creation of some kind of 'solidarity fund' (not related to the trade union of the same name), into which some of the profits of the shops which were working regularly were put, to be paid as compensation to those which were idle. The administration did not deny the existence of such a practice and this provoked a sharp protest on the part of the workers.

Another point of their demands was the system of pay, which had not been changed, despite an agreement from the previous year. (In TsTP-1 pay is not an individual piece-rate, but depends on the production achieved by the shop, as a result of which the workers can shirk.) The representatives of the administration basically referred to the difficult economic situation in which the association found itself. The workers' criticism was very harsh, sometimes to the point of rudeness. Belenko, in his speech, stated that it was the job of the administration to overcome the economic problems the job of the workers, according to the collective agreement, was to work, so references to the difficult circumstances on the part of management were irrelevant.

The position of the 'official' Auto and Agricultural Machinery Workers' Trade Union (Agmash) was represented only by the president of the shop committee in TsTP-1, V.B.Dvortsov. All these events were completely ignored by the factory committee of the trade union. Dvortsov, having supported the demands of the workers in principle, tried to play a kind of conciliatory role, having called on workers to refrain from their sharp attacks on the speech of the head of the economic planning department. However, Dvortsov's speech was received with hostility and was repeatedly interrupted.

The basic outcome of the meeting was a burst of negative emotions and the threat of a strike if pay was low the following month. The tension was somewhat relieved by the announcement read out at the meeting of an increase in pay of 50 per cent for the whole association.

No documents were adopted by the meeting. The meeting was filmed by Samara cable television.

The role of Solidarity in this conflict was not to serve as its inspiration, but amounted only to participation in its more or less peaceful resolution (preparation and conduct of the meeting, invitation to the people's deputy and television, negative attitude to the spontaneous walk-out of the workers). The speeches of Belenko, Lakonov, and Bakhmetov were very well received.

The next episode in the activity of Solidarity was related to the holding of a meeting in shop 8 PSP (production of special bearings — a separate area), in which many workers of shop 7 PSP also took part. The aim of the meeting was to advertise the trade union Solidarity and to provide all the information necessary for this purpose. A city soviet people's deputy was also invited to this meeting, but was unable to come. The meeting took place on 20 October in the corridor of the shop because it was categorically forbidden to hold the meeting in the 'red corner'. The reason for this was that the meeting was held during working time (the leaders of Solidarity did not take into account the fact that this shop worked on a twelve-hour schedule). Despite this, about 70 people participated in the meeting, among them Belenko, Lakonov, V.Zh.Karabaev (the trade union organiser of Solidarity in shop 7). In his speech Belenko laid out the usual set of arguments, which he routinely presents in support of the union, explaining

- the impossibility of common membership in a single trade union with representatives of the owners;
- the absence of a cumbersome administrative structure and of the principle of democratic centralism in the vertical structures of the new trade union;
- related to this, the allocation of by far the largest amount of money to social needs (visiting the sick, funerals and so on).
- other forms of help — legal consultations, refusal to approve sackings to reduce staff;
- benefits, which are erroneously linked in the public mind to membership of the official trade union: holiday passes, sick pay and so on, but which are in fact paid from the social insurance fund and are by law independent of trade union membership.

The meeting was interrupted twice: by the chief of shop 8, who demanded that the workers of his shop should immediately leave the meeting and go back to work (not one person complied), and by the president of the trade union committee of the PSP who entered into a polemic with Belenko as a result of his assessment of the role of the Auto and Agricultural Machinery Workers' Trade Union as a subservient organisation. The participants in the meeting retorted in support of Belenko. The theme of the approaching all-Russian meeting organised by the FNPR for 24 October 1992 was also touched on. Belenko, on behalf of Solidarity, expressed a strongly negative attitude to it, having called it hypocritical and provocative. (Later Solidarity issued an official statement about this, published on 23 October in the local papers.)

The consequences of this meeting show clearly the difference in approach to the defence of workers' rights of Solidarity and of the official union. For participation in this meeting 12 workers of shop 8 were deprived of 50 per cent of their bonus (order of shop N 512). This measure was illegally imposed by the chief of shop because, according to the Labour Code, such an order cannot be issued by the chief of shop, but only by the general director or his deputy. Belenko met the deputy president of the factory trade union committee, Vavilov, about this (because among those punished were members of both Solidarity and Agmash). Vavilov admitted their innocence and tried to persuade the chief of shop to cancel his order, but the latter categorically refused. Subsequently he issued a second order on this theme (N 529a), now drawn up in accordance with the law. But, since they had already fined the workers under the first order, all the actions remained equally illegal. The official union did not take the matter any further, but Solidarity by contrast put the issue of the change in the order to the general director. The director offered to send the order for examination by a lawyer, but he sent only the second, legally corrected, version of the order. Then Solidarity referred the case to the factory Labour Disputes Commission, but since its chair had already characterised their action as 'pettifogging', they simultaneously prepared documents to lay the case before the court. Eventually the ill-starred order was cancelled and the bonuses restored.

During October 1992 activists of Solidarity worked through their own channels (with the support of friendly deputies) to secure 'compromising material' on the general director, A.A.Larin. Evidence in support of many allegations was obtained: the receipt of a large bonus 'for economising on electric power and on the wages fund' in July when the factory was half at a standstill; the purchase of a Volga car at the old price; construction of a garage at the expense of the factory. All this, but above all the incompetence of the administration, which prevented it from doing anything to resolve the financial difficulties of the enterprise, served as the basis for a vote of no confidence in Larin at a general meeting of the collective of the ball shop on 30 October. The meeting took place in the 'red corner'. The president of the shop committee of the official union in the ball shop, N.N.Astashenko, also supported this decision (in Belenko's opinion, in order not to isolate himself from the collective). On 3 November, Belenko and Sergei Ivanov (a tool-setter in the ball shop and member of the shop committee of Solidarity) were interviewed about this meeting on the local television news programme.

As a result, although not in direct response to this, on 4 November Larin held a meeting with workers' representatives, for some reason calling it a 'press conference', although the only correspondents from the press were from the semi-official factory newspaper. The workers' representatives were not elected, but were invited by the administration and trade union functionaries (although Belenko, Lakonov and Ivanov also received invitations). Most of the time was spent answering various production, economic and social questions, during which Larin kept the situation under control. Nobody mentioned the incident in the ball shop until, towards the end of the meeting, dissatisfaction burst through. Sergei Ivanov spoke. Larin tried not to let Belenko speak, but the audience protested. After his speech there was a short, but bitter polemic, then the event was hurriedly wound up.

Further work of Solidarity in November and December 1992 was characterised by the following basic directions:

1. A demand for the indexation of delayed earnings. This form of compensation is laid down in the law, but at the 'press conference' Larin said that the administration was not able to do this, because the delays were not its fault.

   Solidarity put forward this demand at practically all its meetings and was supported by several representatives of the official union (for example, Dvortsov, president of the shop committee of TsTP-1). In November the co-ordinating committee of Solidarity decided to take the matter to court. However, in the middle of

November an order of General Director Larin was issued, satisfying this demand.

2. Solidarity achieved some increase in its membership because it refused to agree, under any circumstances, to sackings to reduce staff, considering that the reasons for such sackings (economic difficulties) should be dealt with by better work on the part of the administration, and not at the expense of the workers. According to the law, workers can only be dismissed with the agreement of that trade union of which they are members. Thus several workers, even in the auxiliary services of the factory, having heard of the possible reduction of staff, hurriedly joined Solidarity.
3. The leadership of Solidarity succeeded in including four of their representatives (Belenko, Lakonov, Ivanov and Karabaev) in the membership of the commission to prepare the collective agreement for 1993.
4. Solidarity succeeded in obtaining the collection of union dues through the ASUP system of check-off, so that in this respect Solidarity acquired equal rights with the Auto and Agricultural Machinery Workers' Trade Union. This was an important step in strengthening the legitimacy of Solidarity not only in the eyes of the workers, but also with the administration.

The next labour conflict in the factory arose once more in TsTP-1, and followed the same pattern as the previous one. On 9 December the workers again received pay packets containing an average of 4,500–5,000 roubles. As a result the machine-tool operators of the second department and half of the eighth spontaneously struck. The workers summoned N.F.Lakonov from administrative vacation. They once more put forward their demands for an increase in pay of 2.5 times and a review of the pay system. (There was only one hand-written copy which was immediately handed over to the chief of shop, Shevtsov, so unfortunately it was not possible to make a copy of these demands.) On 10 December the famous events at the Seventh Congress of People's Deputies of Russia took place, as a result of which many services of the factory administration were not working, as they were listening to the TV and radio transmissions. Belenko and Lakonyi were also extremely worried about a political strike and even tried to contact the *oblast* administration for an explanation of the situation. However, at 3 p.m. Lakonov arranged a meeting in his shop.

During the first half of the day Belenko and Lakonov began to call representatives of the administration (the head of the Department of Economic Planning, head of the Department of Labour and Wages, head of the production complex, and so on) 'to get people to start work'. Only the head of the Department of Labour and Wages, and the head of the production complex agreed to come; the rest refused, saying that they had to listen to the broadcast of the Congress. Again at the factory level of the Auto and Agricultural Machinery Workers' Trade Union there was no reaction to the strike. The behaviour of the president of the TsTP-1 shop committee, Dvortsov, was noteworthy. He learnt about the strike from a telephone call from Belenko. He himself was preoccupied with the organisation of sales in the shop's perfumery and was indifferent to the events, although he responded cordially to Belenko. At 2.50 p.m. a delegation of Dvortsov, Belenko and Lakonov was called to the shop chief. At 3.10 p.m. a meeting took place in the assembly section of the shop, because the red corner was occupied by the perfumery. Lakonov conducted the meeting, Belenko did not speak.

The workers demanded an increase in pay, the answers of the head of the production complex and of the shop came down to the claim that this was unrealistic. The question about the transfer to an individual piece-rate pay system was again put very forcefully. The shop chief Shevtsov said that in TsTP-1 the organisation of technology made it impossible to do this. Lakonov reminded them of the contents of the agreed protocol signed the previous year, where this measure was promised by the administration, and called for them at least to come to some kind of constructive agreement, so that they could resume work. As a result Shevtsov promised as an experiment to introduce individual labour records in the eighth department (assembly) and partially in the second. On the whole he took a tough line. He said that the plan for December had fallen by 22,000 units compared to that of November, that their bearings were not being sold, and that there was no reason to expect a pay increase from anywhere at present.

On the following day the shop started work, the strike having lasted two days. A strike committee was again not elected. In fact the ending of this labour conflict was largely a result of the efforts of the Solidarity leaders. Belenko explained his actions on the grounds that 'a strike in the present situation only serves the interests of the administration', and even stated that there were grounds for believing that it was a provocation from above, in order to stir up the situation in the factory and deepen the impression of general chaos embracing the country, that is to say, it would be one link in a chain of provocations directed at the overthrow of the government. In addition it was not carried out in accordance with the law; the presentation of the demands coincided with their stopping work, and in this sense the remark of the shop chief Shevtsov that 'it is not a strike, but sabotage' had some foundation. The participants in the strike would have to bear their punishment.

At the same time as these events an organisational meeting to establish a new cell of Solidarity was held in the PTP-2 shop, which Belenko did not attend on principle, 'so as not to impose pressure'.

At the beginning of the new year, 1993, there were significant changes in the position of Solidarity in the enterprise, expressed in the practical recognition by the administration of its right to exist. In the second week of January a meeting took place which was attended by the General Director Larin, president of the factory trade union committee, Filatov, and the leader of Solidarity, Belenko. The meeting touched on practical questions (preparation for a new collective agreement) and took place in a good-humoured atmosphere. At the end of the meeting Larin asked Belenko what he could do to help him, and also proposed that Belenko should come directly to him whenever he needed anything. Belenko ascribed such a change of position firstly to the director's desire to conclude an agreement with western partners before whom he wanted to appear as a 'civilised and vanguard manager', and secondly because he had gradually come to understand that it is better not to quarrel with Solidarity. The fact of the matter was that, thanks to Belenko's good relations with the representatives of the press and the democratic wing of the local people's deputies, every conflict in the enterprise quickly received wide publicity throughout the city. One could also assume that the constructive position adopted by Solidarity in the labour conflict the previous month (particularly in TsTP-1) also played some part.

The position of the new trade union was also established on a legal foundation at the lowest administrative levels, in particular, in the relations of Belenko with the director of the ball-bearing production complex, Darkov. Belenko was granted the right not to clock-in, and the right to have the whole day to himself whenever it was necessary to go out of the gate on trade union business. Later he even received a special pass 'with a red border', allowing him to bring in visitors without a pass. An external telephone was installed in the Solidarity office (the trade union office of the ball shop). Belenko was very satisfied with this new situation. It seemed to him that further conflicts would relate to the widening of the influence of Solidarity in other enterprises in the city (they had made preliminary contacts with workers in Progress, GPZ–9 and other plants).

Belenko himself became most concerned with the possibilities of publicising his trade union (he wrote two articles, which were published in the Samara press), and also with theoretical problems. In particular, he said that he was reading Marx's *Das Kapital*, and was also meeting with local economists, trying to resolve the problem of the connection between wages and profits of the enterprise (he thinks that inflationary indexation is insufficient). He considered that wages must be increased alongside the increase in profits (although at the beginning not in a direct percentage relation), which is both just and would give the workers an interest in the prosperity of their enterprise.

The 1993 collective agreement included a clause regulating the relations between the administration and Solidarity, in which the independent trade union was recognised as having the full right to represent its own members. Accordingly the agreement was signed not only by General Director, Larin, and president of the factory trade union committee V.B.Filatov, but also by A.S.Belenko. Belenko was also included in his shop privatisation commission.

By the beginning of 1993 Solidarity had about 500 members (one cannot be precise, because cells did not gather dues). Primary organisations, apart from the ball shop, existed in TsTP-1 (around 150 people), in shops 7, 8, TsPP-1 (quite a new cell of 5 people), TsNSS and so on. The shop organisation in TsTP-1 (organiser Lakonov) had already formalised its separate juridical requisites (stamp, bank account and so on). Beyond the factory a primary cell was in the process of being organised in a tram-trolleybus depot.

In its everyday trade union functions Solidarity provided material help to its members (for instance, 1000 roubles for visiting the sick — this was much more than was allowed by AgMash, and 5000 roubles as a funeral or retirement payment), bought cheap season tickets, received collective passes for 300 people to go to the factory profilaktory, and secured free tickets to the children's entertainment in the Palace of Culture (Agmash paid only 50 per cent of the price). For financial help members could appeal to their shop union organiser or directly to Belenko or the treasurer. The co-ordinating committee discussed these questions only in cases of special expense (for example, one of the union members asked to borrow 10,000 roubles from the trade union for his daughter's wedding: after deliberation his request was satisfied).

From the above chronological account one can draw the following preliminary conclusions about the position and achievements of Solidarity at the beginning of 1993:

1. In the difficult socio-economic situation there was no prospect of the development in Kol'tso of extreme forms of labour conflicts: when there is not enough work, and some of the workers are on administrative vacation (Belenko, Lakonov and Ivanov were on such vacation with 2,500 roubles from October to January), a strike is senseless.
2. The deterioration of the economic situation had a negative influence both on relations of workers with the administration and ITR, and on relations between workers who have regular work and shops and departments which are idle (as, for example, in the case of the 'solidarity fund').
3. The trade union Solidarity, not looking for difficult relations with the administration and high officials of the trade union, in fact plays a constructive role in leading labour conflicts into civilised channels and even resolving them. Many of the demands of Solidarity find support in the shop committees of the AgMash trade union (for example in TsPA, ball shop, TsTP-1).

The position of Solidarity and its leaders in the factory is well illustrated by various people's opinions of them.

President of the factory trade union committee, Vladimir Filatov:

> Belenko was my full-time shop committee president … I said to him: Aleksandr Stepanovich — you are not working. They had already checked him earlier: once, twice they checked — he was not at work. I said to him: you work until 1 July, and then there will be no place for you here. He understood this and created the independent trade union Solidarity. Well, it was created like this: registration is not needed nowadays, they signed a constitution, which virtually coincided with ours, there is even the same wording in theirs as in ours. Belenko and Lakonov were sacked at one time according to article 33, Lakonov's work book was so thick with entries, i.e. he upset people somewhere for something, offended on this level. If one follows his career, he was a deputy in the *oblast* soviet at one time — our trade union committee stuck him there instead of a comrade who retired … the Party organs supported him, the trade

> union was then strongly politicised. And then, after six months, his term expired, it was necessary to have new elections, he tried at first to get elected again, but they said to him at the meeting with the electors, where are you going with this programme, are you not ashamed, withdraw your candidature, hand over to a more suitable comrade.

This judgement calls for some comment. Despite the presence of a certain mutual understanding between Solidarity and the low level trade union committees, the factory leadership of the trade union was sorely aggrieved at the existence on its territory of another trade union, however, small it might be. The leaders of Solidarity were repeatedly accused of all kinds of intrigues and even of working for the western secret services. Ordinary members of the new trade union were regularly denied access to benefits and services to which they were legally entitled, as we will see below, so that literally every question was only resolved with a fight. In fact, opposition on the part of the traditional trade union structures was always significantly fiercer than from the administration of the enterprise itself. The 'factual' information provided by Filatov above does not correspond to the truth, but his interpretation of the image of his rival is interesting.

Chief of ball shop Oleg Polyakov:

> We elected Belenko as president of our shop union committee (he was already president of the strike committee). He was linked to the city's 'informals', and they decided to create a sensation here, in order to increase their role. The workers elected him as a deputy of the *oblast* soviet, they made a good advertisement for him, they did not spare their money: and published leaflets and carried out agitation, saying that he does everything for the workers. He spent 2–3 months there — the workers understood him, that he changed nothing, and on the second round did not elect him. But he organised people skilfully, he was already an able person: he knew whom to call a thief, what slogans to put out ...
>
> He and I were not at daggers drawn, but they held meetings: he has his convictions, we have our arguments with him, he has his interests, we have ours, he goes his own way according to his beliefs. He receives instructions from Moscow, he has contacts there, there is already a whole organisational chain, so he receives such literature from Moscow, even from the Baltics. But Solidarity — this is not only Belenko's circle (though that is what he thinks), this Solidarity already exists somewhere in Donbass or Kuzbass.

It is interesting that in this assessment we find again the idea of Belenko as an 'emissary', of his links with some secret and powerful organisation. Thus their hostility is combined with a certain respect.

President of TsPA shop trade union committee Mikhail Nikolaev:

> I say this about Solidarity: why split, when it is necessary to unite. The trade unions must be one step ahead of the administration, but we are two steps behind. I am in many respects in solidarity with Belenko, but not in everything. Colleagues in the trade union call me the second Belenko, but I am another person.
>
> Belenko takes a lot onto his shoulders. I don't have to carry out all the duties of a trade union activist, there are seven of us on the trade union committee. They still have stable relations, the experience of getting *putevki* and so on. I cannot imagine how one person can cope with all this, while working on a machine at the same time. It is not necessary to break up a complicated system, there is good in it as well.

As one might have expected, the 'idyllic period' of Solidarity's existence did not last long. Relations with the administration did not deteriorate. On the contrary, its pocket newspaper, which in the past had either ignored Solidarity, or printed purely negative material about it, began to publish entirely favourable articles, such as a report on a meeting between the general director and the Solidarity leaders on 29 April, 1993. However, relations with the official trade union remained completely antagonistic. In the same newspaper, articles which followed the trade union line (for example, the text of the report of the regional president of Agmash, or an article written by its Moscow leadership), still called representatives of the alternative trade union 'splitters and renegades', and even hinted at their contacts with the West, and particularly with American trade unions, as intentionally destroying the trade union movement in Russia. But the matter was not confined to ideological struggle, which on its own, given the low authority of the official trade union, would not be very significant. The main lever of influence of the official trade union was its role in the distribution of goods and benefits, which remained in its hands and from which, in violation of the law, Solidarity has been almost entirely excluded. In all his speeches to the workers, Belenko emphasised that *putevki*, sick pay and cheaper groceries distributed through the factory are not financed from trade union funds, but from social insurance funds or from the enterprise's social development fund, and their distribution, according to the law, should not be dependent on trade union membership. In practice, nevertheless, things worked completely differently, and members of Solidarity, with only the rarest exceptions, do not receive *putevki*, or places in pioneer camp, or in the profilaktory, nor even groceries, since the administration of the social insurance fund remained in the hands of the official trade union, the Supreme Soviet having vetoed the President's decree that the money should be withdrawn from FNPR and transferred to a special state fund.

The argument of the apparatus of the Auto and Agricultural Machinery Workers' Trade Union was that although all these goods were bought with common money, in practice their distribution (collecting *putevki* from the tourist office, unloading groceries from boxes, and negotiations with trade organisations) was carried out by the full-time workers of the official trade union, and occupied a lot of their time: 'When Belenko fetches it all himself, then we will share it equally.' This was a well-aimed blow, since Solidarity does not have the full-time workers who could carry out this distribution, nor does it have the network of connections of the official trade union, which has been incorporated into the state system of distribution for a long time.

Although the volume of goods distributed through trade union channels declined considerably, and their prices were not very different from those prevailing in the market, this stream has still not dried up, and will obviously not dry up quickly. The fact that members of Solidarity do not receive anything does not have much impact on their economic situation, but has a heavy moral impact. For example, when the women controllers, members of Solidarity working in the ball shop, tried to get some eggs from the shop trade union committee, the president of the shop committee of Agmash, V.Dvortsov, swore at them in unspeakable language, and told them to 'clear off, democrats!' Such examples, in more or less brutal form, can be observed in all the shops in which there is a Solidarity cell. As Dvortsov, observed: 'You reap what you have sown! I myself got this condensed milk, so let Lakonov get some for you. Think for yourselves where you are better off'. (A woman who came with him to the meeting exclaimed in bewilderment, 'So why have you joined this trade union and democracy?')

Aleksandr Belenko understood the significance of this problem very clearly, and for this reason he stopped trying actively to establish new Solidarity cells: 'I do not want to expose people'. He saw the only solution lay in Solidarity getting control of the management of its share of social insurance funds. For this purpose he established active contacts with the Independent Miners' Union (NPG), which had already made some progress in resolving this problem. Belenko would happily have incorporated his whole organisation into NPG, as there was a complete ideological unity between the two trade unions, but NPG is a trade union of coal miners, and the ball-bearing factory belongs to a completely different industry. Thus Belenko worked in two directions at the same time, on the one hand to establish an agreement with NPG and, on the other, to come to some agreement with the official trade union. According to Belenko, they had agreed to pay 'at least one thousand roubles per signature' for the work of the Agmash bureaucrats. However, this did not correspond at all to the plans of the leaders of the official union. As Belenko sadly joked, leaving a meeting with the president of the factory trade union committee, 'I go down on my knees in front of Fedorov'. The factory administration continued to preserve a benevolent neutrality in relation to all this. If the leaders of Solidarity intervene in any particular case, the administration (and particularly its higher echelons) will, as a rule, meet with them, but not one ordinary member of the independent trade union has any chance of getting, for example, a *putevka*, on his or her own.

As regards NPG, the contacts between the two unions have been developing successfully. Six members of Solidarity, through the channel of NPG, were invited to participate in a week's course in Moscow sponsored by the AFL-CIO. Representatives of the AFL-CIO have subsequently been in touch with the leaders of Solidarity through intermediaries (local journalists) and requested information about the union and promised financial help. Belenko himself accepted an invitation to a meeting of leaders of independent trade unions with Yeltsin during the pre-referendum propaganda campaign of April 1993. At this meeting some of the trade union leaders even put forward the radical proposal for the dissolution of FNPR and nationalisation of its property. However, it was obvious that such an action would not contribute to the stabilisation of the political situation in the country, and so was met by the President only with a sympathetic smile. In December 1993 Aleksandr Belenko stood as a candidate for the *oblast duma* from Samara, although he knew that he had little chance of election, since he had no money to publicise his campaign, and the election campaign was essentially a demonstration of the power of 'sacks of money'.

Eventually it was possible to resolve the question of the transfer of social insurance funds to Solidarity. This immediately made the financial position of the union a bit easier, and enabled it to undertake a larger number of concrete activities (hiring transport to take people to gather mushrooms, renting accommodation for summer vacations). However, the alternative trade union has still not begun to undertake commercial activity — the purchase and sale of goods on behalf of its members.

Despite its limited resources, there has been no significant loss of members from the ranks of Solidarity, whose numbers have remained stable since 1992. Indeed there has even been a small influx of members, although it is true that this is balanced by the fact that, as a result of the difficult economic situation, many workers have left Kol'tso, including members of Solidarity, and automatically drop out of the union when they leave.

Solidarity intervened actively to put its own position in relation to the privatisation of the enterprise. It put forward a demand, in the name of its leadership, for an investigation into the activity of a company called Nika, which had bought a lot of shares very cheaply, so that the workers of the enterprise had been able to buy only a maximum of fourteen shares. However, this demand did not lead anywhere (although formally as a result of it the deputy general director for economics was removed), since the overwhelming majority of workers were far more interested in their pay than in shares, which seemed to them to be unintelligible and useless pieces of paper. At the founding shareholders' meeting the president of Solidarity, having assembled quite a lot of proxy votes, voted against the confirmation of the general director in his post, on the grounds that he was unable, in Belenko's opinion, to provide adequate leadership for the shareholding company in the new conditions. Needless to say, the general director got the votes he needed, but at least Solidarity was able to express and argue its position.

At the end of 1993 we talked to a group of about ten people who had joined Solidarity during 1993 in the ball shop, the main power department and a development shop, to discover their motives for joining. The motives were not very diverse, all coming down to one of the following:

1. Dissatisfaction with the activity of the official trade union: 'In the old trade union nothing got done: they do not give out *putevki*, they only give you ten roubles if you fall ill'; 'they went to Japan and wherever they wanted on our money'; 'Two years ago they had a *putevka* for Vietnam, one for the shop — so who got it? Still nobody knows'; 'and the bosses use the *putevki* every year to go to the South, wherever they want'; 'the trade union never intervened on our behalf'; 'I haven't got anything against the old trade union,

the idea is good, but it is simply that its structure is such that everything gets jammed up on the top floors'.

Here is one example, which well illustrates the situation. Nadya, a control foreman, recalls:

> Somebody stole the purse of a woman in my section. I said to her, 'don't cry, the trade union can help'. She turned to them, but they said to me, 'we don't deal with this kind of thing, and we don't have any money'. How can it be, when she has two children! We talked about it among ourselves and joined Solidarity, nine of the 15 people in our section. Even one pensioner joined, saying, 'I turned to this trade union only once in my whole life, and they refused me'.

2. Evaluation of the activity of Solidarity as fairer and more reasonable: 'At least there is some hope here, but there there are no *putevki*, nothing. And now prices are crazy'; 'Here we know whom to turn to, but there there is nobody'; 'For thirty years nobody knew where our money went, but here we know where it is'; 'you can get a loan if something happens, but in the past money was not allocated for this'; 'Now at least all the money stays with us, we have already set up a special relief fund'.
3. The view that the benefits distributed by the old trade union are insignificant, or, regrettably, do not correspond to the reality or the belief that the members of both trade unions have equal rights (we have nothing to lose).

> If there are redundancies they will cut people and so ...
>
> Interviewer: And do you think that Solidarity will give out *putevki*?
>
> Yurii Zheltkov (milling machine operator, financial organiser and member of the shop committee): Yes I do, and even if they do not give out any, I will still have the money.
>
> Interviewer: Don't you miss out on distribution in the shop?
>
> Zheltkov: What distribution is there now! They gave out some stewing meat — altogether it was 40 roubles cheaper than in the shops, it is a load of rubbish ... They distributed Indian tea for 620 roubles — that is almost as much as it costs on the street.... Many people are afraid that they will not receive *putevki* to the pioneer camp or places in kindergarten, but this does not depend on trade union membership! They try to frighten us by saying that we will receive nothing, we won't even get our season tickets, but they already gave them to us last month. [In fact this was only after Belenko had been to see the Deputy Director for Social Affairs I.T.] But their platforms are pretty much the same, those of FNPR and Solidarity.

4. Emotional motives, connected to the personal authority and charm of the leaders of Solidarity:

> They pay close attention to us ... It was 8 March [International Women's Day], nobody ever gave a damn, but then the lads from Solidarity came along, they congratulated us, gave us chocolates and even kissed us.
> In general they are more attentive, relate to the soul.
>
> We know that Tanya and Sasha are good people, we can trust them.

This last group of motives is basically typical of women.

The recruitment of new members took place in two main ways: either they join, after some time, a cell that already exists in the shop ('we have had a good look at it'), or a new cell is set up in a particular shop after Belenko and other activists have come and spoken about the advantages of the new trade union. Usually the workers discuss it among themselves following such a meeting, and if there is somebody willing and able to head the new organisation, a new cell is established. It should be said that there is no specific 'politics' of Solidarity, in which all its members are expected to participate. The political position of the leaders of Solidarity remains as before (Belenko, for example, spoke very firmly in support of Yeltsin during the Ninth Congress of People's Deputies, and Solidarity issued a special statement on this occasion), but this is the personal position of the activists, so that some of the workers who have only recently joined Solidarity believe that it differs from the Auto and Agricultural Machinery Workers' Trade Union only organisationally. There are no general meetings of Solidarity, but personal contacts between the members of Solidarity remain quite close. However, it is more often the trade union organisers or presidents of the shop committees who interact with the leaders of Solidarity, often going to the latter with financial and similar questions. The ordinary members of a cell relate more closely to their trade union organisers than to the leadership of Solidarity.

This state of affairs, when there were no demonstrative actions taking place, and all activity was directed to the routine organisation of everyday trade union work, did not satisfy all the members of the independent trade union. Beside those who joined the trade union precisely because it was a trade union, inspired by the motives referred to above, there are also people who see it as the prototype of a political party and are still inclined, independently of the real situation, to participate in any kind of resolute actions. The most significant example of such an attitude is that of Nikolai Lakonov, the second most important leader of Solidarity, who is an extremely ambitious person, inclined to populism, with the typical features of a rhetorical workers' leader (as opposed to Belenko, who is a worker-intellectual and connoisseur of the law). At one point Lakonov even threatened to split the union.

Lakonov made his position very clear in an interview with me towards the end of 1993. Referring to Belenko, he said:

> As soon as they gave him a telephone he quietened down, and does not want any conflict with the bosses. To be frank, we do nothing now … He thinks that once he had become president of the co-ordinating committee that was it, he was a big man. I say: in the shop our salary has fallen, I get 13,500, let us stir up the workers, but he says: no, it is not necessary, of course, in the shops their pay is a little more … He says: 'I struck, you did not strike'. I struck too! We even got rid of our shop chief. I created this Solidarity too, and I will tear it down! I only have to say the word in these little cells! And he will be left with 150 or 200 people.
>
> I have not yet decided whether or not to stay at the factory, it is impossible with this pay. A bank has offered me a job paying 50,000, but it is all fetch and carry. I turned it down. But if in the end I stay, I have already decided that there will be two Solidarities, and mine will be very militant. Then we will see, Mr Belenko!
>
> If we do not increase our numbers we will be extinguished like a spent match. People expect some decisive action from us, but he can't even give them *putevki*! His nerves can't take it, do you see … but I don't give a damn what he can't take.… I wanted to go to Moscow to the International Committee for Human Rights, the president is a foreigner, a member of my party [NTS – National Labour Union, a former émigré organisation I.T.], he knows about me, they told him, on account of these *putevki*. But he says: 'Don't go, it's nothing to do with human rights, its simply bureaucrats!' Well, he will not order me, even though he is president, whoever he is … people are constantly held back!
>
> He says: 'you have a juridically independent cell, solve your problems yourself!' So what the hell do we need him for? I spoke to him about pay, he told me to include it in our general demands and give the whole list to the general director. I, like a fool, trusted him, and he settled for all sorts of trifles. Why, just to spit in my face? And what if I spit back?
>
> In general I did not need a trade union, all that was needed was some kind of structure within the enterprise to struggle with the Communists. At first I set up Democratic Russia, but then Yeltsin's decree on the departyisation of enterprises came out, and the trade union had already come along. But in general my interests are more political.
>
> If there are no differences between these unions, what is the point of it?

This long extract brings out very clearly the existence of and conflict between two tendencies in the workers' movement: constructive and confrontational.

However, the development of the economic process turned out to be such that the threat of a split, at least temporarily, receded into the background, with the economic situation making militant action out of the question. Lakonov left Kol'tso, and established a Solidarity cell in the Kirovskii depot of the tram-trolleybus operation, with about twenty members.

By the winter of 1993–4 the situation in the large Samara enterprises had become so difficult that there was some *rapprochement* between workers' organisations with very different political positions, brought together by the need for the basic defence of workers' interests. Thus, in the home enterprise of Solidarity, the joint-stock company Kol'tso, wages were not increased over the summer, and by December 1993 the average salary was only 48,000 roubles. After this payment of wages stopped completely, because of the difficult financial position of the enterprise, with 60 per cent of the January wages being eventually paid in the middle of March. By March 1994 the factory had come to a virtual standstill as it did not have any money to pay for electric power.

The factory stopped again for July and August, and worked only three days a week in September. In November around half the employees were sent on administrative vacation. There was an official declaration of redundancies, which would reduce the number of employees to 74 per cent of its present number. In some months the payment of wages was delayed, so that the holiday pay for July and August was only paid out in September, while only 50 per cent of the August wages were paid. However, some parts of the factory kept working all the time, including ball production, the basis and kernel of Solidarity's organisation.

In the shops which were working the average pay of basic production workers for September and October was around 300,000 roubles, but other categories of workers received considerably less: the controllers for this same period received only 47,000. Nevertheless the administration promised to pay out dividends on its shares for the year as a whole.

In these conditions the struggle to defend the rights of workers appeared almost hopeless: because the factory was frequently stopped, the workers had lost all possible means of putting pressure on the administration. Nevertheless, Solidarity continued to exist and even established new cells in other Samara enterprises, including Lakonov's group in the Kirovskii tram-trolleybus depot noted above. The largest of them is in the northern depot of the tram-trolleybus operation, which was the first Solidarity branch established outside Kol'tso, which at present has about 100 members. The group was established by the fitters, but has now recruited other groups of workers, including the women trolleybus drivers. Workers in transport enterprises in Samara are quite well-paid, which facilitates the activity of the workers' movement. A small primary group, with a handful of people, was also formed on the Samara railway. A cell was also established in the aircraft factory, which was later declared bankrupt. Finally, a primary group was set up in ZiK, another large factory in Samara which is a part of the military-industrial complex. The financial position of ZiK is even more difficult than that of Kol'tso, having already been effectively bankrupt for about a year, the workers dismissed or sent on administrative vacation with miserly pay. It is interesting that Solidarity in ZiK was created on the basis of a small, but extremely active and militant communist-oriented group, the so-called Russian Party of the Dictatorship of the Proletariat, which brands all the better known communist organisations, including the Russian Communist Party, as 'opportunists'.

The association of this group with Solidarity may seem strange when the leaders of Solidarity have always based themselves on supporting democratic forces. However, it shows that in a difficult situation a non-political organisation of the trade union type, oriented to the support of workers, is more attractive and political differences fall into the background in the face of present trials. In connection with the deepening economic crisis in the majority of enterprises in the city the process of expansion of cells of Solidarity has slowed down.

For virtually the whole of the summer of 1994 the aircraft factory and ZiK were at a standstill, so it was impossible for the workers to get together to carry out any organisational work. However, the process of actively organising primary groups continued at another military enterprise, the research and production organisation Slava. This activity came up against strong opposition from the management of Slava, which threatened to sack the leader of the local Solidarity group, a repair fitter. Nevertheless, a primary group was established which maintains close relations with the base organisation of Solidarity. In addition, the entire staff of a sanatorium, located on the outskirts of the city near to Slava, applied to join Solidarity with the support of the chief doctor. Thus at the end of 1994 there were active groups in Kol'tso, Slava, two tram and trolleybus depots (where the situation had stabilised and the primary groups had their own premises), ZiK, the aircraft factory and sanatorium. Negotiations were proceeding to establish a group in the oil refinery at Novokuibyshevsk. All the cells act autonomously, each has its own bank account and stamp, but maintains communication with the president of the co-ordinating committee, often turning to him for advice.

In July 1994 a meeting and discussion group was established in Belenko's apartment, bringing together members of Solidarity and members of the independent trade union Yedinstvo (Unity), based in the VAZ plant in nearby Tol'yatti, which affiliated soon after to Sotsprof. A major line of disagreement emerged, concerning the 'ideological basis of union building'. Belenko criticised Yedinstvo because its constitution allows dual membership, in both the official and the alternative trade union, and because its constitution does not prohibit the common membership of members of management ('representatives of the owners') and workers ('hired labour') in the same trade union. The ideology of Yedinstvo is close to that of Sotsprof which the Solidarity leaders consider to be insufficiently radical in these respects — 'compromising relations' with the traditional trade union structures, in both cases the Auto and Agricultural Machinery Workers' Trade Union. Despite certain differences, an agreement for mutual co-operation and consultation was achieved. Subsequently the leaders of Yedinstvo failed to follow Belenko's advice not to organise a strike at VAZ on the spur of the moment, without observing the legal formalities. The strike took place, was declared illegal (in relation to the legislative norms in force), and many of its participants were sacked.

The leaders of Solidarity continue their sharp criticisms of the activity of the official trade unions, in the factory as well as at regional and national level. Thus, Belenko took part in a television programme on the day of the meeting called by the FNPR on 28 October, 1994 (called by FNPR 'a day of mass action' against the policies of the government), where he called the meeting 'a provocation, aimed at deceiving the workers'. He argued his position thus:

> It is understandable that workers from the budget sphere (teachers, doctors and so on) should participate in this meeting. They receive their money from the government and must resolve their problems with the government. But the overwhelming majority of industrial enterprises are now privatised, they are joint-stock companies, independent economic units, and they have nobody of

> whom to make demands but themselves and their own management, the board of directors. The state has no obligation to support them. The activity of trade unions should be directed against management, which is immediately responsible for the state of affairs in the enterprise. However, how can it happen that in our enterprise the head of the trade union is a member of the board of directors, and the director a member of one and the same trade union! This is a perverse situation.

Recently Solidarity has been building on its connections with the *oblast* administration to prepare a special agreement which would make it the guarantor of the rights of the members of Solidarity. Following initial discussions, a working group has been established to draw up such an agreement. To some extent this agreement would duplicate the existing labour legislation, but in the case of infringements of their legal rights by the factory administration it would allow Solidarity members to appeal to the local authorities rather than to the courts, which may provide a much simpler and more effective channel.

Practical work, as far as is possible, continues. The leaders of the union found summer housing for holidays, paid for from social insurance funds, and the union was still able to provide some things free of charge (for example, beds in military camps, spectacle frames at the expense of the factory, medicines), at the same time as continuing the struggle for the economic rights of its members, which became ever more difficult as the crisis at Kol'tso persisted. Within the factory Solidarity tries to exert pressure on the administration by two methods. First, by drawing the attention of various external forces (press, local administration, prosecutor's office) to the situation in the factory. Second, through direct collective actions within the factory, which in most cases are confined to the ball shop, including Belenko's invention of the two hour fifty-nine minute work stoppage — the maximum length of time people can stop work without facing charges of absenteeism.

In October 1994 a spontaneous strike broke out in the ball shop against the delay in the payment of wages, but Belenko again persuaded the workers not to stop work at once, which would be illegal, but to put forward the necessary demands and to declare a pre-strike situation. Since strikes in the ball shop are usually very well organised, and receive extensive coverage in the local press, that administration rapidly paid the wages due and henceforward the ball shop has always been the first to be paid. (At present in the factory wages are not paid to everyone simultaneously, but according to a flexible schedule so that different subdivisions receive their money in turn.) As one of the members of the trade union committee of Solidarity testified, 'we press for our wages all the time'.

At the beginning of December 1994 another form of pressure on the administration over the delay in payment of wages was undertaken. All the members of Solidarity from the ball shop, and some from the experimental shop, simultaneously made applications to the factory Labour Disputes Commission with the request for prompt payment of salary, indexation for wages not paid on time to take account of inflation, and compensation for moral and material loss. The labour legislation allows only for individual applications in such cases, so the Solidarity trade union committee provided everybody with a sample application which could be used by all those who wished to apply. A total of 180 applications were submitted. There were rumours that some workers who had submitted applications had been put under pressure, being threatened with the sack, although it proved impossible to confirm a single such case. The president of the Labour Disputes Commission said that there were so many applications that it was impossible to interview every single worker separately, so he would receive only a delegation of six or seven people. They were told that the first demand would be satisfied, but the others would not. According to the law the administration then had ten days in which to implement the decision of the commission. However, it did not do so, since the whole factory was stopped from 26 December to 10 January, so Solidarity sent the case to the courts.

The low wages and delays in payment also impede the union's fulfilment of its social support functions, as few members pay their trade union dues. Thus, at the beginning of December 1994 the trade union had only a little over 300,000 roubles, less than $100, in its accounts.

Some practical actions have been taken by Solidarity in collaboration with shop level bodies of the official trade union: for example, a complaint was made about the low quality and high prices of the food provided in the canteen of the ball shop. Following a change in management of the canteen the quality and range of dishes improved.

The employment situation has also remained more or less as before: the Solidarity leaders will only agree to redundancy if the worker himself or herself agrees to leave (for example, to retire or to take another job). However, there is some anxiety in Solidarity that the new draft of the Russian Labour Code does not provide for the trade union to give its consent to dismissals.

The relations of Solidarity with the administration of the factory differs at different levels. Its relations with the factory administration are still marked by more or less latent confrontation, while relations with line management differ in different subdivisions, but in any case are less tense. A special situation has developed in the ball production complex where the director of production has shown himself to be an enterprising and flexible manager. First of all he has managed to provide the division with work, finding customers for 'free balls', that is to say, for production which does not have to go to other shops for assembly. While almost all the rest of the factory has been at a standstill, the ball production complex has had work, and there has even been some reconstruction of the shop, which is appreciated by the workers. Second, although when he first came to this post the director of production struck a very militant pose ('All these Belenkos, Orlovs [Orlov is President of the shop committee of the official union in the ball shop – I.T.] are a result of the miscalculations of management, they have allowed the people to get out of hand'), but he quickly reconsidered his position and established good, even solidary, relations with Solidarity. One expression of this was his active help in finding a vacation centre on an island in the Volga, where Solidarity rented some houses for its members for the summer, paying for them with social insurance funds and membership fees. The chief of production paid from the funds of the production complex for security guards and lent a refrigerator and television set from the shop for the holiday season, which gave rise to a jealous reprimand on the part of the shop leadership of the official trade union, despite the fact that members of the official union were not excluded from using the vacation centre. The production chief also allowed Solidarity to use his fax and even lent Belenko his car.

The change in his position came about as soon as he realised that Solidarity was not a destructive force with regard to production, never engaging in 'populist conflict', not demanding, for example, a wage increase when there was no means of paying for such an increase. For his part Belenko strictly observed all legal procedures and on more than one occasion had stopped 'illegal' spontaneous strikes. At the same time Belenko obviously had great authority in the ball shop, and it was best to maintain good relations with him. Solidarity has 178 members in the ball shop, almost the same number as are members of the official union, but the latter include all management and unproductive workers, such as cleaners and so on.

This populism led the head of the production complex into serious conflict with the factory management, which even threatened to remove him from his post, having combined two production units and nominated the head of the other to direct the new unit, after which he even turned to Belenko for support.

After a truce lasting about eighteen months relations with the factory management have deteriorated sharply. The roots of this deterioration lie in a series of events in the spring of 1994, when the factory was in crisis and payment of wages was delayed while the factory administration appealed to the State Committee for the Management of Strategic Resources for a loan to buy metal to enable it to resume production. When the credit was received some of the money was transferred to the account of a commercial structure, 'Alternativ', which existed within the factory, where it was probably going to be recycled to make more profit. The leaders of Solidarity discovered that the credit was not being used for the purpose for which it had been assigned, and wrote a letter to the Prosecutor which led to an investigation of the financial activities of Alternativ. Leaflets with the text of the letter were pasted up around the factory and the story got into the local newspapers. This whole situation considerably angered the general director. It is typical that he did not attack Belenko directly, but came down on the newspaper which had published details of the financial frauds of the administration. In the factory newspaper a series of articles was published with headlines like 'Do not stop us working!' While avoiding an open confrontation, the director tried to turn public opinion against Solidarity. Thus, for example, at one telephone conference the general director announced that wages had not been paid because 'on the basis of Belenko's accusations the Prosecutor has frozen the factory's accounts'. The general director unexpectedly participated in the report and election meeting of the official trade union in the ball shop in August 1994, which was a completely unprecedented event in trade union practice. The gist of his speech at the meeting was to complain about the intrigues of Solidarity: 'Now it is very difficult to work, various provocations impede us. The recent investigation cost the factory three billion roubles, but it revealed nothing. This was all initiated by Solidarity. Do you never ask yourselves where the money for this organisation comes from? We know this very well, and you would do well to think about it.' Thus, at the time of writing, relations between Solidarity and the factory administration can be described as latent but intense opposition.

Relations with the leadership of the official trade union can be simply described as 'hostile'. The functionaries of the official union still try to discriminate against Solidarity members in the only way at their disposal, in the distribution of various kinds of goods, services and permits.

The president of the factory trade union committee Filatov has repeatedly complained at the difficulty of working with two trade unions. His answer to the question at the August 1994 trade union meeting in the ball shop as to why Solidarity members receive much more financial assistance than members of the official union was typical: 'With our money we have to support kindergartens, sports facilities and so on, but Solidarity does not do any of this. On top of this Belenko himself has said that they have a sponsor. But that will not always be the case.' The last phrase contained a clear threat.

The numbers in Solidarity are gradually increasing at Kol'tso, although the high labour turnover makes this an uphill task. It is indicative that after Solidarity had arranged vacations in the summer of 1994 it was able more actively to recruit women and unskilled workers, such as packers, and even low-grade non-productive workers, whereas for a long time the union had recruited almost exclusively production workers. Despite the fact that at the present moment there is virtually no way to help workers, Solidarity has still not lost a single member, other than those who have left the enterprise and lost their links with the organisation.

This whole text is more an illustration than an example of scientific research. It is difficult to draw any firm conclusions because Solidarity is a unique organisation, by no means typical of the workers' organisations which exist at present in Russia. But the example does go to show that, even though the objective circumstances do not favour the development of trade unionism in Russia, it *is* possible for a normal trade union to exist in a Russian industrial enterprise. At the same time it no more than exists, its experience is of survival without prospects of significant expansion in its activity or growth in its numbers. The development of such structures is impeded by conditions of economic crisis and the difficult situation of workers without rights as well as by the socio-cultural characteristics of the Russian working class and the lack of dedicated, honest and competent leaders.

5. The Changing Status of Workers in the Enterprise

Irina Kozina and Vadim Borisov

Now, here, you see, it takes all the running you can do, to keep in the same place.

Lewis Carrol — *Alice Through the Looking Glass*

This article looks at contemporary changes in the traditional labour force hierarchy in Russian industrial enterprises. Our conclusions are based primarily on case studies conducted in several shops in two Samara enterprises connected to the military-industrial complex, and in a chemical enterprise in Kemerovo. Additional material, obtained from interviews and observation at a number of other enterprises in Samara and in Kuzbass coal enterprises, is also used. The names of the enterprises have been changed, as agreed in advance with the respondents.[1]

The labour force in enterprises has always been organised in an hierarchical manner. We define hierarchy as a complex system of social relations between various socio-professional groups, which occupy particular status positions in relation to each other, as determined by a series of indicators. (In the sociological literature there are various interpretations of the concepts 'status', 'social position' and 'status position', which we regard as being equivalent. This distinguishes our understanding of status from the classical definition, which takes into account style of life, level of education and so on.)

This chapter does not consider the status of the individual as an employee of the enterprise, which is determined by a multi-level hierarchy of status, beginning with that of the industry and its importance in the national economy, and ending with that of the individual in the micro-group. The real social position of the individual and how it changes, which may be characterised by an increase or decrease in

1 An earlier version of this chapter was published as 'Ob izmenenii statusa rabochikh na predpriyatii', *Sotsiologicheskie issledovaniya,* 11, 1994, pp. 16–29.

status, can only be considered in relation to the possible social mobility of the group to which the individual belongs.

We also ignore the social status of the group in society as a whole, and therefore focus on groups of workers within the enterprise. We would like to study status on the basis of five different dimensions:

1. Ideological — i.e. to what extent is the role of one social group or another, in this case the working class, supported by state ideology? This indicator is given priority because under the Soviet system it had a very special significance, which was reflected within the framework of the enterprise.

2. Technological — which characterises the importance of the given group in the activity of the enterprise as a whole and in the production process in particular.

3. Monetary — the features of which are:
   a) the amount earned in wages;
   b) the presence or absence of certain privileges in the production and social spheres, as supported by both official documents and informal norms of behaviour in the enterprise;
   c) the possession of shares in the enterprise (a new feature, indicating participation in the privatisation process).

4. Political — understood by us as the workers' ability to influence management strategy and the administrative decisions taken by the enterprise management. Political indicators include:
   a) the level of strike activity;
   b) the establishment of strike committees and alternative trade unions;
   c) the election of workers to the Shareholders' Council (a new characteristic, indicating participation in privatisation).

5. Social-psychological — i.e. the self evaluation of the socio-professional group in the hierarchical structure — the self-identification of the workers.

These dimensions are all obviously interconnected and, to some extent, dependent on each other. In certain conditions one dimension will acquire more importance in determining status and, correspondingly, influence changes in the others.

In accordance with such representations of status, the position of one or another professional group in the traditional hierarchy of Soviet enterprises is both technologically and socially determined. Thus the appellation 'worker' traditionally determined the rather high status of workers in the enterprise, reflecting the ideological importance of the workers' role in production. Correspondingly the status of intellectual labour was significantly less. This extended even to management, with the exception of top management and chief specialists.

We focus on the status of the socio-professional group of workers in the enterprise, and also on the changing status of individual sub-groups within it, explaining these by changes that are taking place at higher levels, external to the groups under study.

ENTERPRISES — THE CHANGING RULES OF THE GAME

Changes in the labour force hierarchy have been caused primarily by the objective changes to production that resulted from the demise of the centralised system of economic management, the breakdown in the traditional links between enterprises (including those with other republics, following the disintegration of the USSR) and the rejection of the plan as the main functional objective of the administrative system. These changes are now determining the position of various socio-professional groups in the system of production. In this respect it is already possible to speak of certain trends, which are more evident in those enterprises that are actively seeking to adapt to the changing conditions. At those enterprises where the administration remains passive, despite objective changes to the external situation, the traditional hierarchy remains; this allows for an analysis of these issues and a means of comparing several enterprises.

In our opinion the most important reasons for the changing position of various professional groups and for changes to management and production are as follows:

1. A sharp decrease in volumes of production as a result of reduced state orders, confusion in the supply system, price increases and the non-payment crisis. Given an employment policy which still aims to preserve almost all of the enterprises of the former

military-industrial complex (fear of large job cuts, preservation of jobs: for example, at one of the enterprises under study although production had fallen five times during the previous four years, employment had been cut by only nine per cent), only some of the workers in the shops are still engaged in production, while the remainder are either sent on administrative leave or employed in ancillary tasks. Such practices were widespread in the enterprises being studied. In such circumstances the availability of work is becoming something of value. Correspondingly the role of, for example, the foreman, as the distributor of work, is growing. The process of job allocation often proceeds according to the traditional aspiration for fairness, which is often understood as egalitarianism: today one person works on the press, and another sweeps up, the next day the other way around, without any reference to the workers' qualifications. The very real threat of unemployment considerably strengthens the dependence of the workers on the administration.

2. Work is no longer carried out according to the gross output plan, but to specific orders, the receipt of which, to a great extent, depends on the personal initiative of enterprise managers, which also makes the production staff directly dependent on those working in the sales and supply departments. The role of management has thus increased in general, and especially that of the senior management team. Whereas in the past the administration tended to be dependent on the workers, underpinned by the fact that they had to fulfil the plan, as controlled by central bodies, in the absence of 'the plan', enterprise management is now independent of the centre and the workers are finding themselves singularly dependent on the management — those who ensure that orders come in, who are those who give them work. The managers' functions have become more complicated, involving such people as economists, accountants, rate setters and so on, whose role has increased owing to the processes of inflation. All that previously came down from above in a purely mechanical way is now very complex, and different at each enterprise — so that there is real decentralisation. Their work has become more important. At the same time, wages are now calculated in such a way that none of the workers understands on which indicators they are based. There is now a clear tendency not to disclose information about management wage levels.

3. The breakdown of the supply and order system has not advanced the position of those involved in the production process, but rather those involved in sales, supply and marketing. In the past few years one has seen the appearance, within the framework of industrial enterprises, of sub-divisions involved in business, trying to 'make money' for the enterprise by re-selling goods which are entirely unrelated to the enterprise's own production. This means that the role of its own production is knocked from its indisputable pole position in the enterprise's activity to a minor role. As a consequence the role and status of line management has declined in comparison to the position of finance and commercial departments. Accordingly those involved in production are distanced from the administration, as they have different tasks. Line management continues to be in charge of production, while staff management concentrates on marketing and economic tasks. In parallel with the decline in the role of production in the enterprise's activity, the role of the workers engaged in production has also decreased.

4. The appearance of property relations. With the beginning of the privatisation of enterprises, managers are gradually being transformed into owners, while the workers are becoming hired labour. In spite of the fact that one of the administration's main arguments during voting for which variant of privatisation was to be chosen was that 'we must all become the enterprise's proprietors', and that the workers strongly argued for the second variant, once the privatisation process got underway the covert process of redistributing the shares within the labour collective began, concentrating them in the hands of top management.

5. Conversion. As a result of the sharp decrease in government orders for defence production many enterprises have been forced sharply to cut military production, without any possibility of conversion to civil production. An example of such 'collapse conversion' is the Samara Industrial Association (8,000 workers), which produces radio-electronic equipment for military purposes. The production of consumer goods served as a civil cover for defence production. The transition to conversion resulted in a sharp fall in military orders to the enterprise from the Russian government. In 1992 government orders accounted for only 3.4 per cent of the enterprise's total volume of production; in 1993 a further cut was

planned to 1.9 per cent. In comparison government orders accounted for 40–50 per cent of total production in 1991 and almost 80 per cent in 1990. Approximately 50 per cent of the total number of the enterprise's employees are employed in civil production, for which it is already difficult to find markets. Highly qualified workers and ITR (engineering and technical staff), who previously worked on complex military orders, are no longer needed.

All of these objective changes occurring in the enterprise could not but affect the position and status of employees belonging to different socio-professional groups. The most striking changes are the downgrading of the activity of production, at the expense of finance and commerce, the increasing power and status of management as a whole, and the growing insecurity of employment. All three of these processes tend to reduce the status of production workers. This is one of the most painful socio-psychological processes occurring in the framework of production relations within the enterprise.

STATUS CHANGES WITHIN THE WORKING CLASS

Changes are taking place not only in the status of workers as a whole, but also within the working class. With few exceptions we do not consider here the traditional groupings in terms of sex, age, qualifications and so on, but try to divide groups in other less obvious ways, but in which, in our opinion, the more apparent and painful changes are occurring.

Workers in main and 'peripheral' production

The status of any socio-professional group in an enterprise is partly a function of the importance of the group's role in the activity of the enterprise and in the production process. We have already mentioned that, with the appearance of new commercial functions in enterprise activity, the status of staff members in corresponding services has improved. As regards the workers, we observe changes to the status of main and so-called 'peripheral' production workers.

At the enterprises under investigation 'main' production had been sub-divided into elite production and elite orders, so-called 'military' production, and less prestigious 'peripheral' production, the production of consumer goods. There were also various non-productive tasks, such as construction work, work in the social and welfare apparatus, and so on, which had lower status.

Those working in all these subdivisions have the same grade, responsibilities and, therefore, should formally have equal status. However, the reality is that their status is determined by the role played by the subdivisions in the enterprise's activity at any given moment. When the most important measure was gross output, the status of the workers in the basic shops was significantly higher than that of the workers involved in the production of consumer goods. Put very simply those involved in the production of rockets always had a higher status than those involved in the production of teapots and saucepans. With the transition to market relations the situation has changed. It is often the case that shops involved in the production of consumer goods are now the only profitable shops in an enterprise and thus determine its financial capabilities. Such situations often lead to conflict when, on suddenly becoming profitable, the former non-prestigious shops and production units attempt to leave the association or to obtain some measure of independence within its framework. The role of these shops has correspondingly changed in the life of the enterprise as a whole and in the status of the workers, including, for example the allocation of higher wages in comparison with similarly qualified workers in other sections, and other privileges, such as the distribution of barter goods. This leads to a large scale redistribution of the labour force within and between enterprises, as the best qualified workers move in search of higher wages, leading in turn to changes in the age, skill and gender composition of the workforce and in the status hierarchy of different occupations and different branches of industry.

Main and auxiliary workers

A second hierarchy within the working class is related to the workers' position in production; i.e. whether they work in main or auxiliary work within one production unit. Main workers are directly involved in the production of goods, while auxiliary workers serve the production process. The latter are divided into skilled workers — servicing transport vehicles and so on, and unskilled — loaders, cleaners and so on. We, however, are interested in the differences in status between main and auxiliary workers with the same levels of qualification.

In enterprises where the administration is quickly adapting to the new conditions we observed a trend towards higher wages for qualified auxiliary workers such as mechanics and electricians. Their wages are now increasing in comparison with the main workers, who in the past always received more. By August 1993 auxiliary workers' wages at Prokat in Samara were already 10–20 per cent higher than those of the main workers. In our opinion several reasons can be put forward to explain this trend:

- The appearance of a market approach to the evaluation of labour, including the cost of training a qualified worker, depending on his speciality. 'What is a high grade press operator? Someone who has spent a year on the press, but a mechanic or an electrician has to work for 4 or 5 years to obtain the higher grading' (from an interview with a senior foreman of Shop 3 at Prokat).
- In the past, lower wages for qualified auxiliary workers were stipulated ideologically because they didn't 'drive on' the plan. The wages of the main workers, who were directly involved in fulfilling the plan, were, therefore, higher. The situation is now changing; production is falling, volumes are being cut and therefore less attention is paid to the main workers.
- Work on old machinery. As time goes by, machinery becomes increasingly worn out. As it has to be repaired, this puts more demand on the auxiliary workers who service the machines.
- The appearance of a labour market, on which demand for competent auxiliary workers is now rather high. This corresponds to the employment policy conducted by enterprise management in respect of this group of workers. At Prokat, for example, no one has been hired for two years, 'with the exception only of those carrying out auxiliary work — i.e. mechanics, electricians, welders and so on, but only those with high qualifications' (from an interview with the personnel department manager of Prokat).

In other words there is a recomposition taking place within the category of workers, breaking with the traditional hierarchy of main and auxiliary workers, and workers involved in main and peripheral production.

'Kadrovye' and reserve workers

In most departments of almost every large Soviet enterprise there was a layer of so-called '*kadrovye*' workers, who were the *de facto* enterprise elite. The principal socio-industrial characteristics of *kadrovye* workers were long industrial service, higher qualifications and professional experience and job stability (reflected in the continuity of service). To qualify as a *kadrovyi* worker it was usually sufficient to have worked for a sufficiently long period in the department, say ten to fifteen years, to have acquired appropriate skills and qualifications, to have a good disciplinary record, and to have some record of voluntary, 'social' activity. There were also quotas for various types of worker, such as women or those from the provinces.

There would often be a formal list of *kadrovye* workers, who constituted the reserve for recruitment to more senior posts, but others might be informally identified as *kadrovye*. In general, unless invited to take a post elsewhere, a *kadrovyi* worker was obliged to remain in his or her own department, and, if a Party member, would require permission from the Party committee to change jobs. The status of a *kadrovyi* worker would also be affected by that of the department and the job which he or she filled: a *kadrovyi* worker in a main production shop would have higher status than a *kadrovyi* worker in an auxiliary section. Most of the Party organisations were formed from *kadrovye* workers. They were the most socially active layer of workers. The concept of the *kadrovyi* worker was expressed in many symbolic statuses (leading workers, innovators, shock-workers and so on). They correspondingly enjoyed many privileges and occupied a high position in the hierarchy of workers in the enterprise. Once recognised as *kadrovyi* it was very unusual to lose the position, except for the most serious disciplinary offences.

Until quite recently, the military-industrial complex traditionally grabbed hold of the best engineers and scientists, but also the most highly qualified *kadrovye* workers. In conditions of permanent labour shortages, enterprises were engaged in a battle with each other for workers through the provision of various privileges. It was impossible to offer significantly higher wages as an official method, since everything, including the enterprise's wage fund, was decided above, but each enterprise would invent various kinds of incentive, trying on the one hand to formalise them, and on the other, developing a system of 'informal bargaining'. What form did this take?

Formal privileges are those which are laid down in official, more often than not internal, enterprise documents. A typical example is the 'Statement on *Kadrovye* Workers', the main purpose of which was to tie the labour force to the enterprise, where the privileges of the *kadrovye* workers were calculated on a standard basis, providing advantages in the distribution of social favours, which, to a great extent, were provided by the enterprise. However, privileges differed at each enterprise, depending on financial resources and the level of development of the social facilities.

In addition to formal, there also existed informal privileges, for example in the system of work distribution. It is well known that in piece work there are profitable and unprofitable jobs, and that wages correspondingly differ. Informally there was an order for the allocation of this work, establishing a definite queue for the receipt of profitable work. However, highly qualified *kadrovye* workers had a separate queue, which gave them priority. Whereas, for example, an ordinary worker would be allocated a profitable job once a month, the *kadrovye* worker could expect such work two or three times as often.

Other informal privileges existed such as secret quotas, Party membership, awards and promotion to public posts (a place on the presidium), which gave advantages to such workers, as members of 'the ruling class'. As a rule the stratum of '*nomenklatura*' workers, who often had a purely representative role in production, was formed out of such *kadrovye*, 'model workers'. Through such people, who were an integral part of every enterprise, the workers had a chance to exert some influence on the administration, an opportunity to 'demand their rights'. This channel of influence and layer of workers has disappeared, together with the Party committee and the old system of privileges.

The former system of informal relations is disintegrating. Now there are few privileges in the allocation of profitable work, so everyone tries to arrive early at work to ensure that they receive work for the day. The distribution of work is becoming increasingly formalised. Work itself has become something of value and *kadrovye* workers have lost their privileges and, like all other workers, are accepting any job offered to them. This is illustrated by the order in which workers are sent on often paid, but at some enterprises unpaid, leave. Each enterprise has its own queuing system for such leave, which does not provide any privileges for any category of worker. The community closely monitors the observation of social justice. Exceptions are extremely rare, when the entire collective agrees that a particular worker (depending on his or her personal qualities and exceptional family situation) should remain at work and, consequently, receive a wage. This queuing system does not affect management, who are never sent on administrative leave.

The loss of ideological support, the transition to commercial orders and the disintegration of the former system of informal relations are perceived by many workers in defence enterprises as a loss of their special status, with a corresponding loss in privileges and advantages.

A general decline in the level of complexity of work has occurred as a result of the cancellation, or at least reduction, of complex military and space-related orders. The personal craftsmanship of the worker, on which different levels of management, including the director, could personally call if necessary, has ceased to play such a significant role. The importance of highly qualified groups of *kadrovye* workers is waning. This particularly affects production workers, who are on piece-rate bonus payment systems and whose wages have fallen.

Kadrovye workers in the defence complex have experienced a particularly sharp fall in status. The psychology of *kadrovye* workers, who were long accustomed to doing one thing — meeting 'orders of state importance' — greatly influences how they perceive the transition to market relations. Their dependence on commercial orders and the lack of stability at work provides no internal satisfaction nor allows them any self-respect at work.

In contrast there was a whole army of 'reserve' peripheral workers, which in quantity considerably exceeded the genuine needs of the enterprise. In foreign literature peripheral is understood as those categories of workers who do not have a permanent contract and thus can be painlessly dismissed by the enterprise. They do not work on main production, but are engaged on auxiliary work when necessary. It was the practice in Soviet enterprises to maintain on the staff so-called 'reserve' workers, who had few, if any qualifications, and who were used in auxiliary work as manual labour. Those who were recorded as being involved in production, but had virtually nothing to do there, were also included in this category.

In the Western literature this labour 'reserve' is generally regarded as a purely surplus labour force, maintained for the aggrandisement of the enterprise director, or as a reserve to allow for the 'storming' that was regularly required to make the plan at the end of the planning period, indicating the pure irrationality of the planning system. However, the bulk of this reserve had a more important function. Reserve workers were not idle, but nor were they much involved in basic production, even at times of storming, for which they were barely qualified. In fact they were constantly involved in large quantities of auxiliary work: agricultural, building, street cleaning and so on, which the enterprise was responsible for carrying out, usually under the direction of local Party bodies, with its own resources. The standard practice was to redeploy production workers to do this work, but this was obviously very wasteful, and disruptive of production, so enterprise management, and particularly section chiefs, always tried to allow themselves the luxury of having a reserve labour force to avoid having to redeploy any of the main body of workers to meet such demands. The existence of government orders, which guaranteed a constant volume of production, provided the enterprise management with the opportunity to plan for a reserve labour force.

In the past this category of workers caused the most trouble through high labour turnover, drunkenness, theft and so on. However, their surplus number was consciously used by the enterprise management in many ways, for example as a means of social control over the other workers: instead of dismissing workers, they could be transferred to less skilled, and thus less well-paid, work on a temporary or a permanent basis. This category could also be used for more beneficent, paternalistic, purposes, providing continued employment for pensioners, or for those unable to work in more demanding jobs for reasons of ill-health or industrial injury.

Under the new conditions the enterprise obviously first rid itself of this group of workers, and following the first wave of redundancies the category of reserve workers had almost disappeared. It is no longer advantageous for an enterprise to maintain surplus numbers, while there is almost no need to divert workers to auxiliary work, for which the enterprise is no longer responsible. There is also no need to use this group as a means of social control, as this role is successfully carried out by the threat of job cuts and future unemployment.

This does not mean, however, that there is no army of reserve workers maintained by the enterprise. However, its structure and its function has changed radically. Whereas in the past the enterprise could plan its needs for production workers with reasonable certainty, in today's conditions of the collapse of production, instability of supply and of finance, and an uncertain future, each enterprise is concerned with holding on to its skilled workers through slack times, for fear that when conditions improve it will be impossible to recruit and train a new labour force. The reserve army of labour now contains both highly qualified and specialist workers, who are not needed to do their jobs at the enterprise at any given moment and therefore work temporarily on other jobs, alongside unqualified workers such as loaders, crate makers and cleaners, who work in both temporary and permanent positions.

The workers — increasing uniformity

The impact of all these changes in the internal composition of the labour force has been a significant homogenisation of the labour force, as the privileges of the *kadrovye* and core production workers have been eroded, while the reserve of unskilled workers has been displaced. We can sum these processes up as follows:

- From 1989 the most efficient *kadvrovye* workers had already left for co-operatives and other non-state structures, where wages were three times higher than those of similarly qualified workers at state enterprises. Although since 1991 the trend has been to return to the public sector, as a result of the relative levelling in wages and the greater stability of employment in state enterprises, the result has been that the layer of *kadrovye* workers at enterprises has become narrower. On the one hand, this has increased the status (personal worth) of those who remained at the enterprise, who have worked to strengthen their monopoly and indispensability. On the other hand, as the number of military orders has fallen, so too has the importance of the work of *kadrovye* workers in the enterprise. As a result of this, and of the fall in their numbers at enterprises, they have lost some of their influence, and their position in negotiations with the administration has weakened.
- There has been a general trend towards less complicated work resulting from the decline in military and space-related orders, leading to less demand for highly qualified workers.
- The trend towards the commercialisation of services and the consumer sphere is leading to the disappearance of privileges in distribution (including the distribution of favourable work and

orders), and the replacement of the policy of the enterprise granting social benefits to the workers, with a policy of differentiation of pay and security of employment for different categories of workers.

- By not hiring any new workers at the enterprise, or by limiting the hiring to certain categories of highly-qualified workers, there is no influx of young people and fewer workers aged 30 and under. On the other hand, young people, as the most active group of workers, are most likely to leave the factory.
- The dismissal of reserve workers, drunkards, absentees and those who breach labour discipline has resulted in the disappearance of a whole category in the structure of the socio-professional group of workers. This also has purely psychological consequences, in so far as the *kadrovye* workers were looked upon especially favourably against the background of this group. The traditional differentiation among workers gave *kadrovye* workers certain privileges in comparison with the others. The scheduled reduction in the numbers of pensioners and workers with few qualifications is also leading to the disappearance of the special position of *kadrovye* workers.

It therefore seems reasonable to talk of a trend towards an increasingly uniform group of industrial workers, with a reduced role for the highest and the lowest skilled, the removal of the oldest and the failure to recruit young workers. However, it is also worth noting an apparent trend towards a new differentiation between basic production and auxiliary workers, through the gradual strengthening of the latter.

Female workers — the outsiders of structural changes

These processes of homogenisation of the labour force have had a particularly severe impact on women workers, who have suffered most from the production cuts in industrial enterprises. Women have been hit much harder than men by the process of redundancy, particularly from the office jobs which were hardest hit in the first wave of redundancies, but also in the loss of unskilled auxiliary jobs carried out by those of pension age, who are, of course, not recognised as unemployed once they have been induced to retire. However, there has also been a more or less dramatic process of restructuring of the gender division of labour as a part of the recomposition of the labour force. In particular, in the course of our research we have been able to observe a marked tendency for men to take over the better paid occupations, and to move in to the more prosperous enterprises, while women have been left behind, or have moved in the opposite direction.

At Prokat, which was relatively prosperous and where the average wage was rather high, the number of women working in production was cut. The administration was clearly oriented to giving priority to male workers, although this is not mentioned in any factory document, including the draft order on job cuts. 'Women who come to the personnel department for work are immediately rejected without a look at the factory's books.' There is only one argument: 'Work in an engineering enterprise is not for women; they're either on maternity leave, or on sick leave, or on some other type of leave' (from an interview with the executive personnel director at Prokat). No large cuts have yet been made, but gradually, together with pensioners and reserve workers, women are being removed from production. This is partly related to the fact that a significant proportion are engaged in unskilled jobs. However, even those who remain at the enterprise are being dislodged from prestigious highly paid jobs to low paid work, through a redistribution of the labour force within the enterprise. This process of redistribution also occurs between factories. For example, when production was cut at a neighbouring enterprise, some of the highest qualified female press operators were transferred by agreement between the administrations of the two enterprises to analogous work at Prokat. Soon afterwards some presses were, in turn, closed down at this enterprise and the women transferred to the post of cleaners and cloakroom attendants. Many qualified female workers have been downgraded to the grade of 'junior service personnel' (MOP). According to experts who work in shop services directly connected with the personnel policy of the enterprise, there is a trend towards the gradual transition of the former 'female' or 'mixed' occupations to purely 'male' jobs. For example, in shop 3 of Prokat there are almost no women left among the press operators ('a mixed occupation') and jobs in two more traditionally 'female' occupations — annealing and crane operating — are gradually being transferred to men.

At another enterprise — Kol'tso — the picture is the opposite. The enterprise is in a very difficult financial position and wages are among the lowest in town. The number of women working on machine tool production has increased. Whereas in 1990 women accounted for half of all production workers, by 1993 they had increased to 51.5 per cent. Among auxiliary workers the percentage of women was 54 per cent in 1990, and in 1993 57.4 per cent. Among apprentices women accounted for 39.5 per cent in 1990 and 54.3 per cent in 1993. Owing to bad working conditions and low wages men, who had previously formed the backbone of the workforce, are leaving the enterprise and their places are being taken by women.

The general trend is clear — as a result of production cuts women are being dislodged from prestigious highly-paid jobs, which are being taken by men. In contrast men are leaving jobs which are becoming unprofitable and these places are being filled by women.

THE CHANGING POSITION OF WORKERS IN RELATION TO OTHER CATEGORIES OF EMPLOYEES

Alongside changes in the composition of the socio-professional group of workers, it is possible, in our opinion, to talk of an overall decline in the status of workers, in comparison with other categories of employees in the enterprise. This concerns the basic groups at the enterprise — the workers and management. How is this displayed?

Ideology — old and new

An important role is played by the change in the socio-ideological aspect of status, as it appears in the enterprise as a reflection of the re-evaluation of the position of workers in society as a whole. Much of what was said about the hegemony of the working class in the past was propaganda and ritual. At the same time this cannot but have had an effect on the consciousness and self-consciousness of the workers. This moment of self-identification may provide an internal incentive to work, or on the other hand, may be the cause of a fall in discipline in production, through the disappearance of the official ideology of worker-hegemony. State ideology influences the self-identification of various social groups and acts as a lever in the determination of their status (as well as of their perception of their status).

At present in the public consciousness the status of the worker is changing, as a new ideology is created. What was formerly presented by official ideology, and what actually existed in real life doubtless differed fundamentally. However, these ideological clichés to a certain extent influenced the workers' consciousness, their feelings of faith in the future. The worker really believed himself to be an owner. Although he understood completely that, unlike, for example, the general director, he could not control everything, he was still a co-owner of the enterprise. Among the workers — especially those with long service — existed a stereotype: the factory is my life, where I do everything for my family, my flat, my car and my dacha. The factory helps to arrange weddings and military service. The factory ensures medical assistance, holiday vouchers and will even bury you. Almost all vital problems can be solved 'without leaving one's machine'. These ideologies were therefore apparent in the real, daily life of the industrial enterprise worker.

It cannot be said, however, that ideology has, in itself, disappeared from the enterprise. From the old stereotypes ('The workers are the owners of production', and, 'The working class is hegemonic') has evolved over the last 4–5 years the new slogan — 'We must become the owners of the enterprise'. However, new ideologies have not in any way been reflected in the real life of the workers. Although they possess a small number of enterprise shares, these have yet to pay out any significant amount of money in dividends and the workers have little hope of them doing so, at least in the foreseeable future. The reality is low wages, further reductions, and a growing gap between worker and management wages. From this derives the feeling of hopelessness and pessimism. New ideologies, therefore, 'don't work'.

The status of workers in production was also supported by the fact that demand for what was produced was guaranteed. Now that there is over-production this status is falling, as if in direct dependence on the filling of factory warehouses with products for which there is no demand. Because products lie in the warehouse, and no one needs them, the worker begins to sense that he or she is not needed and that his or her work is senseless. Moreover this gives a clear understanding of the inevitability of production cuts and subsequent job cuts. Under the new conditions the worker feels the loss of stability in his existence, to which he had become accustomed in previous years. In this sense it is possible to say that the Russian worker has already met the problems raised by the western models of the market:

when the worker's employment depends on the needs of production and the requirements of the market, his job is always in danger. The greatest threat to the worker undoubtedly lies in the ever-present possibilities of unemployment. (Schneider, E.V., *Industrial Society*, 2nd ed., McGraw-Hill, New York, 1969, pp. 221–3.)

Privatisation — the struggle for status

As practice has shown, the transition of the enterprise from state ownership to a share-holding company is usually accompanied by an increase in the differentiation between ITR and management, on the one hand, and the workers on the other. At the Plastmass factory in Kemerovo, for example, which was a pioneer of privatisation, in October 1992 the workers' salary was R19,703, while the ITR made R51,314: a coefficient of 3 was applied to ITR (on one unit of workers' salary), while chief specialists received a coefficient of 5. Another example concerns the Kol'tso joint-stock company in Samara, where in April 1993 (on the eve of privatisation) the average wage of production workers was R38,600, of chiefs and ITR R29,600 and of auxiliary workers R19,792, which represented a hierarchy characteristic of the traditional Soviet enterprise. According to the chairman of the enterprise's independent trade union, by May, i.e. only one month after privatisation, the wages of ITR had sharply increased in comparison with the workers' wages. The enterprise Prokat was privatised in Autumn 1992: in July 1993 the average salary was R92,500 for management, R85,000 for specialists and R60,300 for workers.

From the start of privatisation a distinct tendency has been observed of growing differences between the incomes of various categories of workers (we are not taking into account the possibility of shadow incomes because they are difficult to assess). In contrast to management, the workers' wages and real income are almost identical, as the possession of a small number of shares provides no real increase in income by dividend payments in comparison with wages.

The enterprise management become the proprietors and their role in the company increases. Correspondingly the workers' dependence on the administration increases even further, as the former now have a controlling stake in the company.

The differentiation between shareholders will continue to increase in the future. It is possible that the income to be received by a shareholder at the end of the year as a dividend payment could exceed his real wage for the whole of the previous year. A typical example is the situation with the management of the Plastmass factory. At the end of the year it received a 100 per cent dividend pay-out on its shares. If we take into account the inequality of share distribution (general director – 10 per cent, management board – 10 per cent, other levels of management, including shop chiefs – 15 per cent, remainder (workers) 65 per cent), it becomes obvious that some senior managers' income in respect of their shares could significantly exceed their officially declared wages.

New indicators of status, which are directly related to privatisation, have recently appeared. First of all there is participation in privatisation, which presupposes the participation of the workers in such forms as the choice of privatisation variant, subscription to shares and representation on the Shareholders' Council.

At all the enterprises studied, under pressure from the administration, or thanks to their persuasion, the second variant of privatisation was chosen, giving 51 per cent of shares to the labour collective, which protects the management from attempts being made by outsiders to attempt to take control, as is possible under the first variant, if a significant quantity of shares are sold at auction.

Once the choice of variant has been made the labour collective begins to subscribe to the shares. Different trends are discernible at this stage. For example, at Prokat some of the old ideology was preserved, and such factors as the length of service at the enterprise were taken into account in the allocation of shares, although senior management received additional privileges through the application of special coefficients, of between two and five, covering a total of 52 people.

Length of service was not taken into account at Plastmass. Shares were allocated in proportion to wages, which for management and ITR were three to five times higher than workers.

At Kol'tso the levelling principle was applied to the allocation of shares. However, the administration, being afraid that the labour collective would not be in a position to buy up all of the shares on offer to them, enlisted the financial support of a 'commercial structure', which bought up rather a large number of shares. A few months after the privatisation of the enterprise the management of this commercial structure became a part of the enterprise's management team.

As a result of the subscription campaign at those enterprises where a levelling principle of share distribution to the workers was applied there are now many 'small' shareholders (there are about 20,000 workers at these factories). For example, at Kol'tso the maximum number of shares is 14. At Prokat most workers have bought only the number of shares that could be bought with vouchers and have not paid anything more. This has amounted, on average, to between 10 and 20 shares. Our interviews show that one reason why workers subscribe for shares is the fear that those who did not sign up for shares would be the first to be dismissed.

It is important to note that almost immediately following the share subscription the administration in all of these enterprises adopted a policy of redistribution of shares and concentration of a controlling interest in their hands. The distribution of shares in the enterprise thus sets up a new hierarchy of status, in some ways more complex and different to that which traditionally existed in Soviet enterprises.

Similar variations can be observed in the tactics used by the administration in defining the structure of the Shareholders' Council. At Prokat the administration openly recommended during the election of representatives to the Shareholders' Council, that the workers should not participate. In an internal enterprise document entitled 'Temporary rules on the transfer of (voting) shares to the trust of plenipotentiary representatives of the collective', it was recommended that 'the shareholders in large structural divisions entrust the management of their shares to members of the enterprise administration'. As a result there is not one worker among the 12 members of the Shareholders' Council. The management of Plastmass, sensing the increase in discontent among the workers, allocated three places to workers, to be elected from the shops where 'those who breached the peace' worked. As a result the initiators of most conflicts in these shops were elected to the Shareholders' Council, where they are in the minority and, as such, in no position to influence its policies. They are now constantly have to justify themselves to their colleagues for not being able to defend their interests. Their authority in the eyes of the workers has fallen sharply and the general opinion is that 'management has bought them off'. The leaders of the fledgling workers' organisation were neutralised and the administration once again controls the situation at the enterprise. At Kol'tso several workers have been allowed onto the Shareholders' Council, under pressure from the independent trade union, but they have no real influence on the policies conducted.

On the basis of what has been said we may conclude that a new form of status is appearing. This is the relation to property, a measure of the position and role of socio-professional groups in the process of privatisation. New hierarchies are taking shape and new relations are beginning to appear between new subjects: the hired workers, the proprietors, and management: those that for decades existed as protogroups. Thanks to privatisation they are acquiring legal rights to property, to manage and to sell their labour power. The structure of the enterprise and the structure of the Shareholders' Council are not one and the same. The management determines the policy and fate of the enterprise, apparently less dependent on the labour collective and more dependent on the owners, who typically give preference to commerce, as a more profitable occupation than production, and are quite ready to insist on the closure of an enterprise for reasons of financial expediency. There are almost no workers on the Shareholders' Council. Their influence over management has fallen, even in comparison with former times, when STKs and trade union committees (self-management organisations, ideologically involved in production) existed. These bodies are not included in the structure of the joint-stock company and accordingly have no influence supported by law.

Radical changes to the position of enterprises and also to the role and position of workers at enterprises has led to the loss of the workers' traditional basis of self identification. Privatisation is now creating a basis for self-identification, as the owner of the enterprise. However, our observations have shown that in the privatisation process the different levels of management have been able to preserve and to increase their status by acquiring property, while the workers have obtained no significant share of property, nor any real opportunity to participate in the running of the joint-stock company. The problem of preserving their status in the course of privatisation for the workers has been transformed not into a problem of property, as is the case for the managers, but one of preserving their jobs. This depends on the strategy employed by the joint-stock company and the extent to which the workers are able to influence management decisions, i.e. primarily on the political component of status.

SOME NEW TRENDS

The indices of the political component of status

Evidence of real change to the status of workers is provided by the strengthening of their political activity, as apparent in the growth in the number of strikes and the establishment of new workers' organisations. Nevertheless it is worth noting that such a trend was observed only in coal industry enterprises. No such trend was apparent in the enterprises mentioned above. The existence at coal industry enterprises of the independent miners' union (NPG) forces management to take account of the problems troubling the workers. Whereas previously it was almost impossible to gain access to management, the latter is now compelled to sit down with the trade union leaders at the negotiation table, which testifies to a reverse trend, i.e. an increase in the role of the workers. Such a position, however, is not typical of other branches of industry, nor even in the coal mining industry. Of the ten coal enterprises included in our research project, the alternative trade union exists at only one.

Strikes — testimony to the realisation of falling status

Money has played a definite and increasingly significant role in the weakening of the ideological aspect of status. It is possible, therefore, that the reaction of workers to a decline in their status is displayed in conflict over wages. Perceptions of changes in the level of wages are not based only on real changes, but are also significantly distorted. Sometimes workers talk of wage cuts which never actually occur. This occurred in two conflicts at the Bratchenko mine in the Kuzbass. In the first case, the workers claimed that wages at the mine had fallen in comparison with others. The director responded with objective statistics, which showed that not only had wages not fallen, they were in fact an average of 40 per cent higher than at other enterprises. In another case there was a dispute between the director and one of the sections, in which the workers were indignant that salaries were too high in the offices. It ended when the director jumped out in front of one of the most irrepressible workers and shouted: 'If we find one such case, you punch me, if we don't, I punch you'. They went to the accounts department to compare the wages of workers and those who worked in offices (in this case no comparison was made of the wages of workers and chief specialists, but rather of workers and administrative department staff, accountants, wage department staff and so on). The result was that no such cases were found. Nevertheless it is widely held in mining circles that office staff receive considerably higher wages than underground workers.

Such displacements of conflict into demands for wage increases occur regularly under the conditions of the market transformation of the Russian economy and are widespread. In our opinion conflicts in Russian enterprises testify to the workers' lack of consciousness of the real causes of the fall in their status. The spontaneous bursts of discontent, the many conflicts about wages, as a result of which it is discovered that the wages of the ITR and management do not greatly differ from those of the workers, do not leave the workers satisfied. Discontent remains among the workers, as does the feeling that they are being deceived by management. It appears that the workers are trying to control the traditional financial indicators of status (wages), not yet understanding that new characteristics are acquiring much greater significance. The vague sensation of deceit and hopelessness leads to suspicion and an openly hostile attitude on the part of the workers to all types of proposed reforms issuing from the administration. Wages change, and may even increase in some cases. The workers, however, sense the fall in their status, even if it is not evident in wages. They want to compensate the loss in status through their wages, seeing it as a traditional indicator of status.

To be fair, it should be noted that the period of December 1993–March 1994 was characterised by an increase in strike activity at the enterprises under study. The reason in all cases was delay in the payment of wages. In one enterprise this led to the director being forced to resign, at another to a court case over the breaking of one of the terms of the collective agreement concerning the period within which wages should be paid. In both cases wages, which were two months overdue, were paid immediately. In these disputes no demands for wage increases, nor any political demands, were put forward. On the contrary, the workers rejected all attempts to divert the issue politically.

Irrespective of wage levels, the workers still feel the fall in their status and consequently that the ITR and enterprise management are better integrated in the new conditions and have better opportunities to receive income from shares, hidden incomes and so on, from which the workers are deprived. Thus the further down the road to privatisation, and the more involved the group is in privatisation, the less important are wages, in the narrowest sense of the word, as an indicator of status. At the Plastmass factory, for example, it is evident that although managerial wages are relatively low, a more significant amount is received in the form of dividends, owing to the concentration of shares in the hands of the administration.

CONCLUSIONS

Despite contradictory trends, which express a combination of the weakening and even disappearance of some and the strengthening of other indicators of status, we believe it correct to talk of the falling status of workers as a whole. This also explains the fact that increased strike activity of the workers and the appearance of alternative trade unions, although it increases their influence on the decisions taken by the administration, merely represents the necessary reaction of the workers to the weakening of the above mentioned indicators of status. The increase in their political and trade union activity cannot compensate for the loss of those socio-economic guarantees which were previously provided by the government. By the whole artificial process of creating the status of the worker, official ideology guaranteed a minimum for all. The government now refuses to fulfil the guarantees it previously gave: the national wealth is being redistributed, which is not to the workers' advantage and thus their situation is worsening. Under such conditions the workers are forced to strengthen their politically formed status to prevent it from falling sharply. In so far as new trade unions only exist at very few enterprises, the increase in political activity among the workers may only be considered as an embryonic trend.

The changing status of workers is directly connected to the changing status of labour within society, to its value in the public consciousness. The status of labour is changing: from a perception of it as the sphere of the self-realisation of the vital powers of the person, to labour as a commodity. The social value of labour, as set by official ideology ('Work makes man beautiful and glorious!', 'Glory to Labour' and so on), is being replaced by a new ideology — which does not even mention labour and for which the most valuable quality is the skill to make money ('We'll turn your vouchers into gold', 'Bet on the leader!', 'Play and win!'). The value of intense daily labour is being replaced by the values of a period of primitive accumulation of capital, the perception of life as a lottery, enabling a person, if lucky, to become a millionaire in a few hours (a television advert showing how a tramp finds a winning ticket and is instantly transformed in to a smartly dressed person with the keys to a new car) and is beginning to be shaped into the new ideology of 'Russian business'.

During the period of CPSU domination, when the status of the working class was ideologically defined, all laws and directives were subordinated to the prevailing ideology to give the widest rights to the workers. (In essence these laws were the 'most progressive in the world', the only qualification being that the workers could not use them without management sanction. Attempts by the new trade unions to use their legal rights have led to attempts by both legislative and executive bodies to change existing labour legislation, having removed from it the formally established rights of the workers: this is further evidence of the state's approach to the rights of hired labour.) Ideological influence also had an effect on determining the workers' level of wages. As the former ideology has disappeared, so too have the status privileges it determined, including the monetary privileges expressed in wage levels. The new ideology is derived from the real situation and leads to a gradual legitimisation of informal (including shadow) relations and the status indicators together with the hierarchy inherent in them.

The domination of working class ideology meant the domination of the CPSU, as the bearer of this ideology. Politically the working class was suppressed. Only one side of activity — industrial, was encouraged, and only to a certain degree, to ensure that plans were filled and bonuses and awards received, but no more. Now there is no state ideology of the working class. A new ideology is beginning to form, determined by the economic and social conditions of the workers' lives and work. The workers are beginning to be aware of their interests, as distinct from the interests of the enterprise management. Evidence of this is provided by the fact that demands that wages be paid on time are addressed exclusively to the management of the enterprise. Outside coal mining, attempts by management to re-address these demands to the government or references to the general payment crisis have not been successful. This situation differs significantly from the situation just one year previously, when, as a result of a spontaneous strike at any enterprise, both the workers and the administration would go amicably side by side to their local 'White House' to demand solutions to their problems 'from them'. An awareness of trade unionism is also gradually forming, but so far only apparent in the activity of enterprise trade union committees. Many attempts have been made by numerous political organisations to bring elements of party consciousness to the work environment. However, at this stage the workers are unreceptive to the idea of creating a workers' party.

At the same time conflicts are of an open and mass nature, as individuals turn to mass action. There is, therefore, a need for the creation of workers' organisations which are capable of expressing collective demands. The ideology of the Soviet state never extended to the individual; it covered only classes and social groups. The workers always confronted the social system, which they didn't like, one-to-one, so that they solved problems that arose individually, moving from one place of work to another within the same system. Labour turnover at enterprises was high and reflected the level of dissatisfaction of the workers. Production cuts and subsequent job cuts, i.e. the threat of unemployment, deprive the workers of the opportunity to solve labour conflicts in the traditional individual manner. There is nowhere to go. Work as such, and consequently the preservation of jobs at a given enterprise, becomes a new value. The result is that the accumulated discontent of individuals begins to form a collective consciousness, which demands expression in collective action and either the restructuring of the ideology of the official trade unions or the creation of alternative structures to official organisations, such as the strike committees and new trade unions, although it has to be acknowledged that this tendency is only in its infancy.

6. Gender Differentiation and Industrial Relations

Galina Monousova

THE ORIGINS OF THE RESEARCH

The social and labour policy of enterprise management is in many respects determined by macroeconomic factors. However, equally important, alongside these external factors, are the social situation within the enterprise and the particular patterns of behaviour of the employees, which may be conditioned by a number of different factors, including the social characteristics of the employees. One can distinguish various groups of employees working in a particular enterprise by such factors as sex, age, qualifications, education and length of service, and analyse the ways in which the behaviour of the workers and the employment policy of management are influenced by such factors, trying to discover to what extent management has a conscious policy of forming a labour collective with particular qualitative characteristics. Correspondingly, one can analyse the extent to which the social characteristics of the workers are reflected in the development of labour relations in the enterprise. The point is to try to identify various models of the formation of uninstitutionalised labour relations and the mechanisms of their appearance in labour collectives with different social characteristics.

The main problem addressed in this chapter is that of the influence of gender on the pattern and development of industrial relations in Russian industrial enterprises. This is not by any means a simple issue. While Western sociologists, informed by feminism, believe that gender is one of the most fundamental determinants of patterns of social relations, Soviet sociology, under the domination of Marxism-Leninism, denied the independent influence of gender as a social factor, although it rested on a firm belief in natural psychological and emotional differences between men and women, that suited them for different jobs and different social roles. The scientific problem is that there tends to be a strict gender division of labour within and between Russian enterprises, so that gender differences coincide with a range of other social, demographic and technological characteristics of the labour force, the job and the working conditions. This means that it is not immediately obvious that behavioural differences between different groups of workers can be attributed to their gender difference, since men and women might behave in similar ways in the same situation. At one level it may be possible to explain behavioural differences in terms of specific characteristics of the job and the worker, regardless of gender. But at another level, gender may prove to be the decisive factor.

This chapter tries to address these issues on the basis of case studies of four enterprises which include both those with a predominantly female labour force and those with a mixed male and female labour force, in which conflicts have arisen related to the different attitudes of management to male and female labour. In three the action of female workers has gone as far as the threat of a strike, the threat even being realised in one case. The question logically arose of investigating and comparing the mechanisms of labour relations in enterprises with a female labour force with those in enterprises with a mixed labour force. One of the tasks of the research is to try to determine and explain the problem of women's employment in industrial production.

METHOD OF ANALYSIS

The analysis presented here is based on materials drawn from case studies of four Moscow enterprises, one of which was studied as part of a project financed by the Russian-American Fund. In each enterprise conflict or potential conflict situations have been identified in which, to a greater or lesser extent, there have been reactions, or even no reactions at all, from various groups of workers to changes in the labour policy of the administration in relation to the workers. An attempt is then made to analyse the factors which determine the corresponding behaviour of the workers and actions of the enterprise administration.

Particular attention is paid to the question of whether gender has an influence on the labour behaviour of the collective and correspondingly on labour relations within the enterprise. To answer this question a comparative analysis of patterns of labour relations in enterprises dominated by women and enterprises which employ men and women equally is carried out, in order to determine whether the different enterprises display particular characteristics. If they do, then the question arises of how and why they arise.

The research is constructed on the basis of material gathered through interviews with managers at various levels and with workers, as well as through questionnaire surveys of workers. The comparison of labour relations is carried out at two levels: at the level of the personnel policy of higher management, and at the level of workplace labour relations. Above all we are trying to characterise the situation. In the course of the analysis the following questions were posed. What are the social characteristics of the workers employed in the various factories? What are the particular features of the employment policy conducted by management in those factories? How are the relations between the workers and their immediate managers in the workplace constructed? What type of labour behaviour (collective/individual; inclined to conflict/oriented to compromise; independent/paternalistic) prevails among the workers in each type of factory?

SITUATION ONE: THE ENTERPRISE PIZZA

Principal socio-economic characteristics of the enterprise

The research in the food combine Pizza was carried out at the beginning of 1994, just after Pizza had been privatised as an open joint-stock company in December 1993. Eighty per cent of the employees of Pizza are women. The average number of employees during 1993, according to the records, was 2823, of whom 2488 were workers. In the Soviet period this enterprise belonged to group B, enterprises which did not enjoy priority in state financing and support, with lower wages than at the priority group A enterprises. This historical fact is one of the reasons for the predominance of female labour in the enterprise. However, today the financial and economic position of the enterprise is very secure. There has been a growth in the volume of production by more than 50 per cent in 1993 over 1992, and an increase in the number of employees by 15 per cent in 1993 over 1992. According to experts, the financial condition of the joint-stock company is sound and profitable, distinguishing it from the condition of the Russian economy as a whole. The level of pay is above the average for the branch of industry, the lowest wage in December 1993 amounting to 60,000 roubles. The high demand for its products is kept up by barter relations, which allows the administration to sell groceries and consumer goods to the employees of the combine at prices which are significantly lower than those in retail outlets.

Although it is predominantly a women's enterprise, all the senior managers are men, with women found only in the accounts department. The average age of the managerial employees is 40–45. There have been substantial changes in managerial work, including the extensive computerisation of office work and the recruitment of a number of young male specialists, but there has so far been no structural change in the management apparatus, and no redundancy among the white-collar workers, although it is clear that changes will come in future.

The research was carried out in the four main production shops, varying in number from 174 to 451 employees. Three of the four shops have male shop chiefs, aged between 40 and 45, while the fourth has a woman chief, aged about 60, who has been in post since 1986 and is now the president of the trade union committee of the enterprise. Each shop chief has two deputies, one of whom is responsible for personnel matters, the other for technical matters. The shop chief is responsible for all matters that arise, but above all for the fulfilment of the plan. Beneath the shop chief are the foremen, who act as section heads, and brigadiers. Practically all the foremen and the specialists in the shop office are female, and their status is closer to the workers than to shop management. The foremen are in regular contact with the workers, frequently stand in for women workers when they are absent, and in general enjoy the workers' confidence. Their main task is to allocate work to the brigades for each shift. The character and working conditions of each of the shops is almost identical, although they differ in the operations that they carry out.

One brigade works on each stage of the production process, with payment in accordance with the final product. Each brigade is set its plan tasks to fulfil, but the shop chief assigns bonuses to the workers individually, on the basis of the profits earned by the factory. There is a system of penalties and fines which have been agreed with the trade union and which are incorporated in the collective agreement.

In the main operations manual-mechanised labour is predominant. In all shops the work takes place on production lines. The labour is rigidly interconnected. The work is very monotonous and intensive, with difficult working conditions, often exceeding the legal limits. In all shops the basic workers are women on grades three or four, while the auxiliary workers, mainly involved in carrying and loading, are mainly men on grades two and three, many of whom give the impression of not being in the best mental health. Each shop has its own repair brigade (on average 40–50 people), which repairs and maintains the equipment. These are exclusively men with high grades (five or six). Since the equipment is old and often breaks down, the basic workers are very dependent on the repair service.

The one exception to this general scheme is one automated section of one shop. One year ago an automatic production line, imported from West Germany, was installed here. The age and gender profile of the workers here is significantly different from that in the other sections in the factory. The shop chief and shift foremen are all men, with half the production workers being men and half women, but the women operators here are on grade four, while the men are on grade five. The fitters are exclusively men on grades five and six. In this section 40 per cent of the workers are under 25 years old.

In general one can conclude that the women workers are predominantly engaged in the more monotonous, less skilled work, in difficult working conditions, which often exceed the health and safety norms. Men, on the other hand, dominate the more skilled jobs and are graded higher than the women. Even when a man and a woman work on the same grade, the shop chief tries to ensure that the man is paid more (each grade has three pay levels, with the shop chief having the right to change the payment level within the grade). Women see this situation as perfectly normal, and it is not the source of any real discontent. Indeed, the women workers say explicitly that men should be paid more. Their dissatisfaction with the level of their pay is not connected in any way with a comparison with the pay of the men.

Shop-floor relations and the intensification of labour

The main emphasis of management policy has been on increasing profits by increasing sales of the products and increasing production by increasing the intensity of the labour of the workers. The social and labour policy of the administration of the combine is clearly stated, and consists of the following: First and foremost we should mention the high level of pay, supported by the management, and the extensive social privileges, the importance of which is remarked on by all the workers. However, alongside this the combine is distinguished by a very high intensity of labour and a constant tendency to increase the length of the working week. The factory works a two shift system, but once or twice a week it will work a night shift, and three of the four Saturdays a month are working days. The normal working week is around 46 hours. One should also note the high degree of authoritarianism of the director — the workers call him 'Papa' — which is felt at all points in the hierarchical chain of management, including in the workplace.

Against the background of the high intensity of labour, the enterprise administration decided at the end of 1993 to change the system of sending workers on their regular vacations from the following year, compulsorily splitting the time into two halves, allowing the workers to take half in the summer, and the other half at some other time of the year, according to a schedule agreed with their shop chief. The administration explained the reasons for this in terms of technological constraints and the need to earn increased profits. The response to a question regarding the legality of this course of action was that the enterprise had been privatised: in its statutes it is laid down that the basic aim of the joint-stock company is to earn profits.[1]

The interesting point for our investigation is the reaction of the workers to what was a clear violation of their rights on the part of management. The behaviour of the workers, their reaction to this situation, provides definite evidence of a particular pattern of labour relations that exists within the enterprise. We will attempt to analyse the behaviour of the workers in this situation. First we observed that the workers behaved in various ways, although according to their responses to the questionnaire survey they had virtually identical attitudes to the situation that had arisen.

One can define three categories of workers, working in various positions in the enterprise. The management of the enterprise estab-

1 It is by no means uncommon for the management of privatised companies to violate the Labour Code, and to justify this violation with the argument that the law does not apply to private companies, reflecting a common view of the law as a bureaucratic impediment to entrepreneurial freedom, rather than as the basis of a market economy.

lishes different relationships with each of these different categories. It turns out that this factor to a considerable extent determines the behaviour of the workers.

In looking at labour relations on the shop-floor, we begin with the automated section. Those working here have a fairly autonomous position. The impact of the authoritarianism of the director is significantly less here, since in this work the relations between people are much less significant than the work of the machinery. The chief of this section feels more independent than the heads of all the other sections. In an interview he was very frank in speaking of the policy of management:

> A lot depends on the work of our section. We are at the beginning of the technological process. I do not know what our director is thinking about introducing a new vacation schedule. It is useless saying anything to him, because he will not listen. I think that we will work something out for ourselves, we are in a special position because of our equipment, with it on a continuous cycle.

The repairmen in the production departments are in a specially privileged position, because the work of the equipment depends on them. The chiefs of the sections and the women workers both experience this dependence. This category of workers feels very self-confident. Their earnings are higher than those of the women production workers. The new vacation schedule does not concern them. Their confidence is to be explained primarily by the fact that their high qualifications mean that they can always expect to find work elsewhere. Management is anxious about this situation and has to take the wishes of this category of worker into account. As one repairman said:

> I will go on vacation when I want to. If I leave, with whom will they [meaning the management of the factory] replace me? The old equipment here depends a lot on me.

The shop chief said,

> There is a brigade of repairmen in the shop. Of course we are very dependent on them. The women workers often complain that nobody comes when they call. Their earnings do not depend much on the work of the basic equipment.

One of the chiefs of the combine said,

> The new vacation schedule will not affect the repairmen. They will carry out preventative maintenance, and then go on vacation. We are relaxed about the behaviour of this category of workers. They are highly skilled workers, and we value them.

The third category of workers is the women with middle-level qualifications who do the basic production work. The work of these women is strictly dependent on the production line, on the repair workers, on one another and on managers of all levels. It is precisely this category of workers which is exposed to the most intensive exploitation. It is precisely this category of workers which is affected by the new vacation schedule. And it is precisely this category of workers which is most inclined to non-conflictual behaviour. Although the results of the questionnaire survey showed that these workers completely disagreed with the new vacation schedule and were dissatisfied with the work regime, the high intensity of work and the working conditions, they did not either in their attitudes or their action reveal any desire, aspiration or attempt to take any collective action against the decision of the director, despite the fact that, according to the law, women with school-age children have the right to take their vacations whenever they want. We should note that in interviews the women workers expressed themselves very clearly and categorically:

> They wear us out with Saturday work. Look at us, do we look like women? And what working conditions — the weight we carry about, and the draughts! Nobody bothers about us. We have to take time off sick to have a rest.

> We are hardly ever at home, but we still have to do housework. There is never enough time to give to the children. If they break up the holiday as well we shall not be able to bear it.

At the same time the women asked us to preserve their anonymity, being afraid of the management.

Possible variants of behaviour of the workers

With a realistic appreciation of the possible courses of action in this situation, the women workers said that they could not change anything. The trade union completely supported the administration. This was confirmed in an interview with members of the trade union committee, who considered that their principal task was to try to convince the workers of the need for changes in the vacation schedule for the sake of production. The possibility of collective action was completely rejected.

In practice the women's discontent was expressed only in talk at the level of the brigade:

> We made a fuss at the meeting. But what is the point? The management knows our views, but they are not interested in them. And really, we are afraid to speak out openly. Some are waiting for an apartment, some for an allotment.

Individualistic types of behaviour prevail. There are no tendencies to collective behaviour. Even the changes in their vacation entitlement, which cause obvious inconvenience for the women and give rise to a great deal of dissatisfaction, do not give rise to any desire among them to resist the decision of the director. Interviews showed that they prefer to resolve problems on an individual level. Practically every woman worker is sure that she will resolve the problem for herself. The majority consider that they will resolve the problem of the summer vacation by going on the sick list, which many of the women are able to do in order to prolong their vacation, an unorthodox but legal way of solving the problem. They identify the principal basis of their dissatisfaction at the level of the shop chief, on whom the women workers depend not only for their earnings, but also for the receipt of apartments, garden plots and barter goods.

As one of the women said in an interview:

> At present I do not say anything against any kind of actions on the part of management — management has given me an incentive. I was one of the first to receive a refrigerator. Then their attitude to me changed sharply. It happened after I spoke at the meeting.

The workers consider their foremen to be the real defenders of their interests.

In general this is explained by the usual system of labour relations at the level of the shop. Strong economic levers at the level of the shop (calculation of bonuses, application of the system of penalties and fines, distribution of cheap goods and groceries) have created a system of informal individualised relations between line managers and women workers. This can be seen by contrasting the three shops headed by men with the shop which is headed by a woman. Labour relations in these shops are constructed in different ways. In the shop which has a woman chief relations are more authoritarian. She has established mutual relations with the workers herself. The foremen carry out their functions at the formal level, while at the informal level mutual relationships are determined at the level of the shop chief. In this shop the workers' position, their payment, and the distribution of barter, are found to be strictly dependent on their relationship with the shop chief. In the other shops the situation is different. The informal level of relationships is established at the level of the foreman. The male shop chiefs prefer to resolve all questions of labour relations at the formal level with the foremen. All the foremen in the women's collectives are women, while in the men's collectives they are men.

The basic feature of employment in the combine is related to the specific characteristics of a women's collective. One can observe a high rate of turnover of the collective. Every year 140–190 young women join the enterprise from technical college. This situation arises because women go on maternity leave, not all of whom want to return. As one woman worker said,

> Those women whose husbands are earning do not come back. People who work here are those with nowhere to disappear to.

The other feature is that a high proportion of the collective are not natives of Moscow. This aspect strengthens the dependence of the workers on their place of work.

Despite the fact that the combine has a fairly high level of wages (about 2.5 times the average for the branch and for the industry as a whole), the women workers do not try to hold on to their jobs in the enterprise. This is expressed in the fact that many women do not come back to the factory after maternity leave. The labour turnover in the various production units is around 15 per cent. In addition about 40–50 people are away from each shop every day because of temporary incapacity. These features lead to a shortage of labour in the enterprise. One has the impression that the administration of the enterprise is not particularly surprised by this. They have devised their own methods of getting hold of temporary workers. The problem of the shortage of labour is resolved at the level of the shop. In the combine there is a high proportion of temporary workers, comprising students from technical college, pensioners who had earlier worked in the combine and women workers who are on leave to care for their children. As the line managers explained, they have a list of telephone numbers of people who are ready to come to work when necessary. They have worked out a special system of payment for this category of employee.

Assessing the situation as a whole, we should note that the enterprise management conducts an employment policy which is differentiated according to the different categories of worker. Management increases the level of pay, introduces various social privileges (a large subsidy in the canteen, free transport, and so on), so that to some degree it cares for its workers. In interviews, managers appeared completely confident that the enterprise has no problems with its basic workers. As one manager said,

> They are women. Where are they going to disappear to? They always come running to me.

It appears that the behaviour of the workers can in general be explained by their appreciation of what they can do in the given situation. In this enterprise the women workers prefer to resolve their problems on the individual level. Some individuals try to preserve good relations with management, while others can leave, or at any time go onto the sick list.

SITUATION TWO: THE ENTERPRISE DEVICE

This is a closed joint-stock company, manufacturing watches. The research took place in the early summer of 1994. The total number of employees is 5,500, although this number is steadily declining as people leave as a result of delays in the payment of wages. Sixty-five per cent of the employees are women. The age and gender composition of the labour force varies between shops. There are shops with 85 per cent women workers, shops with 40 per cent women, and some particular sections with no women at all.

The general economic situation of the factory is one of crisis. The main reason for the crisis is the problem of sales. As a result there are frequent stoppages. The absence of money for pay and for the purchase of raw materials has resulted in large debts, as a result of which the factory is now under the administration of the tax inspectorate. All financial transactions are frozen. Money arriving in the enterprise's accounts is automatically transferred to pay its debts to the state. The only exception to this is the payment of wages which is long delayed and naturally leads to discontent among the workers. The directorate pays hourly rates and tries to shift the problem of selling the product onto the workers. The workers understand the situation. As one of the women workers said to me in an interview:

> My job is to work. If they do not provide me with work, then I also have to carry out the functions of the sales department and sell watches. Is that normal?

The main feature of the present situation is the crisis in the management of the enterprise following a sharp conflict in 1993, including a strike, as a result of which the former director was removed. At the present time some of the workers support the former director, others support the new one.

We will try to analyse the behaviour of the workers in various subdivisions at the time of the open conflict a year ago, and at the present moment. We can construct our analysis of the situation in this enterprise by comparing the attitudes of the workers to the previous situation and to the present, since the previous and the new directors constructed their relations with the collective differently. The previous director had a strongly authoritarian personality, supporting strict hierarchical relationships in the enterprise. The present director tries to be democratic, often speaking on the radio, trying to keep the whole collective in touch with the development of the economic and financial situation.

The analysis is based on two workshops. The assembly shop has 2,000 employees, 80 per cent of whom are women. The basic operations are predominantly manual, organised on the principle of a soft conveyor, with flexible flow. Pay is according to a single scale, differing according to the price of the watch that is being assembled. There are sections whose workers are assembling watches that sell for hard currency, for about $50. The workers in these sections earn about five times as much as those doing similar work, but assembling cheaper watches.

The workshop which makes the outer casings of the watches employs 600 people, 73 per cent of whom are women. This work is basically mechanised. The main equipment consists of a bank of machines. Some of the equipment is traditional universal Soviet machinery, some of it is modern Western automatic lines. We can see a very sharp age and gender differentiation between the workers using the different types of equipment. The automatic equipment is used by young men up to the age of 30, while the old equipment is used by women and men of pre-pension and pension age.

We can observe similar tendencies in the formation of labour relations in this enterprise and the one considered previously. The automated section is fairly autonomous. The workers said in interviews that it did not make any difference to them who was the director, the head of the section was very confident and independent. The automated equipment enables them to make high quality products. The workers in this section took a neutral position in relation to the situation in the factory. There had been no significant organisational changes in their relations with line management with the change of director.

As one of the workers in the automated section said in an interview:

> My job is to work. It makes no difference to me who is the director. We are pretty detached from the factory as a whole.

As regards the other sections in the shop, the workers take much more interest in the situation in the factory as a whole. A series of interviews with representatives of various levels in the hierarchical chain of management in various workplaces (plant managers, shop chiefs, foremen and workers) revealed very different evaluations of the system of labour relations.

Let us look at two stages in the development of the situation in the factory. The conflict in 1993 arose as a result of dissatisfaction with organisational changes which had been introduced at the factory. Two years earlier the so-called 'Yel'chaninov Production System' had been introduced, according to which all production processes were broken down into production complexes, each resulting in some kind of final product. Internal prices were introduced. Changes were made in the chain of responsibility of various services, concerning the technical services in particular. All technologists were removed from subordination to the shop chiefs and combined in an independent technological department, serving the factory as a whole. The production complexes were given their economic independence and their own funds. The form of payment of wages in the factory was fundamentally changed. The new system was based on the establishment of a wages fund for the workers dependent on their output, and a system of coefficients which determined the pay of the foremen, shop chiefs and senior management in relation to the size of the workers' wages fund. The differentials were set at a very high level. The system included additional pay for foremen and shop chiefs for entrepreneurial activity. Those who had serious opportunities to engage in independent economic activities welcomed the changes, while those who had fewer such opportunities rejected them.

Discontent began to grow in the factory, both among managers at various levels and among workers, who were outraged at the differentials opened up between the pay of the foremen and their own pay. The real reasons for the conflict require some further analysis. However, at first sight it appeared that the open discontent of the workers was provoked by certain managers in the immediate entourage of the director, who wanted to replace him. This was stated directly by workers, foremen and shop chiefs, and is supported by the facts. For example, leaflets were distributed among the workers itemising the level of wages and the income of the director and his deputies, access to which information was available only to senior managers. It has subsequently become clear who distributed these leaflets — the chiefs of the information department. The result was that a strike was organised in the factory, in whose organisation the independent trade union Sotsprof, which had two groups in the enterprise, organising (predominantly female) assembly workers and (predominantly male) workers on the automatic lines, played a significant role.

The basic demands of the strike were to change the Yel'chaninov system and to call a conference of the labour collective. Differentiation among the workers appeared at the time of the strike. Many workers signed the strike demands, but it was only the workers in the assembly plant who actually participated in the strike. Moreover, even the president of the Sotsprof group organising workers on the automatic lines did not join the strike. In interviews, many workers explained their failure to participate in the strike in the following way:

> There was a lot of work. This was not a time for fooling around.
>
> This was all wrong. Those who had work did not participate in the strike.

In the assembly plant it was basically those who worked on the assembly of the cheap quartz watches who joined the strike. The brigade of high skilled workers who assembled the high precision watches did not participate in the strike.

The conflict took on increasingly sharp forms. The social situation was heated. The Sotsprof representative managed to collect the number of signatures required to call a conference to re-elect the director, which took place in the autumn of 1993. A new director was elected by a small majority, with the votes of the state property fund, which held 20 per cent of the shares, proving decisive, indicating that even at the time of the election a significant proportion of the employees supported the former director.

At the time of the open conflict the most active workers were those working on the assembly of quartz watches. The production of these watches was unprofitable for the factory. Indeed, the warehouse was still full of quartz watches which had remained unsold since 1987. These were the lowest qualified and the lowest paid workers. Their activism was expressed in their joining Sotsprof and their participating in the strike. Considering that it is only women who work on the assembly of quartz watches, the strike was effectively a women's strike. The Sotsprof group on the automatic lines, representing exclusively men, did not back participation in the strike. (The fact that the Sotsprof group on the automatic lines did not want to unite with the Sotsprof cell created in the assembly shop is interesting in itself.)

One should note that in the casing plant, where many low-qualified women work on low-paid operations, the women workers took no interest either in the new trade union, or in the strike, or in the election of a new director. As one of these women said in an interview:

> Our shop did not participate either in the strike or in the work of the conference. At that time we had a lot of work. I do not understand a lot of things that happened to us at that time. Samsonov [the former director] was good for me. Of course he fiddled with the foremen's pay. They say that he stole a lot, but things were better for us then.

A number of factors contributed to the activism of the women assembly workers. At first sight a decisive factor might appear to be the presence in the shop of people who were able to organise such activism. However, this was not a sufficient condition, since the high-skilled workers, who were also organised in the independent trade union, did not participate in the strike, which involved only the women working on low-paid operations. The most important role was the pressure put on the relations between workers and foremen as a result of the increased pay differentials in favour of the foremen, but this again was not sufficient to lead to a breakdown in relations, since it was only a minority of workers who joined the strike. Nor was an increase in differentials combined with low pay sufficient to provoke a strike, since the women making the watch cases were also low-paid, but did not join the strike because they had work. It would seem therefore that it was the combination of low wages and the increasingly insecure position of the women assembling the cheap watches that initially disposed them to act collectively, while it was the growing differentials which led them to act on their own, without involving their foremen. It was when the women workers began to act collectively and developed an aspiration to unity that the link in the chain between foreman and worker finally snapped. The strike, with the demand to change the new system and ultimately to replace the director, was the result.

Practically everybody saw the cause of the management crisis as lying in the new system of economic organisation, introduced by the former director, resulting in the large differentials in pay between different categories of employee. Both workers and foremen spoke about this discontent. As one foreman said:

> We were forced to hide the list of wages, distrust arose among the workers. We began to lose the manageability of the collective.

However, removing the Yel'chaninov system by no means removed the sources of discontent, although there is almost no active collective behaviour on the part of the workers. Many people now talk about their desire for the return of the former director, a strong owner (*khozyain*). A considerable number of workers in the assembly shop are now leaving Sotsprof, which continues to support the new director. One should stress that nostalgia for the former style of management was notable not only in interviews with line managers, but also with workers. Among its merits the line managers mentioned the clarity of instructions, the feeling of stability, the existence of a strategy for action.

The majority of workers are pessimistic and do not have confidence in the present management, expressing a preference for the former authoritarian style of management. The women workers referred to the fact that before there was a steady supply of work, and so of earnings and various social privileges, which they have no more. Some women workers said in an interview, 'Before they took care of us, now nobody needs us.' Many women workers said that they had changed their mind and regretted having voted against Samsonov. 'We hoped that it would be better, but it turned out worse!' However, although the women working on the assembly of the quartz watches continue to maintain a fairly active position, they do not express their dissatisfaction openly; their behaviour, like that of their colleagues, is now marked by its individualism, particularly now that the assembly of quartz watches is at a standstill and the women workers have been sent on vacation. The highly skilled workers have responded to the crisis by seeking jobs elsewhere, while those who remain preserve the traditional orientation to securing their position on the basis of their individual relations with the foreman.

Despite the completely different economic positions of Pizza and Device, and the different degrees of social tension, there are some close similarities in the relation between the character of labour relations and the technical and economic characteristics of production in the two enterprises. Workers on identical operations tend to have identical skill, age and gender characteristics, and to behave in similar ways. The similar attitude of the workers in these two enterprises to the strong management style is interesting, workers in both cases regarding it as both natural and desirable. In Device many workers called and continue to call the former director by the same term used in Pizza, 'Papa'. It seems that such a style of relationship was fairly widespread in collectives in which workers with a middle level of qualification working at manual-mechanical labour on various kinds of production line predominated. The crisis at Device would seem to show that when the traditional style of labour relations, based on individualised relationships between workers and line manager, is destroyed there are no real mechanisms of management to replace it; there is no new system of labour relations, and so one sees a crisis in the system of management.

SITUATION THREE: THE ENTERPRISE LENKON

Lenkon is an enterprise in the heavy engineering industry, which has been a joint-stock company since 1991, employing around 400 people. Research in Lenkon has been carried out continuously since 1991.[2]

2 Research in Lenkon has been conducted in collaboration with Valentina Vedeneeva and Veronika Kabalina.

Traditionally men have predominated in the enterprise. The management body is entirely male, apart from the accounts department, and no women participate in managerial decision-making. The economic and financial position is considered to be stable. There is now a growth in the volume of production and significant changes in the structure of management. The main features of the social situation are as follows.

The system of labour relations at Lenkon differs from the previous enterprises in being less authoritarian at the level of top management. Shop chiefs here have considerably more economic independence. The organisation of labour in this enterprise also differs from the others. The work is basically mechanised, has a more individual character, there is no rigid dependence of workers on one another or on the flow of work. The women here, in comparison with the previous enterprises, are mainly engaged in auxiliary operations.

The enterprise is marked by a very dynamic senior management team, which has pursued a firm and innovative management strategy ever since the arrival of the director in 1987, with special emphasis on employment policy as the management tries to upgrade the labour force, and frequent review of the wages system. The enterprise was a pioneer of privatisation with shareownership being concentrated in management hands. While the workers initially had illusions about the virtues of shareownership, these have long been dissipated, and there has been a growing sense of distance from management and rising social tension within the enterprise. At the same time, workers have retained some confidence in the long-term strategy of the management, and positively evaluate the fact that senior management relates to the factory as an owner (*khozyain*).

The research in this enterprise is based on the press-stamp section, which is interesting because it has a mixed collective, two-thirds men and one-third women. The press-stamp section appears at an early stage of the production cycle, stamping out and assembling metal casings. Metal is cut, some parts are stamped and then the parts are polished and electrically or gas welded. There are also repair-fitters and adjusters in the section. A work study exercise at the beginning of 1993 concluded that the workers in this section were overgraded, and the section was heavily over-staffed. There is a rigid gender division of labour within the section. Work on the stamping machines is considered to be women's work, because of its monotony, and it is paid at average rates, in this case at grade four. All the other operations are paid at higher rates.

Unlike the case in Pizza, this inequality, which means that the women earn significantly less than the men, gives rise to a great deal of discontent among the women, and has led to sharp conflict. The situation was aggravated by the management style of the section chief, which was perhaps not unconnected with her position as the only female section chief in charge of a section dominated by men. The section chief was a young woman, who had been brought in by the director in 1990 from a reinforced concrete factory, where she had worked as a shop chief since 1985. Her arrival coincided with the reorganisation of the section, in the course of which she replaced virtually the whole of the labour collective, only four of the original staff remaining following a wave of redundancies in 1992. She brought most of the women stamp operators with her from her previous enterprise.

The section chief was a strict authoritarian manager, who concentrated all power and decision-making in her own hands. This tendency was reinforced by the fact that she was suspicious of the foreman, frankly acknowleding that she saw him as a competitor for her post, although in fact he was a rather passive person with weak professional skills. As a result she reduced the functions of the foreman to a minimum in order to keep him under control which, at the same time, reduced his status in the eyes of the male workers because of his inability to stand up to the chief. One result of this was that almost everything took place at the level of formal relations, and informal relationships were almost completely absent in this shop. The section chief has absolute control over the determination of wages and the distribution of money from the incentive fund. This gives her very strong economic levers of management over the collective which in turn serves to inhibit protest. The male workers were unhappy with what they saw as the dictatorial style of the section chief, and refused to recognise that she could have the technical or professional competence required to do her job, simply because she was a woman. There was thus a very clear division, and even antagonism, within the collective along gender lines, which was also expressed socially, as the male foreman spent his breaks smoking and playing cards with the male workers.

As everywhere, the women in the shop were unhappy with their pay. For a year, between 1989 and 1990, this section had been an independent co-operative, with wages around double those elsewhere in the factory. This situation ended when the section was re-absorbed into the enterprise, and wages had since fallen owing to the shortage of work. The enterprise had also been through a series of reforms of the pay system, which also disrupted the established rates and relativities and provoked widespread conflict. In this case the women in the shop were particularly aggrieved that the men were paid more than them because they contrasted this with what they regarded as the poor quality of the work of the male cutters, who provided them with blanks, and auxiliary workers who repaired their machines. Discontent led to open conflict when the women lost out yet again with a wage regrading, in response to which they appealed to the factory management to review the grades, threatening to strike over the issue. In an attempt to smooth over the situation, the shop chief gave the stamp operators large bonuses in order to make up for their losses and to carry them with her. This action in its turn gave rise to strong discontent among the men, although this was less obvious and was not expressed openly.

The section chief realised that this conflict had been intensified by the overt gender divisions within the section, which she believed had been reinforced by her own management strategy. She therefore revised her approach to management of the section, drawing the foreman into a more active managerial role and, in particular, giving him responsibility for the women working the stamp machines. She meanwhile has become more involved in supervising the mechanical operations, partly as a means of imposing her authority as a specialist over the men.

SITUATION FOUR: THE ENTERPRISE MICRON

The fourth example is an enterprise in the electronics industry, the former defence complex Micron, which was studied in 1993. This enterprise employs around 6,000 people, and is now in crisis. The reduction in the volume of production, and the cessation of production of its principal products, has led the enterprise into a difficult financial position. This situation has led to an exodus of high-skilled male workers, leading to a sharp change in the age and gender composition of the workforce, which now has a large proportion of working women pensioners. This has hit some shops, which have lost experienced foremen and section chiefs, very hard.

The management structure is typical, with no structural changes, although there have been some reductions. The director and his deputies are men, most of the management services employ women, and it is particularly against these female office workers that the discontent of production workers, both men and women, is directed. The situation in the shops is similar, with most of the shop chiefs being men, while the deputy shop chiefs and office workers are women, and it was precisely this group of employees who were affected by the first wave of redundancies.

The loss of skilled male foremen and section heads has led to considerable changes in the composition of line management, with many women, who had previously worked as technologists, replacing them. However, many of these women were not very happy to be in the position of managers, complaining that it was difficult to manage men.

Social characteristics of the enterprise

The social situation in the enterprise can be characterised by a number of points:

1. The closure of particular workshops and the reduction in output has made it necessary to find new types of production, which frequently require less skilled labour than before.
2. Very unhealthy working conditions.
3. Practice of sending people on compulsory vacation.
4. Significant proportion of working pensioners.
5. High level of social tension.
6. Dissatisfaction of workers with the policy of the factory administration.

The present analysis is based on one shop producing electric circuit boards, whose labour force is 60 per cent female. The shop used to have a central role in the enterprise, making circuits for military equipment. But with the collapse of military orders the shop found itself in a more peripheral position, with cuts in employment and the need to develop new kinds of production. These changes could not but have an impact on the life of the shop.

Conflict in the shop arose in the first instance as a result of the differential relationship of the shop chief to various categories of worker. It seems that the male shop chief deliberately constructs the labour force according to what he considers to be the requirements for new kinds of production. He exercises all the management functions at the level of the shop, sections and individual work places. The foremen are regarded as his assistants, and have no real authority of their own, their status being close to that of the workers. The situation of men and women in the shop is sharply differentiated. This is expressed in their working conditions, the kind of work they do, their qualifications and, correspondingly, the level of their wages.

The women are mostly young with incomplete secondary education (eighth class) or elderly women, past pension age, who are happy to do any work to eke out their pitiful pensions. Most of the women are engaged in manual low-paid operations on the third and fourth grades. Interviews show that they are basically content to do monotonous manual work, their discontent arising exclusively from the level of their pay. The men in the shop are setters, fitters and tool makers with middle education. They can earn good money, not only carrying out their main responsibilities for repair and adjustment, but also producing various parts and components. They are better qualified and better paid than the women, earning about double the women's wages.

Wages are made up of two parts. The basic wage is calculated by the foreman in accordance with the grade of the worker, their output and scale bonuses. The other part is a bonus out of profits which is allocated by the shop chief on his own initiative. Informal relations are created at this level. The foremen are completely separated from the economic levers of management, which are concentrated in the hands of the chief. This means that the wage of a worker basically depends directly on the shop chief's attitude to him or her. There are no clear criteria which relate earnings to the work done. The pay structure allows the shop chief to determine the level of wages of each worker on his own initiative, and he uses this to carry out a deliberate personnel policy. The different position of men and women in the shop is a result of this policy. It is obvious that the plan of the shop chief is to use this policy to create a collective with two characteristics: with high skill levels and personally devoted to the shop chief. The principal motive of the shop chief in his relation to the workers is his attempt to differentiate them into core and peripheral workers in the face of the prospect of reductions in production and its reorganisation to produce different kinds of products.

Behaviour of the workers

The behaviour of the workers is sharply differentiated. Some of the workers, basically the high-paid male adjusters, are in a privileged position. They do not express any dissatisfaction and see themselves as having a future in the factory, while their skills are generally in demand so that they can always find a well-paid job elsewhere. This gives them a high degree of independence. However, the mechanism of distribution of wages is a serious source of tension in the shop. Many workers are unhappy with the policy pursued by the shop chief.

One can distinguish three categories of workers who express their discontent with what they consider to be the unjust distribution of pay, according to the level of their activity. The least active are the women engaged in low-paid manual work. They express their discontent with the actions of the shop chief quite frankly, but this expression is basically restricted to the verbal level, and it is most unlikely that they will engage in open conflict, because these women are not essential for the shop, and the shop chief does not try to hold onto them. Moreover, the working pensioners understand that they can be dismissed at any time.

The second category is the better-paid and more experienced women machine operators. These are women in the age group 40–50, whose skills are specific to this equipment and this enterprise, so who have little chance of finding comparable work elsewhere, but who risk losing their jobs with the planned restructuring of production in the enterprise. These women actively express their dissatisfaction with their level of wages, and this discontent was expressed openly in the spring of 1993 in the formation of an initiative group which sent a collective letter to the director demanding a pay increase for all groups of workers, the replacement of the shop chief, and the threat of a strike if their demands were not met: in effect the declaration of a pre-strike situation. The protest had been provoked by the very low level of pay in the face of growing inflation, and also by the fact that managers, beginning with the deputy shop chief, were transferred to individual contracts, the result of which was that their wages came to exceed those of the low-skilled workers by more than five times. The protest was not supported by the privileged male workers, nor did the low-paid women participate actively in it. Nevertheless, it resulted in the general indexation of wages in the factory although the conflict did not develop any further. The shop chief took a neutral position in this situation. He answered the women's demand for higher wages by saying, 'if you don't like it, you can leave'.

The third category is those male machine operators who have not for one reason or another established personal relations with the shop chief. The reasons may be that they do not like his management style, or that they have been infringers of discipline or absentees or drinkers. These people express their discontent in a passive form, although they declare their willingness to participate in any kind of protest, including strikes.

We can see here that a policy of management directed at the stratification and differentiation of various professional groups leads to the attachment of high-skilled workers to the enterprise, on the one hand, and to the squeezing out of low-skilled workers, short of redundancy, on the other hand. At the same time, the different socio-economic position of the different groups of workers form different interests and, correspondingly, different kinds of behaviour.

GENDER DIFFERENTIATION AND INDUSTRIAL RELATIONS

What lessons can we draw from these examples regarding the position of women in conflicts within the sphere of production? Firstly, one should note the importance of this question. There is a large number of women working in industry, and it seems that it will be particularly these workers who will be subjected to the most radical change in their situation. However, this is not simply because they are women, victims of male discrimination at every level, although neither is it accidental that such victims are women. Women workers tend to have specific social characteristics, occupying quite specific positions in industrial production. Women production workers are to be found predominantly in routine, and usually monotonous, jobs with a medium skill grade, correspondingly low levels of pay, and relatively low levels of mechanisation. Changes in the technological organisation of production will, it seems, have their primary impact on this category of employees. On the one hand, mechanisation and automation will lead to the regrading of these jobs, and their simultaneous reclassification as male jobs. On the other hand, where mechanisation does not take place, productivity will be increased by intensifying labour and lengthening the working day. In both cases, women workers will be threatened with losing their jobs, or being pushed aside into less attractive and low-paid kinds of work, while those who remain will find it increasingly difficult to combine their waged work with their domestic labour, so that this work will increasingly be dominated by young women, who will leave their jobs when they have children, while older women will increasingly be marginalised in the labour force. All these tendencies are most clearly demonstrated by the example of Pizza. Thus, in the present period of economic transition the position of women workers with middle level qualifications is rather weak. One has the impression that in the future these factors will be aggravated, and this category of women will be hit hard by the processes of change.

These changes will not be expected to affect women uniformly, but to have a differential impact, depending particularly on skill levels and age. Young women will be more in demand when it comes to selecting workers for jobs. The intensification of labour and the pressure to increase productivity will probably increase the demands made on women's skill, although more highly skilled jobs will most likely continue to be dominated by men, and the overall reduction in demand for labour of average skill will force large numbers of women back into unskilled, casual and temporary work. It is probable that there will be some outflow of older and lower skilled women from paid employment altogether, although this might only be temporary. Although most women have to work both in the home and in paid employment, in some families it may be financially possible for the woman to give up the latter and choose to concentrate on her domestic work. The situation in the labour market may be expected to reinforce this tendency as pay differentials between male and female jobs increase further. However, once again we should emphasise that this is likely to be only temporary, with a subsequent stage of a further restructuring of the age and gender structure of employment.

It should be stressed that at one level these changes are a direct expression of changes in the economic pressures and technological structure of production whose impact is most keenly felt by medium skilled workers in routine jobs, regardless of the gender of these workers. In this sense the fate of women is not a matter of discrimination against women as such, and indeed in the enterprises researched we found no evidence of such direct discrimination against women. However, at another level it is not mere chance that such jobs are dominated by women, for such jobs are considered to be particularly appropriate to women, given the supposed social and psychological characteristics of women workers. Again it should be stressed that this characterisation of women is not simply something imposed on women by men, but is something with which most women identify themselves. Surveys, interviews and observation repeatedly show that women are less inclined than men to follow a career, to improve their technical qualifications, to seek to seek to fulfil themselves through their work. This is hardly surprising since, on the one hand, women are under strong social and ideological pressure to fulfil themselves through marriage and motherhood and since, on the other hand, women's career prospects are so limited when the higher skilled and better paid work is monopolised by men.

These changes are mostly in the future, although it may not be far ahead. At present a significant proportion of women industrial workers have middle levels of qualification, and so the behaviour of this category of workers, their reactions to this or that action of the administration, is of some interest and has a significant influence on the social situation in the enterprise.

What determines the reaction of women workers to change? One conclusion that we can draw immediately is that women's reaction is not determined by any supposedly inherent features of women's psychology, but is determined primarily by characteristics of the social situation in which they find themselves. Thus women workers are not necessarily passive and submissive employees who will endure every hardship imposed on them. In particular circumstances women can be at least as militant in asserting their rights as can men, while men can be absolutely docile and submissive in the appropriate circumstances.

Nevertheless, there is no doubt that women have lower aspirations than men with regard to their kinds of work and the size of their earnings. The fact that in enterprises in which the economic situation is deteriorating the age structure changes, with some feminisation. By contrast, in those successful enterprises traditionally considered women's, the management apparatus at practically all levels becomes male, showing the strong dependence of the age and gender structure of the labour force on the economic and financial prospects of the enterprise.

Various sources show that the main dissatisfaction of women arises from the low level of their wages, but this dissatisfaction is not related to their position relative to the men. Many women workers consider, for example, that men ought to earn more. There was no indication of any direct discrimination against women in the enterprises in which the research was conducted. Moreover, there was no sign of serious dissatisfaction with the working conditions, even though they were very heavy, for example, with frequent violation of the norms laid down for the amount of weight that could be carried during one shift. Many women workers are willing to put up with high health risks or to work in heavy and unpleasant conditions in order to be able to earn more and to qualify for a pension at the age of 45 (although the financial compensation is often quite small). Women are motivated to take this kind of work, although it is likely that the proportion of women oriented to it will fall over time. The problem with this category of women workers is not the fact that their socio-economic position is different from that of men, but that they consider their position to be normal and they do not try to change it.

The differentiated position of men and women does not give rise to conflict in itself. Conflict is created by the differential attitude of management to various categories of workers, in particular towards workers with middle levels of qualification. One should note that in predominantly female enterprises we have observed a policy of the intensification of labour. In enterprises where men work on the basic operations, we see a policy of pushing women into a peripheral role. In both cases management takes into account the position of women in production and in society, distinguished by their greater dependence both in the particular character of their jobs and in their family roles.

Workplaces which are predominantly female have a number of specific features. At the level of higher management there is a very marked tendency to exploit the established structure, procedures, connections, a tendency to a conservative type of management and to authoritarianism. Strict relationships of one-man-management at all levels of the hierarchical management chain are typical. The director's social and labour policy derives from the simple principle of intensifying labour, while increasing pay and social privileges. There is direct bribery to get the workers to work harder and they are manipulated in various ways. The directors are confident that they can manipulate women in this way. In particular industries they encourage the employment of this category of workers.

The position of women in society is used when the majority of women have a dual role, working in industry and fulfilling their domestic work. Many women in the enterprises researched are bringing up children on their own so that, on the one hand, they need their earnings and, on the other, they need the various kinds of commodities that they can obtain in the enterprise, so that the distribution of goods through the enterprise is a great help to them. The workers accept this style of management, and many of them prefer it. Surveys in particular show that in predominantly female collectives, where most of the workers work on medium skilled jobs, there is an appreciation of a strong paternalistic regime, and little feeling of a need for independent action, and especially collective action. Eighty per cent of those questioned in Pizza answered that if problems arose that worried them but were not resolved, they would refer to management at some level, while in Mikron, with a mixed collective, 40 per cent of the women considered that this was the way to act, while only 10 per cent of men answered in this way. A readiness to organise independent activity was expressed by only 4 per cent in the primarily women's collective, but 12 per cent among the women and 26 per cent among the men at Mikron.

It is clear that the aspiration of women to defend their rights and interests actively is lower than among men. They prefer individual types of behaviour, loading themselves with work, pay, various sorts of social privileges. This way they take care of themselves. To a certain extent this can simply be related to the psychology of wage labour: the director perceives the workers as an owner. It is difficult to establish a direct dependence of the management style of senior management on the gender composition of the labour force of the enterprise, and it may be that this kind of behaviour is more related to the skill level of the workers, and in particular to the type of production. Enterprises dominated by women's labour are usually of the traditional kind of production, in whose costs wages take a high proportion, that is to say they have a high proportion of living labour. Interviews show that the management of the enterprise often thinks not of technical re-equipment to increase income and profitability, but controlling an obedient collective. In particular, one of the chiefs of Pizza openly declared that it was unprofitable for the enterprise to automate production. It is much more profitable to use workers of average skill. That is the view of top management.

At the lower levels of management it is necessary to focus on the special role of the foreman. If the influence of gender on the specific character of labour relations in general is not clear, at the lower levels its influence is more obvious. But even here it is not a matter of whether the collective is male or female, but of the coincidence of the gender of the foreman and the workers. In particular, male shop chiefs in female collectives frequently insist that the foremen in such shops should be women. Nevertheless, it seems that in enterprises with women workers these factors have a greater effect, which is connected with the fact that at the lower levels the system of informal labour relations is more highly developed, corresponding to the greater significance of personal contacts and gender at this level. The foreman often takes on the trade union function of defending the interests of the labour force. And if this really is possible, many conflicts are extinguished. The enterprise Device shows this clearly. The consequence of a breakdown in the relation between foreman and workers was a strike. The rise of an independent trade union expressed these tendencies to act collectively. Now, six months later, the situation has reverted to the previous channels, confidence in the foreman has increased, and workers have left Sotsprof. It seems, then, that conflict arises when the shop chiefs and foremen are not able to develop informal labour relations in the workplace. The examples show that as often as not conflict is provoked by the destruction of the usual system of labour relations at the level of the shop. It seems that in the transition period the labour behaviour of workers will depend to a high degree on the system of labour relations established at shop level.

The position of men and women is clearly differentiated in industry. However, in my view this is not the main problem. The main problem is that at the level of social consciousness this situation is perceived as normal, so that women accept this situation without serious complaint.

7. Gender Stereotyping and the Gender Division of Labour in Russia

Elain Bowers

In this chapter I want to examine the relationship between the gender stereotyping of jobs and women's experience of work in Russia. The chapter is based on fieldwork carried out in 1993 and 1994 in Samara, Moscow and Syktyvkar, and concentrates on case studies of two printing enterprises in Syktyvkar. These enterprises are interesting because although the basic production jobs are defined as stereotypically male jobs, the majority of the workers are in fact women.[1]

GENDER STEREOTYPES AND THE GENDER DIVISION OF LABOUR

How do we explain the gender division of labour? Popular explanations refer to stereotypes which are beliefs which define the kinds of work that men and women can do or should do in terms of supposedly essential differences between them.

These stereotypes are deeply ingrained in both Russia and the West, and in their basic outlines they are very similar.[2] However:

1. There are big differences in the jobs which are thought to be appropriate for men and women in Russia and in the West. In Russia

[1] An earlier version of this chapter was presented to the conference of the British Association of Slavonic and East European Studies, Fitzwilliam College, Cambridge, 26 March, 1995.

[2] In addition to the research quoted in this chapter, I regularly asked people on as many occasions as possible during my stay in Russia to explain to me why particular jobs were men's jobs or women's jobs. While the specific explanations would vary considerably, the stereotypes underlying them were remarkably constant and, in general, very familiar.

women have long worked as doctors, engineers, economists, construction workers, manual labourers, street sweepers and in coal mines — jobs which in the West were traditionally identified as men's work.

So, although the stereotypes of what it is to be a man or a woman are in broad outline very similar in Britain and Russia, the characterisation of the jobs which are done differ, depending on whether they are done by men or by women.

In the same way, apparently very similar jobs are characterised very differently if one is done by men and another by women.

2. Stereotypes are held to apply to all men and all women. But we know that in reality individuals are very different one from another. Although men may, on average, be stronger than women, a lot of women are stronger than a lot of men. So many women can do 'men's jobs' as well as many men, and vice versa.

   However, women are not supposed to do such jobs, not because they cannot do them, but because they are not 'suitable' for women: to do a man's job is to betray one's femininity and to undermine a man's masculinity.

   So the argument often shifts from the claim that women *cannot* do certain jobs to the claim that women *should not* do such jobs.

3. Stereotypes often refer not only to supposed physical or psychological characteristics of men and women, but also to their supposed moral qualities, which are directly related to their gender roles. Thus, for example, high paid work is appropriate for men because men are supposed to be the breadwinners.

4. Stereotypes tend to be self-validating. If women do not have the chance to do a particular kind of job, they are not able to acquire the skills required by that job. If a job is considered to be a man's job it will be designed around what are supposed to be men's capabilities, and conversely if it is a woman's job.

5. Many women do in fact do jobs which are supposed to be men's jobs, and do them as well as men do. However, in such circumstances these jobs continue to be thought of as men's jobs, and particular reasons are given to explain why these jobs are not being done by men.

GENDER STEREOTYPES IN BRITAIN AND RUSSIA

Surveying the Western literature, we find that there are broadly two kinds of argument put forward to justify the gender stereotyping of jobs.[3] The first is the argument that a job is appropriate to a particular sex because the other sex *cannot* do the particular job — they do not have the physical or psychological capacities required to do the job. The second is the argument that a job is appropriate to a particular sex because the other sex *should not* do the particular job — because the job has features or makes demands that are inconsistent with the social and/or moral role of the particular sex. In both cases the arguments tend to be self-validating, so that both the gender division of labour and the gender stereotypes are simultaneously reproduced, the continued exclusion of women from particular jobs justifying the argument that women cannot or should not do those jobs.

Women can't do it

Lack of physical strength

This is often the first reason given for women's inability to do a particular job, for example that the work is too heavy or that there is too much standing. It clearly is the case that women are less strong than men on average, but men contribute to women's lack of 'knack' or strength by denying them the ability to develop their physical capacities:

- By excluding women from the experience needed to develop physical strength and confidence.
- Men are influential in designing labour processes, so that the job specification and design of equipment is conditioned by the gender stereotyping of the work — whether lifting gear will be used, the height of machines, for example.

3 See, for example, Cynthia Cockburn, *Brothers: Male Dominance and Technological Change*, Pluto, London, 1983. Cynthia Cockburn, *Machinery of Dominance: Women, Men and Technical Knowledge*, Pluto, London, 1985. Ruth Cavendish, *Women on the Line*, Routledge and Kegan Paul, London, 1982. Miriam Glucksman, *Women Assemble: Women Workers and the New Industries in Inter-war Britain*, Routledge, London, 1990. Ann Game and Rosemary Pringle: *Gender at Work*, Pluto, London, 1984. Fiona M. Wilson, *Organisational Behaviour and Gender*, McGraw Hill, Maidenhead, 1995.

Health hazards

Particular jobs are said to present gender-specific health hazards. Dangers for women's fertility are frequently cited, but dangers for men are ignored in these arguments.[4] The stereotyping of the jobs is reproduced by the failure to take measures to counter such real or imagined health hazards.

Mental ability

Men are seen as being pre-eminently rational beings, while women are dominated by emotion. On this basis women are seen as stupid, inadequate or illiterate, lacking the capacity for initiative and independent thinking, and so incapable of doing jobs which require the independent exercise of intellectual faculties.

Conversely, some work is seen as women's because men are too intelligent to do it and because it utilises some of women's specifically feminine attributes. For example:.

- Only women can stand to do boring work because they are more patient and conscientious in carrying out routine and intellectually undemanding tasks.
- Women are said to be:
  more persuasive,
  more caring,
  more attractive and
  foster a co-operative and non-threatening atmosphere.

These psychological stereotypes are self-validating in the sense that they condition the socialisation patterns of boys and girls. However, they are also self-validating in the sense that departures from the stereotype are characterised as individual and exceptional deviations from the norm — a rational woman is 'hard', an emotional man is 'soft'. Thus the qualities of every individual are defined in relation to the norm — identical behaviour in a man or in a woman will be described very differently, and the norm persists However, many counter-examples are identified.

4 In the Russian case folk medicine, sometimes institutionalised in official regulations, leads to what seem to us bizarre arguments. For example, people will tell you that women cannot be airline pilots because of the gynaecological risks imposed by vibrations, although the same vibrations apparently neither harm men's fertility nor affect the female cabin staff!

The rational/affective distinction

The rational/affective distinction is linked to women's supposed innate aversion to machinery and technology. Women are often said to be too temperamental to work with machinery, which men's more rational temperament is better suited to. But:

- Men as a sex have appropriated technology. They design it, maintain it and often operate it.
- The educational and occupational structure teaches boys to be scientifically and technologically capable while disqualifying girls in this respect.
- Men identify themselves with technology and identify technology with masculinity.

Where women do work on machines it is usually in a routine operational relationship, while men have an 'informed and interactive relationship' to their machines — women are only 'lent' machinery by men.

Natural temperament

- Women are said to be too emotional to cope with male working environments, and could not take criticism from supervisors or stand up to them, so that women are assigned to supposedly low-stress occupations.
- Women are said to be naturally unreliable, because after years of training they then leave to have babies. Menstruation is also cited as a problem.
- Women have an instrumental and temporary attitude to work. They fluctuate or get bored with the work.
- Women are fly-by-nights.
- At a certain age women are more concerned with their looks and then with getting married and having babies and looking after children.
- Women's main centre of interest is assumed to be the family and this is seen as a negative attribute in regard to work. For men, marriage and children on the other hand are seen as advantages and signs of increased responsibility and stability.

- So women are seen as partial workers, as incomplete, temporary, choosy or flawed workers.
- They may have nimble fingers and dexterity but they are not all-rounders.
- Even if women are diligent workers they are not able to take responsibility.

All these stereotypes are self-validating and self-reproducing, and relate not to the reality of men's and women's experience of work, but to the ideological typification of that experience, linking the definition of the different gender identities of men and women to the characterisation of a particular job in terms of those qualities which supposedly define those gender identities. These typifications are so powerful that they are almost impervious to critical empirical evaluation:

1. The characterisation of a particular job is not based on a detailed examination of precisely what skills are in fact necessary for the performance of the job. A particular job is regarded as being almost self-evidently a man's job or a woman's job. Should a closer examination of the skills used challenge the gender assignment of the job, it is more likely that the definition of the job will be changed, rather than its gender assignment, as new features are discovered to confirm its self-evident gender definition.
2. Evidence that men can successfully do women's jobs and vice versa does not necessarily challenge the gender stereotyping of the jobs. Women who do men's jobs are seen as exceptional in some way, so that it is still asserted that merely average women could not do the job.

Nevertheless, when women do successfully perform men's jobs, this constitutes some kind of an affront to the manhood of the men who do those same jobs. Men's sense of prestige and machismo rests on the exclusion of women from the same jobs.

If women do the same work it is seen as devalued and may come to be defined as 'women's work'. Everything women touch is tarnished. Thus, when the gender division of labour cannot be sustained by arguments that women cannot do the particular jobs, the argument tends to move towards the assertion that women should not do those jobs.

Women should not do it

Even if women prove that they can do men's jobs, it is still argued that they should not do them. The supposed psychological characteristics and social roles of men and women are transformed into moral qualities attached to gender identity.

1. Ideas about masculinity and respect are linked to the fact that men are supposed to be able to support women. The man should be the head of the family and breadwinner. Having a wife at home was seen as a privilege and as a status symbol and a man's degree of manliness could be gauged by the size of his wage — the man should earn a family wage. If his wife works, her earnings are seen as peripheral to those of her husband. It is an affront to his manhood if she earns more than he does.

   These moral arguments mutually reinforce the characterisation of women as inherently fickle, unreliable and uncommitted to their work. Thus a woman who violates these supposed psychological features of womanhood by displaying commitment to her work stands morally condemned for betraying her femininity.

2. The issue of sexual morality. Women are sexual creatures and are exposed to bad moral influences by entering male occupations. They would be coarsened by men's bad language and lose their femininity. Married women in particular are seen to be at risk of forming liaisons with men at work if they work in too close contact with them. Exposure to men's male/male intercourse would damage his woman in a man's eyes. They would be spoiled by men/for men.

These moral arguments interact with the characterisation of women as emotional and caring by setting strict boundaries to their expression of their emotions. A woman who works in a competitive male environment risks breaking beyond the boundary between emotion and sexuality and, if she is too successful, risks condemnation for exploiting her sexuality. These arguments rest on two contradictory images that men hold of women:

- Women are seen either as pure and unsullied beings, who do not swear, are clean and caring, look nice and smell nice. That is, woman's sexuality is her husband's alone to define and exploit in the comfort of his own home.

- On the other hand, men also want women's sexuality as free currency and women are routinely besmirched and belittled at work (for example, pin ups).

These contrary positions rest on the ambiguity in the definition of women as an object for men, as wife/mother and as whore, as property and as free currency, which is linked to the separation of home and work. The man knows that if his woman works in a male environment she will be the object of the condescension, sexual fantasies and lust of her male colleagues, because he knows that this is how he relates to his female colleagues. At the same time he knows that the female colleagues whom he demeans are, or should be, the property of another man. Thus the woman is branded as guilty of arousing the lust of the man because she does not know her proper place.

On the other hand, if women do turn up in male workplaces it implies that they are asserting their own estimation of their worth in opposition to men's definition of their sexuality. Women are competing with men and demanding that they be taken seriously, that they are not reduced either to something to protect and cherish, or treated as a sexual pawn. But this implicit demand challenges the gender differentiation that is the basis of men's self-identification.

The underlying principle behind these contradictory positions is that of complementarity. The appeal to essential qualities in men and women celebrate difference, but not randomly. Each is seen as the complement to each other. Thus, if women step out of their position, they challenge the identity of men.

This leads to two further contrary positions:

- On the one hand, women are seen to have an adverse effect on men. 'Men are not men in the company of women.'
- But on the other hand 'men are more like men when they are with women'. Men together behave more like women — narrow minded and spiteful — women bring out the best in men.

In other words women are seen as a catalyst and a threat to men, whether present or absent.

The gender stereotyping of jobs is not simply an ideological rationalisation of an historically developed gender division of labour. It is a very powerful means by which men defend their own gender identity by confining women within their own subordination. If women violate this gender stereotyping in or at work, they find themselves morally condemned for straying beyond their proper role. This also means that, to the extent that women themselves continue to accept these stereotypical categories, they are denied any collective means of challenging their subordination, since any attempt to move beyond the role assigned to them is conceived, by women as much as by men, as an exceptional and purely individual action, that may be justified by the particular circumstances or the particular qualities of that individual. Women are thereby allowed through the barriers individually, and each woman has to find her own way forward individually, but the barriers themselves remain intact.

GENDER STEREOTYPES AND WORK IN RUSSIA

In the Russian context I will examine whether these types of stereotypes are also prevalent or whether there are differences. Is it only men who present these stereotypes, or do women subscribe to these stereotypes as well? I will finish by looking at the contradiction between practices and meanings and at conflicting interpretations of events and practices.

Men's work, women's work

All the interviews quoted here are from two printing enterprises in Syktyvkar. One of the reasons for this is that it provides a clear comparison with Cynthia Cockburn's work on printing in Britain.[5] Cockburn's book looks specifically at compositors, mainly linotype operators, who were regarded as the most highly skilled workers in print and were exclusively male. In 1977 for example, there were no women employed in any of the main production areas in the national newspaper industry, including printing.

The gender division of labour in the printing industry in Syktyvkar was very different however. At the small enterprise (14 workers) all the workers were women and at the large enterprise (260 people) 90

5 Cynthia Cockburn, *Brothers: Male Dominance and Technological Change*, 1983.

per cent of the workforce was female and both enterprises were known as 'women's enterprises'. Most of the printers and all of the compositors were women. That is, they were doing jobs which were very clearly demarcated as men's work in the West. However, it immediately became very clear that in Syktyvkar too these jobs were regarded as men's jobs, even though they were being done by women. The gender characterisation of the job was, at least at one level, independent of who was doing that job. For example, as one woman said, 'much heavy work in Russia is done by women but it is still men's work'.

Both men and women that I talked to gave a very clear statement of the differences between what men and women should do, and that they should do different work. The stereotypes that were invoked to characterise work as men's and women's work turned out to be very similar to those in the West, even where women were clearly doing work that was designated as men's work.

The most common perception was the distinction drawn between heavy work (men's) and light work (women's). In the small enterprise there were no men employed full-time (apart from one fitter from the large printing enterprise who came to service and repair the machinery), yet the stereotype was still invoked. In contrast, in the large enterprise men and women are working in different areas, and here the stereotype was not only invoked but also given concrete reference. For example, the gendering of work in terms of heavy and light was also mentioned by one of the women printers in the large print enterprise:

> Women and men should do different work. Women should do light work and men the heavy work. Operating the computers and in photocomposition is women's work of course, but here with the machinery it should be men. Really I'm doing a man's job. Women should be shop assistants and hairdressers or doctors, and managers if you have a good mind, or teachers. Because the jobs are easy and light. Fitters and turners should be men's work.

This woman drew the distinction between heavy and light work and insisted that she was doing a man's job even though she had worked as a printer for 20 years and earlier had said that the work was not that heavy or tiring.

One of the sub-themes running through many of the accounts is that women only work in the dirty and heavy areas because of the low pay. One frequently mentioned view is illustrated by the chief of the trade union committee who said that: 'if they paid enough I'd work in any conditions'. The same point was referred to by the woman director of the small printing enterprise:

> It's heavy work and I don't like to see women working here, especially the linotype which is very harmful, and cutting. The printers should be men, really it just turned out long ago that it was low-paid and not very important perhaps. They pay us, but only enough not to let us die.

The director refers to the idea that heavy work should be done by men, presumably because they have the physical attributes to do such work. She then explains the fact that women do this work by reference to the low pay, invoking another gender stereotype, which identifies women with low-paid work. The implication is that if the pay system were different then the employment policy in the enterprise would also change.

Many of the respondents' comments were presented in terms of what ought to happen rather than what does happen. This is illustrated by the chief of the trade union committee who went on to say:

> Printing should be men's work and we are trying to get rid of the most harmful work [linotype] because women as future mothers should not work in harmful conditions ... and it has large equipment and only men should work on it.

Here she is referring to an idealisation of the difference between men's work and women's work explicitly in terms of harmful working conditions and women's place in society as mothers, as well as implicitly in terms of relative strength.

The danger to women's fertility was frequently cited as one of the reasons why women should not work with harmful chemicals. For example:

> women should not do harmful or heavy work, especially at my age [23] because they can bear children. Women have another role, a more difficult role as a mother — and there are harmful conditions here and already two women are ill and have stomach problems.

The difference between men's and women's supposed mental capacities or their temperaments were also often used to justify the differences in their work. As one woman argued:

> Working with a machine is not like washing dishes. It is more technical work, and working with machines is male work. From the point of view of the

> structure of people's minds; women's minds are more inclined to humanitarian sciences and men to technical and men are more able to work on the technical side.

Women frequently argued that 'men have a different kind of mind to women. They are more analytical', or that men were more logical. This was often accompanied by the view that 'women are not like men, they don't leave everything at home, but men do'. This view was expressed by both men and women, though rather more frequently by men. So one man stated that women

> shouldn't be pilots or bus drivers. I don't trust women in this position — a woman driving a car is very dangerous ... because women depend on their mood and if something is wrong at home it's always on their minds and women never leave home behind ... Men are very dependent on women at home but at work men think only of work ...Women always think of their children and what condition their husband will come home from work in ... drunk or sober.

In general the men stated these views even more forcefully than did the women, and while the women tended to concentrate on the physical aspect, i.e. that women couldn't physically do such heavy work, some of the men emphasised women's more decorative purpose in life!

> Men and women should do different work, and heavy work is men's work — and work which has long hours and night shifts and harmful conditions because women must be beautiful and weak and must not look like horses ... — for example bus drivers. Bus no 4 has a woman driver, but imagine her in dirty overalls under the bus, covered in oil and then preparing to go to the theatre. She would smell. On the other hand, men must be proud of their position and profession and that he earns the money for them to go to the theatre.

Or another man:

> Printing is men's work and I don't understand why it's women here. Women must be women and you can't be or feel yourself as a woman working here.

In talking about 'women's work' both men and women tended to bring out other supposed innate attributes, such as women's dexterity or patience. For example one man said that it was women working in the binding shop because:

> Men couldn't do this work because you need to be accurate and neat and the men are not so patient.

Or another man:

> Women should do sitting work because men can't sit down for long periods. They need to be able to move around. Women are more patient. Physical work is men's, and women's hands are more useful for cloth and foodstuffs. Men are more rough.

Or as one woman put it, these jobs are 'women's jobs because men would look very funny just sitting here collating papers', and 'the work is too boring for men'.

Similar arguments were used about the linotype operators:

> It's like typing and men just wouldn't like to sit and work with their fingers all day long.

And:

> Men can't cope with this work. They are more suited to more crude work because we work with very small pieces.

As the chief of one shop put it:

> Women are the perfect performers … it's a sort of discrimination but it's right because of the nature of women.

It was argued by most people that

> Women should do all the work that needs to be done carefully, thoroughly, cleanly or neatly … because of their nature.

However, it was also argued in certain cases that women were not attentive enough for other jobs. So for example, women could not work on the larger and most modern printing machines because women were not as attentive as men.

> Well it's not very heavy but it is more intellectual and you need imagination — printing needs some very delicate regulation of the equipment and women can't do it by nature … they are brought up in a different way … more like housewives … when they are working they think always about their families and men think more about their machines first of all.

Another point that often came up was the '10 per cent formula'. That is, the men would describe some small aspect of the job that would definitely prevent women from doing it, even if they could do the rest of the job. So, for example, one of the men working on the large offset machines said:

> Women could not do this work because it is too heavy. You need to insert large format paper. If it wasn't for this they could do it. It is complicated, but they could do it.

Stereotypes about men's role as providers were not as pronounced as in the West, but nevertheless existed. This was most clearly linked with wages, and people often said that men would not do this work because the wages were not high enough and they would not be able to support their families. As one man said:

> Maybe it's just a tradition that men must do the heavy work and take the burden of life on their shoulders.

Women as well as men generally thought that men should earn more. While the principle of equal pay for equal work was more or less taken for granted, in practice, because men and women were working on different machines with supposedly different, and in the women's case, lower skill levels, it was expected that men would earn more.

The one thing that is slightly different from Britain is the attitude to women working at all. While some men expressed the wish that their wives would stay at home, even they acknowledged that it was up to the women themselves and that most of their wives actually wanted to work. However, the idea that being able to support a wife at home as a mark of status is increasingly gaining ground, especially amongst entrepreneurs and businessmen.

Women's attitudes to their work

Despite the fact that the workforce in these plants was overwhelmingly female, and always had been, printing was still seen as men's work. Jobs within the enterprise that were described as women's work were very similar to those in the West, for example typing, computer operators, and fiddly work like binding. Furthermore, both men and women justified describing other operations as men's work in ways that were again similar, and as contradictory, as in the West.

However, the ways in which these stereotypes related to the actual lives of the women in particular was also contradictory. Despite the identification of heavy work with men and low pay with women, some women did comment that:

> Our husbands don't earn much more than us and in any case we work like men, sometimes even harder and besides we do all the housework.

Most of the distinctions that identified work as men's work made little sense, especially the distinction between heavy/dirty work and light/clean work. Most of the women worked in precisely those areas which were amongst the heaviest. For example, nearly all the printers on the old letterpress technology were women. When new technology had been introduced men were employed on the new planetas (offset machines). But as one of the women pointed out:

> Conditions are often bad. Sometimes they install equipment with no ventilation, but the workers are pressed for time and ignore the conditions ... they know about them but they don't have any time to worry about them ... I have worked here for 20 years and it's difficult to imagine anything else. I liked the work as a printer but it should be men really ... the older equipment is heavier but you need higher qualifications on the planetas because it is more complicated production.

The women working on the linotype also provide a good example of how different aspects of a job are stressed, depending on who is doing it. What is conventionally known as the most skilled and highly paid work in the West is done by women here.

In the West the work is described as making demands on numeracy, literacy, aesthetic sense, dexterity and physical strength and the men are said to have an interactive and informed relationship with their machines.

In the enterprise in Syktyvkar however, the work was most often described as being suitable for women because it was like 'typing' and involved accuracy, patience, and a lot of sitting still. The women were also described by most men as having a fairly basic relationship to the machinery:

> A man can't bear it when his machine doesn't work ... he must win the fight against the machine ... women will just say that it doesn't work and go get a mechanic.

Many women on the other hand when talking about their own work displayed as much attachment to 'their' machines as any of the men:

> As a printer I could repair my machine and I loved my machine. Everyday I stayed behind after work to clean it and do small repairs and even when we had *Subbotniks* [extra work on Saturdays] I still tried to clean my machine even when I wasn't supposed to.

> Women can work with machines — they do here and do small repairs themselves and clean them and so on. ... There is a special time set aside for it and the mechanics guide them and give them the parts they need. ... There is one machine that works only for one woman ... It takes time to learn a machine and if you do it for a long time with one machine then you can hear if it's working properly and you know if you need to stop it ... They know when something is wrong and what repairs are needed and can feel by the quality of the paper if a machine will work well or needs to be adjusted.

Some of the women clearly still gained pleasure from the content of the work:

> This work is quite interesting and it's very pleasant when you do something beautiful and it is not too difficult ... it is an art work. There is a sense of producing something tangible, artistic ... and as a woman I think all women feel satisfaction when they do something creative.

Others, however, described how the work had changed. In the past they had done colour printing, but this was only done now on the new technology. Most of the women's work now was printing blank forms and one woman said:

> We used to print posters and pictures and I liked the work, I liked mixing the colours to match the original, but we don't have this work now. Working with the forms 'cools' you because it is more simple and you don't have to worry about the quality so much and your soul doesn't work.

However, for most of the women work was an essential element in their lives:

If you love your job you can't stay at home, and two days on the weekend is enough for a rest ... I probably wouldn't give up work even if I could ... it's my character ... I can't live without people ... I'm a very sociable person ... I was home for 18 months with both the children ... when children are small they need a lot more attention and 18 months is not so long ... it just flew by and I was soon back at work. ... Most women want to work, although the conditions are not so good ... you need something else ... and it depends on us to make things change ... if there are problems at work it's up to us to change them, and if all women stayed at home who would do the work? ... I can't even take a holiday.

While many women said that they worked primarily for financial reasons, most followed this by saying that it would be difficult not to work at all because it was boring to stay at home with children all the time, and also because of the social contacts:

I wouldn't give up work now even if we had enough money ... because I always have fresh news ... We publish nine newspapers ... you can buy them but I have the news today and you only tomorrow ... I would die at home of boredom ... I would have only the TV set for company ... and I would miss the company here ... I have spent so many years here I couldn't live without it ... even when I was at the professional school all our practical lessons were here and I have been here over 20 years.

Another woman said:

I'm used to working here and seeing the people and I couldn't be at home all the time ... maybe women should work only 4 hours a day ... but in Russia we like to spend time with each other in large groups ... it's a national habit ... and we need the wages as well because not everyone has a husband or one who earns enough ... I think that at least half the women here would continue to work even if they didn't need to.

And another:

I'd go mad staring at four walls all day ... We work at home as well but without any thanks ... not that we're thanked here either but at least here we feel needed, but not at home.

It was not only that women did not live up to the stereotypes. Many of them felt that men did not either:

Earlier 'men were like men' ... now they are too delicate ... they are physically strong but they are afraid of physical work, afraid to overdo it ... and they are busy in commerce and trade ... men are lazy and don't want to work ... they have everything.

CONCLUSION

In broad outline, the stereotypes which define the appropriateness of particular jobs for men and women are very similar in Britain and in Russia, despite the fact that the actual jobs done by men and women are different. When work that is considered men's work in Britain, but women's work in Russia (for example linotype operators, or, in the coal mining industry, work in coal preparation plants), it is the description of the key features of the job that differs, not the gender stereotype to which it is related. When women do work that is considered to be stereotypically men's work, this is justified in relation to a stereotype that is not attached to the job itself, that the work is low-paid, but the work continues to be thought of as men's work. When new technology makes it possible to raise wages, men take over the new jobs.

When women describe the general characteristics of their work, they do so in terms of the gender stereotypes. However, these stereotypical descriptions are contradicted by their more detailed and concrete descriptions of their work, when it becomes clear that they are perfectly capable of performing intricate, demanding and heavy work as well as the men, that they are as concerned about and committed to their work as the men, and that they carry a heavy domestic burden on top of this, without their domestic cares disrupting their work.

This disjunction between stereotypes and reality serves to separate women from their experience as they talk about work in a highly gendered and evaluative language which does not bear any relation to what women actually do or what is actually important to them. However long women have been working at their jobs, and however important their jobs may be to them, they still speak of their own work as though they are intruders who have no right to be where they are, and speak about their collective experience in ways which diverge fundamentally from their individual experience.

This disjunction makes any kind of collective resistance on the part of women *as women* extremely difficult, because the language within which they speak of their experience is not theirs.[6] This is perhaps one reason why resistance tends to be very contradictory and often self-defeating, diverted into acquiescence and compliance and a disenchantment. This is perhaps also one reason why women seek highly individualistic solutions to their individual problems, which again leads to compliance, resignation and indifference. Indeed, unless the framework of gender stereotypes itself is challenged, resistance can easily serve to reproduce the conditions it was intended to overcome as it serves to legitimise and reproduce ideological rationalisations of women's subordination. On the other hand, gender stereotypes can only be challenged effectively by precisely that collective action that they serve to inhibit.

6 Of course, women workers have played a very important role in collective actions at all points in Russia's history, often giving a lead to the men. However, in general women have been active in the workers' movement *as workers*, and not specifically as women. The whole iconography and ideology of the revolution conspired to de-sex women as workers, and to link their feminity to their role as mothers.

8. The Regional Elite in the Epoch of Bankruptcy

Pavel Romanov

In this chapter I intend to explore the social forces underlying the implementation of Russian bankruptcy legislation at regional level, with particular reference to the relationship between economic and political power. The chapter is written at what is still an early stage in the bankruptcy process. It is based primarily on research carried out in the Samara region, whose giant aircraft factory is still, at the time of writing, the only major enterpise in Russia to have been put through the bankruptcy process (*Financial Times*, London, February 7, 1995). It is, therefore, premature to claim that my findings can be applied to all regions of Russia, or extrapolated into the future. Nevertheless, various other sources of information support the supposition that events in Samara, apart from regionally specific features, also incorporate certain general features which are important to the understanding of the current stage of economic life in Russia.[1]

A POLITICAL TURNING POINT

Samara *oblast* is one of the top ten regions in Russia, measured by their contribution to the gross national product. Situated in the Middle Volga region, a significant industrial potential — large aerospace, engineering and metallurgical enterprises — is concentrated in Samara. A substantial part of this potential always had a marked military-industrial orientation and, in addition to the general problems of the

1 This chapter has been written on the basis of monitoring of the local press and interviews with a large number of informants in local and regional administration, banks and industrial enterprises during the period October to December 1994, supplemented by research material gathered by Veronika Kabalina in Moscow and Vladimir *oblast*. An earlier version of the chapter was presented to the conference of the British Association of Slavonic and East European Studies, Fitzwilliam College, Cambridge, 26 March, 1995.

current period, they are enduring the consequences of a sharp reduction in military orders.

But it is not only the reduction in military orders which acutely poses the question of the efficiency of this or that enterprise, but also the low levels of productivity, ageing machinery and the fall in industrial production (in the factories of Samara *oblast* over the past five years it has amounted to up to 70 per cent). Government economists have been arguing for a long time that it is necessary to bring order into industry, having taken active steps to restore the most unprofitable enterprises to health. During the autumn of 1993 there was already widespread discussion about plans to bring several enterprises into what was called 'indicative bankruptcy'. However, nothing had come of any of these plans in reality. The reason for this was the absence of a properly worked out normative basis for the application of the law on insolvency.

By August 1994 industry in the Samara region found itself in an extremely difficult situation. During discussion in the *oblast* Duma of the results of economic developments in the *oblast* in the first half of 1994, the deepening crisis in the local economy was plain for all to see. The pace of the decline in the volume of production had been even greater than anticipated (28 per cent, instead of the 18 per cent forecast). Production in the military-industrial complex and in light industry had fallen by almost half. Agricultural production had fallen by 15.9 per cent. Only ten per cent of enterprises had not reported a fall in production. Fifteen per cent of enterprises faced a real threat of bankruptcy, since they were unprofitable. Production had stopped at 162 enterprises, 397 enterprises were in arrears in the payment of wages, the total sum of which in the *oblast* amounted to 98.6 billion roubles (*Samarskie izvestiya*, 26 August, 1994).

Such a situation was not specific to Samara, so nobody was surprised at the revival of experiments in the sphere of bankruptcy by the central authorities. The first sign of the strengthening of policy was the visit of the general director of the Federal Bankruptcy Administration, Sergei Belyaev, to Samara. He defined the main technical task of his department: 'bankruptcy as a factor in the reorganisation of enterprises'. In Samara the bankruptcy chief participated in regional meetings with leaders and representatives of trade union committees from chemical industry enterprises in the *oblast* and then in the *oblast* administration he met with representatives of the Union of Industrialists and Entrepreneurs. At a press conference reporting on the results of his visit Belyaev said that according to the records of the State Property Committee, thousands of people were working in factories in various branches, but in fact only a handful were working there. That is to say, the enterprises in practice had been liquidated, but their debts continued to grow. This tendency to 'soft liquidation' was very dangerous, and the government was going to force the process of bankruptcy ahead.[2]

The director of the Samara territorial bankruptcy agency (one of 83 such agencies established throughout Russia), A. Bakhmurov, announced that 16,000 enterprises in the region had been inspected, including all forms of property, and that documents had been signed recognising 21 of them as insolvent:

> These are enterprises with an unsatisfactory (negative) balance structure, whose liquidity is below the average for the *oblast*. However, one could count on one's fingers the number of creditors who have submitted cases for the collection of debts to the arbitration court, which is slowing down the process of bankruptcy. In the near future the Samara agency will finish the formation of a databank concerning the financial condition of enterprises, so as to decide what to do with them — whether to take account of the complaints of the enterprise administration about objective difficulties, or to refer the matter to arbitration (*Samarskie izvestiya*, 25 August, 1994).

2 Yeltsin issued a decree on insolvency in August 1992, following the debt crisis that was precipitated by price liberalisation and the illiquidity of the banking system, and that was temporarily resolved by an effective debt write-off. However, this decree proved singularly ineffective, with only about fifty small enterprises being taken to court, around ten of which were declared bankrupt (*Izvestiya*, 29 June, 1994). A further Presidential Decree of December 1993 was followed by a government resolution in May 1994, implemented in subsequent Presidential Decrees, to get tough on bankruptcy. The main principle of the policy remained that of the 1992 decree, to use bankruptcy proceedings as far as possible to provide the space for the reconstruction of the enterprise as a going concern, with liquidation only as a last resort (Sergei Belyaev, *Rossiiskii Ekonomicheskii Zhurnal*, 8, 1994, p. 23). Thus the decree provided that the contract of the existing enterprise director would be terminated, and a new director appointed by the appropriate bankruptcy committee (usually on the basis of nomination by the creditors). The enterprise's debts would then be frozen for a period of up to eighteen months, during which time it would have an opportunity to restructure itself. At the end of the period the enterprise would be sold as a going concern or, if restructuring failed to establish solvency, the enterprise would be liquidated and its assets sold off. The decree also provided for an injection of new funds for enterprise restructuring, although no provision was made for such funding in the government budget, and Sergei Belyaev, head of the Federal Bankruptcy Administration, announced in August that only private funds would be available for this purpose (*Izvestiya*, 25 August 1994). The existing decrees do not clearly distinguish bankruptcy from insolvency.

DO FACTORIES WANT TO BE BANKRUPT?

To be declared bankrupt is a serious, unusual and, for the administration of the enterprise, humiliating process. However, in a number of cases the management team itself declares its bankruptcy and takes the initiative in presenting the case to the arbitration court. One case of such an initiative is that of the large Samara factory Gidroavtomatika. There was no way in which this enterprise was going to be able to rectify its economic position following the collapse of military orders. In the first half of 1994 it repeatedly stopped production. In July, according to official data, 85 per cent of the Gidroavtomatika workers were on compulsory leave.

But what forced the administration of the factory to ask to be recognised as insolvent? The answer to the question is contained in the Law on Insolvency. According to the law, once an enterprise has been declared insolvent, all its debts are frozen, and the money coming into its bank accounts is allocated not to the payment of its debts to its suppliers or banks — of its creditors — but to its reorganisation. This period can last as long as eighteen months, during which time attempts are made to correct the situation. Where such attempts are unsuccessful, it is anticipated that the enterprise will be sold. However, the possibility of this occurring is purely hypothetical, taking into account a whole series of circumstances, some of which we will discuss below.

It seems to us that many managers in present conditions would choose insolvency as the way out of a permanent crisis.[3] In doing so they would possibly have to sacrifice their own comfortable position — since the administration of the enterprise is for this period put into the hands of external management nominated by the creditors. One can anticipate that for some this would be a form of self-sacrifice, but for others a certain informal arrangement with the banks and local administration would guarantee the stability of the position of the factory bosses.

In the case of Gidroavtomatika the arbitration court, having considered the case, refused to declare the enterprise insolvent. Despite the existence of debts to its creditors, the court ruled that the enterprise

3 Aleksandr Shumilin, director of the Vladimir oblast bankruptcy administration, reported that he was frequently approached by directors seeking protection from creditors, restructuring funds, and help in finding outside investors, which he provided if the enterprise has a packet of shares available for sale (interview with Veronika Kabalina, 16 November, 1994).

was sufficiently liquid and could not, according to the law, be considered bankrupt. According to various sources, this was a purely formal reason for refusal, because the regional authorities had no interest in bankrupting this factory, and was not prepared to meet its management halfway.

Reference to the arbitration court may not necessarily be made by the senior managers responsible for the condition of the enterprise. It is quite obvious that for many of them such recourse would imply the loss of their job and nothing more. One can see a number of cases over the summer and autumn of 1994 in which conflict within the senior management team of an industrial enterprise culminated in the opposition referring a plea to declare the enterprise bankrupt to the arbitration court. The episode at Syzransel'mash is indicative in this respect, where the bankruptcy plea was submitted in the name of the trade union committee of the enterprise.

Syzran' is a city in Samara *oblast*. In 1997 the enterprise Syzransel'mash will celebrate its centenary. But the enterprise has never in its entire history found itself in such a difficult position. Its trade union committee appealed to the *oblast* administration in a letter in which it pleaded for the enterprise to be declared bankrupt (*Samarskie izvestiya*, 9 September, 1994). There was a serious reason for this plea. The 2,500 workers had been on compulsory leave for several months, more than 1,000 workers had left the enterprise in the previous year because of the lack of prospects and the banks had refused it credit. The examination of the solvency of the enterprise, conducted by employees of the regional tax and financial services in April 1994, showed that the net indebtedness of the enterprise amounted to 3.5 billion roubles, a figure which will have increased by the end of the year. And it transpired that the production cost of one agricultural machine in 1993 was 1,167,000 roubles, while it sold for only 1,157,000.

According to a trade union representative, 'the factory management is in complete disarray — the loss of material assets in April amounted to 316 million roubles, on top of the losses made by the factory'.[4] Another no less important argument in his opinion was that 'the bulk

4 Reports of the loss of material assets from enterprises in a pre-bankrupt situation are in fairly common circulation around the enterprise. Unofficial sources mention in particular the plundering of raw materials and parts (paint, carpets) from one of the aviation factories. The names of those responsible are well-known to many of the workers in this factory, but criminal prosecutions have hardly ever occurred.

of the shares are concentrated in the hands of various legal persons and the factory administration, while the labour collective has only seven ordinary (voting) shares'.[5] The trade union activists are also angered by the fact that in conditions of 'economic failure the administration has bought an armoured car for the enterprise to transport cash, for 35 million roubles, and seven automobiles'.

BANKS ARE INCLUDED IN THE GAME

As one can see, up to a certain point the initiative in the matter of bankruptcy belongs, basically, to the enterprises themselves. Their main creditors, the banks, including commercial banks, which have lent them huge sums of money for the purchase of raw materials and payment of wages, have up to now remained passive. This can probably be explained by the fact that both sides — banks and factories — are playing a waiting game. Both sides have been waiting for the government to take the actions promised to unravel the crisis of mutual non-payment which has already paralysed Russian industry. There have been broad announcements of a number of different ways of resolving this problem: in the form of the centralised covering of debts or through a system of mutual accounting, or maybe through the issue of bills. The latter method would appear to be preferable to the banks, which could operate with bills instead of suffering the losses that would arise in the event of widespread bankruptcies.

The government's solution appears to have been for its representatives to hold behind the scenes negotiations with leaders of the regions and local banks (as with the visit of Sergei Belyaev to Samara), which have activated the creditors of industrial enterprises. It has become clear that neither the new financial institutions, nor state bodies on their own can find an effective solution to the looming problems.

5 A typical feature of this appeal is the fact that a) the authors appeal directly to the oblast administration - thus indicating the real distribution of power in the region; b) it uses the phraseology of justice, emphasising the 'unjust' distribution of shares (although, in essence, this signifies that the trade union stood aside during the process of privatisation and only remembered the workers' rights when it suited it).
It seems to us that the most probable reasons for the conflict with the top management of the enterprise (considering its traditional venality) are power and money. The trade union activists, having missed out during privatisation, want to get hold of some of the property which they seemed to have lost as a result of privatisation.

The main bank operating in the industrial sphere in the Samara region is the Middle Volga Commercial Bank (SVKB).[6] Its representatives are included on the boards of the largest privatised enterprises in the *oblast* (the largest producer of rolled aluminium, Sameko, the aircraft building factory AVI.S and many others). Some commentators connect the decision of SVKB to refer cases of debtors to the court with the appointment of a new manager to the bank, Danya Vagapov, who officially took up his post on 29 August, 1994. They also comment on the significant influence which several bureaucrats of the regional administration exert on its progress. Among the first steps taken by Vagapov in his new post were to refer insolvency cases to the arbitration court concerning the individual private enterprise Garant (declared bankrupt), the state enterprise ZiM (Zavod imeni Maslennikov) and joint-stock company AVI.S (so covering a private enterprise, a state enterprise and a privatised enterprise) (*Volzhskaya kommuna*, 7 September, 1994).

The hearing of the ZiM case was postponed on a petition from the *oblast* bankruptcy committee. According to representatives of the *oblast* administration, the government was expected to take a decision in the very near future about so-called 'enterprises of state importance', which would include all military factories. Since in ZiM military production takes place side by side with shops which produce consumer goods (electronic equipment for motor vehicles, watches, sewing machines) the division of the enterprise had been proposed (*Volzhskaya zarya*, 19 August, 1994). In the future, in place of one factory, there would be two — a 'state' enterprise producing military equipment, and a peaceful enterprise, which would be sold at auction

6 The Russian banking system is fully represented in the Samara region. This means that within the oblast banks of various types are active: both state and commercial. The latter include both branches of financial structures based in other cities and local Samara banks. It is also necessary to bear in mind that some of them are based on the capital of businessmen, entrepreneurial structures (for example Inkombank, Volzhsko-Kamskii Kommercheskii Bank), others were created in the form of 'pocket' banks of industrial enterprises (such as AvtoVAZbank, Inzhenerbank), while a third group are essentially splinters from the former Soviet banking system, reorganised out of the system of branch affiliates of the State Bank after the restructuring of the latter (SVKB, for example, developed out of the Samara branch of Promstroibank). The activities of the SVKB financiers often demonstrate the usefulness of traditional informal contacts. These contacts, with a high degree of continuity, connect such banks by hundreds of strings with the local administration and state structures. Local analysts take the view that each of the three or four leading banks in the oblast lobbies at the regional level through its own particular bureaucrats, in practice the leading personalities in the region.

immediately the decision was implemented.[7]

However, it should be noted that no such division has taken place, and nobody knows when or whether it will happen, but the decision about insolvency is blocked. One can see in this a tactic of the regional administration and industrialists who do not want to see the property of a factory, which is quite competitive in market conditions and has a huge potential, going under the hammer. The results of privatisation in such circumstances would be quite unpredictable. This contrasts with the more usual variant of privatisation when shares are formally transferred to the labour collective, which in practice means that control remains in the hands of the existing management of the enterprise, with whom the local authorities already have well developed relationships.[8]

The banks, as if wakened by the change in state policy, seemed ready to follow the new course. In this respect the Samara autumn agricultural fair was indicative. Its programme included an auction, sponsored by the *oblast* administration and the state property fund. Shares of 19 privatised enterprises were put on sale, but there was also a phenomenon which was new to Samara, the sale of the liabilities and mortgaged property of enterprises. The latter comprised primarily agricultural machinery and equipment and building materials required by peasant owners and farmers. Here the *oblast* administration was

7 Shumilin, the chief of the bankruptcy administration in Vladimir oblast, complained that the regional administration saw bankruptcy as just another way of channelling state funds to local enterprises. Takamak, a local military enterprise, was heavily in debt with a very weak management. Shumilin proposed putting the enterprise out to tender to bring in a stronger management, but the Director had close personal connections in the oblast and secured its inclusion on the list of military enterprises to receive priority support from the Federal budget (Veronika Kabalina interview, 16 November, 1994).

8 Bankruptcy is an effective mechanism for the forced privatisation of enterprises which are either potentially viable or have valuable assets. Such a forced privatisation is being contemplated for the giant AZLK auto factory in Moscow, whose privatisation has been blocked for over four years by political conflicts. The director of the Vladimir oblast bankruptcy administration regards this as the 'gentlest' solution, but it is not easy to find a buyer, particularly because the conditions of sale normally include the requirement to maintain employment and to continue to support the social sphere. The one Vladimir enterprise declared bankrupt was the joint-stock company Undol'skaya Manufaktura, with debts of 27 billion roubles against a valuation of 15 billion, of which the main creditor and initiator of the suit, a branch of the Moscow-based Agroprombank, was owed 15 billion. The enterprise was placed in administration for 6 months from December 15th 1994, at the end of which period it would be auctioned. However, the director of the bankruptcy administration proposed to define the reserve price of the enterprise on the basis of the sum of its indebtedness, plus the amount required to invest in restructuring (more than 21 billion) (interview with Veronika Kabalina, 16.11.94).

expressing its approval of the new types of relationship between agriculture, banks and industrial enterprises, such as were established through this fair. Only in July there had been a trial auction for the compulsory sale of mortgaged property of enterprises indebted to SVKB. The experiment was considered a success and according to the management of the bank will be repeated in future. For example, at this auction property to the value of 9.5 billion roubles was put up for sale. The Krest'yanskii bank also took part in the sale, putting up for auction a small cheese factory in Orlovka, a village in the Koshkinskii district (*Volzhskaya zarya*, 19 August, 1994).

CHRONICLE OF THE CRISIS OF THE AIRCRAFT FACTORY

As has already been said, the Samara aircraft factory (AO AVI.S) is one of the enterprises which fell into the category of completely hopeless industrial enterprises, against which SVKB decided to submit an insolvency case to the arbitration court. The local mass media reports on the case are rather inconsistent. Some sources (such as *Samarskie izvestiya*, 27 August, 1994), for example, reported that the management of AVI.S itself decided not to wait for a decision of the regional bankruptcy agency and, seeing no possibility of restoring its solvency, declared itself bankrupt, having asked the chief of the federal bankruptcy administration, Sergei Belyaev, to speed up the procedure. Whatever may have been the case, until the end of August the situation was still rather uncertain. AO AVI.S should have started work on 1 September, following a one and a half month shut-down, when all the workers were sent on compulsory leave (some shops had not worked since April). However, when the workers came in to work they found an order of the administration posted at the entrance extending the compulsory leave with minimal pay (in practice with no pay at all) until at least 19 September. The factory had already experienced enormous difficulty with the sale of planes over a long period (almost a full year's programme of finished planes remained unsold), and as a result of huge indebtedness production had been practically paralysed (*Samarskie izvestiya*, 2 September, 1994).

Economics, politics and the unprofessionalism of management

The speed of the collapse of an enterprise, which was in the past one of the leaders in domestic aircraft construction, should not cause any surprise. Even in 1992 and 1993 work at the aircraft factory was considered prestigious among the inhabitants of the city. The reduction of military orders could not overturn it, as was the case in the majority of enterprises in the region. The production of civilian aircraft appeared at first to be quite a profitable sphere of activity. Everybody spoke about the extraordinarily high wages of the workers, compared to other industrial enterprises, the strong system of social welfare — kindergartens, rest homes, sports palace and so on. Non-monetary means of payment of labour were especially valued, the distribution of barter goods which were provided at much lower prices than they could be obtained outside the enterprise. Most of these goods (clothes, toys, domestic appliances) were produced in China, arriving in payment for planes delivered to China.

At the end of 1993 the negative tendencies, which had been building up for a long time, resulted in a sharp deterioration in the economic position of the enterprise. The workers were the first to experience the change in the situation, when they went as usual to collect their wages at the window of the cash office. The wages of basic workers were cut, in connection with the fall in the amount of work. This reduction was accompanied by delays in the payment of wages. The workers, used to their prosperous position, reacted sharply to signs of sickness in their own enterprise, which hit them in the pocket. Discontent at the difficulties in receiving their honourably earned money flared up and was expressed in spontaneous meetings at which the workers confronted the factory management with reproaches addressed to the senior managers. Indignation was so great that the general director of the enterprise, a charismatic leader who had been in the post for many years, had to endure a humiliating torrent of snowballs in response to his attempt to justify himself and to calm the people. Soon after this the director resigned and retired.

In the spring of 1994 there had been a fight in the office of the chief accountant and one of the shop chiefs was taken to hospital. This incident happened when he tried to collect his pay, jumping his place in an irritated queue of people who had been waiting hopelessly for a long time to receive their money. The position of the victim was made worse by the fact that the workers found out how much he was paid (the salaries of managers from the chief of shop upwards are not usually disclosed) which amounted to several millions of roubles.

These episodes provide only a weak indication of the level of social tension which had arisen in the machine shops. Nobody knew how everything would turn out, but the new factory administration changed its employment policy. Instead of working on the principle of a partial working week, workers in the basic production shops were sent on extended leave on minimum pay. Each person was given a certain period after which he or she should return, if the situation improved. Over the summer people could work on their allotments, which moderated the tension and quietened passions somewhat. Some of the skilled workers found other jobs and ways of making additional earnings.

The managers of the enterprise gave various explanations for the production crisis. The majority saw the source of all the problems outside the factory, identifying a series of negative factors. Among the most common explanations heard were the following:

1. Bad publicity arising from incidents in Russia and abroad involving the modified TU-154 aeroplane produced by the factory. The crash of a plane at Irkutsk in January 1994 was very widely publicised. The factory's specialists insisted that the source of the problems was not the poor quality of engineering, but mistakes on the part of the crew. However, they did not manage to counter the bad publicity. As a consequence they not only lost long-term agreements, but customers even refused to pay for aircraft which were being assembled. This revealed mistakes on the part of the sales representatives of AO AVI.S, since the sales contracts were drawn up in such a way that it was not possible to demand the payment of penalties.
2. Another factor in the crisis was said to be 'the government's civil aviation policy. The fact is that priority has been given to international transport — they are buying Boeings, which are the same type of aircraft' (interview with a department chief, November 1994).
3. Changes in the organisational structure of Aeroflot, the main domestic customer, which has been privatised into a series of quite small independent companies. Seventy per cent of the planes produced by the factory are destined for the use of these firms on internal flights. Many of the planes have been flying for a long

time, but the companies which use them are not in a financial position to update their fleet, taking into account also the demand of the manufacturer for payment in advance and the sharp increase in the price of the planes (interview with shop chief, November 1994).

4. Inflation has also reduced the ability to pay of the new commercial structures, who are the other customers for planes. According to several specialists, two or three years ago these structures, in conditions of a stable dollar exchange rate and high bank interest rates, could quite easily invest in the purchase of aircraft. The enterprise had even developed a programme to produce a very small plane for business flights, a project which has been frozen. Now that all signs of stability have disappeared, new Russian businessmen have lost interest in aviation (interview with manager, November 1994).

For an objective appraisal of the state of affairs in the enterprise it is impossible to ignore the opinion of those sober-minded middle managers who criticise the lack of professionalism of senior management. One can hear, for example, that the enterprise management, having achieved reasonable economic results in 1993, lived from day to day, concentrating on a familiar sector of the market, without developing any long-term perspective. When the situation was destabilised by the wave of non-payment, the sales department was not ready for it.

The active appearance of competition from the aircraft factories of Ul'yanovsk, Voronezh and Tashkent also came as a surprise to the monopolistically minded administration. They quickly took over the traditional niches of the Samara factory, helped by the latter's passive marketing policy. The basic error here, the middle managers believe, was the orientation to an established circle of large customers, inflexibly scorning any interest in the small new firms (interview with shop chief, November 1994).[9]

The level of preparation of deals with foreign partners is also considered to be very low. Planes were sold to China and Egypt on a direct basis, without any government guarantees from these states, without payment in advance and on a barter basis — for consumer goods and toothpaste. Egypt now owes the factory three million dollars and China, thirteen million. The private Kirgizian aviation company Zvezda Vostoka owes the Samara factory 69 billion roubles.

9 These interviews were conducted by my colleague Lena Lapshova.

When one takes other debtors into account, the debts owed to the enterprise more than cover its own debt (*Volzhskaya Zarya*, 2 November, 1994).

The most significant miscalculation of the factory administration, and apparently the main reason for the increased attention paid to it by the *oblast* authorities, was its connections with Moscow financial circles, at a time when the bureaucrats of the regional administration were trying by every means to concentrate the maximum power in their own hands, having grabbed it from the centre! It is difficult to imagine that in its effort to protect the home market from the Moscow sharks, the local bureaucratic elite would allow any external unpredictable financial forces to penetrate the territory subordinate to it.[10]

The actual canvas of events only became known after the external arbitration board was imposed on the management of the factory. A regular flow of information about the implausible activities of the previous administration appeared in management submissions, which were leaked to the local press. It was reported, for example, that in the summer of 1994 the general director of the aircraft factory signed an agreement with the Moscow financial concern Stolitsa to collaborate on extremely unprofitable terms. According to this agreement Stolitsa committed itself to 'attract external investors' and promised 'to invest its money in the development of production, co-operate in widening the market for the products, carry out market research and participate in the modernisation of production'.

In return for these illusory promises, AVI.S 'guarantees to co-operate with the concern in realising its control of the financial activities of the enterprise, to provide it with any information necessary for this, including financial records and pre-contract documents'. Moreover, every contract for the sale of planes would be considered to be invalid without the signed agreement of Stolitsa. Alongside this,

10 The concentration of power in the hands of the oblast administration is a process which does not have anything to do with the decentralisation of the Russian Federation. Even for those oblasts in the Urals region or in the Far East, which some time ago spoke about establishing some kind of republics, the loud demands for sovereignty were no more than ways of pointing to a problem. The problem consisted of the unequal position of republics and oblasts (or krais), in the unjust redistribution of federal money between the regions which paid the taxes and those who received grants from the federal budget. One cannot say that these contradictions had been resolved by the end of 1994. At least not in the Samara region where the constitution of the oblast, regulating its relations with the centre, has still not been adopted. This does not mean, however, that many powers and concessions are not extended from Moscow in an ad hoc way, through personal meetings and informal negotiations.

conditions for the cancellation of the agreement were stipulated, that the agreement is permanent and can only be terminated with the agreement of both parties. The unilateral abrogation of the agreement by one party would incur a penalty to be paid to the other of 50 billion roubles.

Official commentators assume that this is merely a mechanism through which to transfer the factory to a new owner, which only failed because of the intervention of the regional insolvency agency and the case in the arbitration court. It is possible that the existence of such a contract was also a reason for the delay in the decision of the arbitration court, which only reached a decision at the second attempt (*Moya gazeta* 5 November, 1994).

Bankruptcy

On 19 September the fate of the enterprise was determined. By a decision of the arbitration court AO AVI.S was declared insolvent and transferred to external management, in the results of which 40 of its creditors registered a special interest, the largest of which was SVKB. The general financial picture, with the inevitable gaps which arise when one does not have access to the primary documents, is as follows:

Basic indicators of the financial situation of AO AVI.S

Creditors (All figures in billion roubles):

SVKB	115	
Avia-bank	8	
federal budget	30	
wages	5	
other	20	
not indicated	22	(This may be AvtoVAZbank)
Total:	200	

Debtors:

China	13	million dollars ('barter' dollars)
Egypt	3	million dollars
Kirgizia	69	billion roubles
Other	13	billion roubles

Other Assets:

Uncompleted planes	60	billion roubles
Stocks	12	billion roubles

All the debts of the enterprise after the decision of the court are frozen and that money which it receives as profit will go to new investment in production and the payment of wages to the workers, who had not been paid since March.

Why was the aircraft factory not declared bankrupt? Where has the term of twelve months come from? Was the possibility of the immediate sale of the enterprise to cover its debts considered? Some clarification of the reasons for this decision are provided by an interview with the deputy chief of the regional administration Vladimir Moskovskii. In his statement it is clear that the reason for the decision was more political than economic (officially the reason for the delay was, in the words of the judicial verdict, 'the real possibility of the enterprise's restoring its solvency'). Describing the negative social consequences of declaring the factory bankrupt today V. Moskovskii said:

> First, the whole enormous social sphere of the enterprise (357 apartment blocks, 22 kindergartens and so on) would be left without any stable source of financing. Second, at least 8,000 workers would be laid off, adding to the ranks of the unemployed. Third, the *raion* and the city would lose ten billion roubles in taxes from their budgets. Fourth, if the factory changed its production over time, and made something else instead of aeroplanes, this would have a very bad impact on the regional economy, since 22 per cent of the raw materials and parts are supplied by local enterprises, who would immediately lose their markets. Fifth, it will become impossible to carry out mobilisations in the event of natural disasters or emergencies (*Samarskie izvestiya*, 27 September, 1994).

It seems to us that it was the expectation of such possible negative consequences for the economic and social stability of the region that was one of the most important reasons for the delay in bankrupting AO AVI.S. The fear of a social explosion is constantly visible in many public statements of both local and national leaders.

The decision of the Creditors' Council about the candidate to be the external manager of the enterprise turned out to be a surprise for the conservative-minded circles of the industrial administration of the city. On 28 September it was announced that the new manager would be the young manager of the Samara branch of AvtoVAZbank, Lev Aronovich Khasis, an appointment that was unexpected even by him. The new manager of the aircraft factory has managed to build a meteoric career in his 28 years, having been for several years the head of the AO Samarskii Torgovyi Dom, an enterprise which imported large quantities of mass consumption goods from Israel. Khasis was well known for his close contacts with the *oblast* administration which, possibly, was also one of the main reasons for his nomination. It is interesting that the new head of the factory was a graduate of the Samara Aviation Institute, and had carried out his pre-diploma placement in one of the shops of this enterprise.

It turned out, following the nomination of Khasis as head of AVI.S, that the arbitration court only confirmed his appointment at the second attempt. It is also interesting that it was Khasis who went forward, while the chief creditor, having the largest interest in the enterprise, SVKB, did not put forward a candidate at all. The new chief of AVI.S explains this by the fact that by this time active negotiations were being conducted about the purchase of the enterprise's debts by AvtoVAZbank.

At the moment it is not clear who will hold the controlling interest in the Samara aircraft building giant, which currently is not in the hands of anybody. The shares are at present distributed as follows: the state holds 25.5 per cent, the labour collective holds 50 per cent, while various investment funds hold the rest.

To keep control of this issue, Khasis invited the deputy president of the regional state property administration, A.Osipov, to join the management team he was assembling. Osipov became the deputy director for legal matters. The record of the other members of the team commands similar respect. The former head of the city tax inspectorate, A.Antamokhin, was appointed 'to strengthen the accounts department'; L.Terent'ev, a colleague of Khasis from AvtoVAZbank, became deputy for marketing, and another colleague, V. Ryzhkov, would handle relations with the press, which would acquire considerable significance.

At the press conference to introduce Khasis as the new director there was talk of reorganising the management team, and of at least increasing the profitability of aircraft production. Speaking about the long-term future of production, Khasis declared that the TU-154 is a perfectly reliable and competitive plane, and that the accidents which had taken place recently and had adversely affected sales had arisen exclusively as a result of the human factor.

The former general director of AVI.S, E. Kornev, explained that the decision 'to close ranks' with the financial world had not been an easy one for him:

> But circumstances required it, it was necessary to subordinate ourselves.... The biggest loss at this time is the two thousand core workers who have left... However, it is comforting that the majority of them have kept their labour books in the personnel department of the factory. Having learned that production levels will be restored over the period 1995–7, I am sure that they will return despite the easy money which many of them are now making (*Volzhskaya kommuna*, 2 November, 1994).

First steps of the new administration

The arrival of the external management at the aircraft factory became an event not only in the life of the enterprise, but also in the life of the city. The interests of tens of thousands of people, many organisations and enterprises are very closely connected with the fate of the aircraft building giant. Great hopes rested on its revival. Taking this factor into account, an intensive advertising campaign was developed, during which press conferences followed interviews and statements to the press alternated with communiqués about the course of overcoming the crisis. The main emphasis of the single-minded information campaign was put on optimistic forecasts and promises of the new administration and the discussion of positive changes.

People did not have to wait long for the first news. On 3 November the first plane sold after the arrival of the new management departed for Tyumen'. This sale, the first for six months, was hailed by the new manager Khasis as evidence of the revival of aircraft production (*Moya gazeta*, 5 November, 1994). This news coincided with the confirmation of an arrangement achieved between the two largest banks in the city: AvtoVAZbank had redeemed all the liabilities of AVI.S to SVKB for 42 billion roubles. The contract was concluded in the form of a credit extended by the seller to the buyer with gradual payment of the capital sum and a fixed percentage rate of interest.

Commenting on this event, Lev Khasis expressed optimism and the hope that the credit would be liquidated in a short time and the factory would soon return to its former financial prosperity. He announced, in particular, that 'contracts for the delivery of 18 planes by the end of the year had now been concluded, demand for them is huge' (*Volzhskaya zarya*, 2 November, 1994). A new method of selling had been worked out — a kind of leasing or instalment plan. Among the buyers were RAO 'Unified Power System', the Sakha Republic and the Tomsk, Ekaterinburg and Tyumen' aviation companies. Firms from Belarus, China and Bulgaria had expressed interest, but foreign sales would only be made on the basis of prepayment in hard currency. According to Khasis these contracts would provide uninterrupted work for the factory until the second quarter of 1995.

One should note, however, that no miracle had taken place — Tyumen' had been ready to buy the planes in May (interview with shop chief, November 1994). However, at that time the enterprise had no interest in selling the planes, as was shown by the unfortunate experience of the sale of two completed machines — all the money received for them immediately went to cover the interest on the debts to SVKB. It was only the freezing of debts and opening of the accounts that has given any sense to commercial activity.

In the future the new administration plans to make considerable changes in the system of sales, introducing an instalment plan and a system of discounts, based on world experience. Moreover, information has appeared about a new economic scheme of work of the enterprise, to be introduced at the end of 1994, and about the rapid structural reorganisation of the factory, with its subsequent decentralisation. The character of future restructuring is limited to calling a halt to the creation of new services and subdivisions. According to an order, already sent for approval by the arbitration board, there are and will continue to be reductions in the administrative staff, small shops will be amalgamated, some divisions and departments will be liquidated, and the process of establishing separate structures for social services and capital construction has begun, with the factory retaining a 50 per cent controlling interest. The new management is going to make more intensive efforts to transfer housing and kindergartens to the municipal authorities. The sports palace is to be transferred to an independent enterprise to earn money. In December the issue of the separation of subsidiary agricultural activities and a public catering combine, with the factory retaining a controlling interest, was studied. The middle managers in the factory support these imminent decisions, achieved long ago in many enterprises in the city, one commenting thus: 'For a long time all this has been imposed on us, now we will get rid of it all, like in Western countries' (interview with department head, November 1994).

Living with bankruptcy

Up to the summer of 1995, although the company continued to be in a difficult position, there were some marked improvements in its situation. It declared that it had paid off half of all the debts of the factory and had high hopes of paying off the remainder during the period of external management (*Volzhskaya kommuna*, 5 July, 1995). Delays in the payment of wages ceased, the most important sign, in the eyes of the public, that the crisis had been overcome. However, the most important changes in the enterprise have been those in its system of management, where the team of young financiers joined the large team of experienced industrialists.

There were probably few people who expected that the arrival of a new administration in such a large enterprise with a complex system of relationships, developed norms and values such as the aircraft factory, could proceed without difficulty. However, it is very difficult to discover in practice what difficulties the team of outside managers encountered in the process of 'getting used to' the existing managerial machine. One has the impression that this process has been one of the creation of a new mechanism of control, sometimes carefully groping, or sometimes with sharp thrusts of the bayonet. One can suggest that the work of the arbitration management is developing on the basis of shadowy agreements about the limits of its interference.

The original plan of introducing external management did not in general anticipate, on the basis of the statements of the representative of the *oblast* administration, the manager and general director of the factory, how much there would be serious intervention in the management apparatus and how much structural reorganisation there would be. Nine months after this event, the then general director commented on this decision, in which he had been an immediate participant, thus:

> It became clear that without the help of a well-disposed bank we would not get out of the situation, ... I turned to our main creditors ... The main task of the arbitration manager and his team is to make money from production, and from the money to make more money. That is what they came for ...

This was a very widespread view and many members of the factory administration considered that sales was the weakest part of management since the old chiefs 'were pure producers, not economists, and even less financiers. But today that is what we need. But unfortunately they are very scarce.' Several months of development have led precisely to this scenario. Agreements about the completion of old deals have been reached, and new ones concluded, under the system of leasing discussed above. Energetic sales activity has expanded in all directions, including representation at the Paris air show at Le Bourget etc. The old administration has stayed in place, representatives of the arbitration team declare aloud: 'We are not producers and we do not intend to get into that business. But finance and marketing are needed and must be adapted to the level of contemporary demands — with this we will be concerned'. No criticisms of the old management have been heard, the new managers are completely loyal and do not allow careless comments, indeed they fairly often speak of the old traditions and the need to preserve them. Against this background the only important event turns out to be a further change in the name of the enterprise, from AO AVI.S it has become AO Aviakor (Aviation Corporation). In the press the arbitration management is stated to have become only 'a superstructure over the external structure of management' (*Volzhskaya kommuna*, 1 August, 1995).

Personnel changes proceeded almost unnoticeably for the outside observer. The former general director was fairly publicly removed from his post. However, this was presented as a voluntary self-sacrifice in the interests of the factory. This was followed by serious declarations of immediate plans to transfer the whole social and welfare apparatus, which had traditionally been a feature of the aircraft factory, with its sports complex famous throughout the city, its tourist bases, kindergartens, rest homes, profilaktories and so on.

The most important step of the administration was the reorganisation of the management of the factory. Until this reform, according to one member of the administration, a head of the personnel service (interview, 15 August, 1995), the management of the activities of the factory was organised into eight different spheres, each headed by a deputy of the general director: general questions; social questions; capital construction; economics and so on. The chief accountant and chief engineer had equal rank with the deputies and were directly subordinate to the general director. There is nothing in principle novel in this scheme, it reproduces the senior management of any large Soviet enterprise. Nor is the aircraft factory exceptional in the size of this apparatus — it was a consequence of the number of office posts occupied, many of which duplicated one another functionally, while the functions of others had already been eliminated with the collapse of the planned economy.

In general, therefore, and this is the most important point, that in order to confirm its control over the factory management, the reform was carried out with great speed and on a large scale. Now three departments have been created: production, financial-economic and administrative-legal. All the former departments, apart from those which have been liquidated, have been divided among these three. 'We have followed the path of structural amalgamation in order to reduce the management of the enterprise' (*Volzhskaya kommuna*, 1 August 1995). This structural amalgamation was accompanied by a significant reduction in the number of office staff. According to the administration, as a result of this reorganisation around 80 per cent of the employees of the management apparatus left (interview with vice-president for personnel work, 15 August, 1995).

All heads of departments, and also some key subdivisions (public relations, social policy and so on), are directly subordinate to L. Khasis. Two of the three departments are headed by members of his team, but production questions remain entirely in the sphere of competence of the 'radical' factory managers and this department is even headed by the same person in charge in the past. Nor has the reform extended to the system of line and shop management. Despite the fact that the shop structure of management in general reproduced on a smaller scale the higher level structure of the factory administration, to touch it would imply interference in production questions, which the arbitration management, evidently, cannot at the moment allow itself to do. This does not imply that there has been no managerial reorganisation. The enterprise administration is discussing immediate plans to create an industrial structure of a holding type. This would imply combining several technically related shops to form separate factories with a defined status.

Attempts of this kind had been undertaken in the past. Several years ago, for example, a consumer goods factory and a sanatorium-profilaktory, Reatsentr, were separated from the factory and given their economic independence. After the imposition of the arbitration management their independent status was annulled — the new administration considered that they had been given too much independence.

According to the conception which is being considered today the new factories will consist of parts of a common structure, possessing a determinate amount of financial freedom and with powers which are not strictly controlled by the administration of the holding company, which will still monopolise many functions.

An awareness of the new structure of the joint-stock company, Aviakor-servis, which was widely publicised in July 1995, is very important in discussing this scheme (*Volzhskaya kommuna*, 19 July, 1995). L. Khasis announced that 'the aim of the new structure is qualitatively to improve the guaranteed servicing of passenger planes produced by the factory, and also to supply aviation companies in Russia and the CIS countries to the fullest extent with necessary spare parts and complete assemblies'. To realise this project they plan to create a network of aircraft servicing centres throughout the CIS countries.

Up to the summer of 1995 there were various changes in the policy of the administration of Aviakor which affected a number of strategic questions. Representatives of the arbitration management began to speak less of the magical sales and more about the need for the state to support the aviation industry. This was related to the objective conditions of work in the industry at present, whose realities had to be taken into account. The basic reality was the very long time required to produce an aircraft and as a consequence the need to have substantial reserves of working capital which Aviakor, with its old debts, did not have at its disposal. The position of the Samara factory was not an isolated case in this respect.

For example, in 1994 the production of aircraft and helicopters had fallen to 151 from 505 in 1991 and 378 in 1993 (*Volzhskaya kommuna*, 5 July, 1995). At present there are 25 long-haul aircraft of the latest type, valued at 380 billion roubles, waiting for buyers. As a result the aircraft factories in Ul'yanovsk, Voronezh, Saratov, Perm and other places are on the verge of stopping work. The industry employs 778,000 workers, and if one takes account of neighbouring industries and the service sector the total employed is more than 3 million. The new types of passenger aircraft developed by the design offices, which are considered to be competitive with Western aircraft, cannot be produced in any quantity because there is not the money.

Analysts consider that state assistance provides the only way out of the situation, although the state has only reduced it, from 31 per cent in 1992 and 14 per cent in 1993 to 8 per cent in 1994. The aircraft producers have strengthened their demands for this support to be increased and for access of Western aircraft to Russia to be restricted. A whole range of arguments, including patriotic ones, have been put forward in support of these demands.

The aim of expanding state support began to be taken up in the policy of the administration of the Samara aircraft factory. A new push towards the next stage of the relationship between the factory and the state was provided by the visit of Prime Minister Chernomyrdin to Samara. Chernomyrdin came to the city on a semi-official visit, to celebrate the anniversary of the Samara Technological University (formerly the Kuibyshev Polytechnical Institute, of which he was a graduate), and met with the directors of the key Samara factories. He had a particularly long meeting with L. Khasis.

The result of these conversations, according to several sources (*Volzhskaya zarya*, 5th July, 1995), was a programme for the production of new types of long-haul aircraft supported by state financing. The new types of aircraft will be equipped with engines and navigation equipment produced by European and American firms.

The financial support of the state, obviously, cannot cover all the demands for money to put the new aircraft into production. Thus the principal of joint financing is envisaged, with investment capital coming from outside companies. Chernomyrdin promised that it would be possible to attract this money with state guarantees from the Russian government.

Another important indicator of this turn around in the internal policy of the factory was the reassessment of the plans to transfer the social and welfare apparatus to the municipality. This, of course, does not concern the substantial housing stock, the transfer of which to the local authority is legally obligatory. It was decided that the sports centre, rest homes, tourist bases and kindergartens would remain inviolable. The argument in support of this was the need for the social and welfare apparatus for the preservation of the collective and its importance as a factor in the cultural tradition of the factory.

Many people in the factory administration of Aviakor now speak about the preservation of tradition and this is represented as very important to the understanding of the present situation. In our view, this is a reflection of the wider problems connected with the reconstruction of Russian industrial enterprises (remembering that arbitration management, as a recognition of insolvency, in the view of those who organise the bankruptcy process is merely a lever of reconstruction). Those management teams which replace the so-called 'red directorate', which is really only a name for the traditional technocratically minded management team, oriented to the receipt of government support, run into similar problems and often have to fall back on similar patterns of behaviour. Other factors also complicate the situation — certain expectations and demands on the part of the local authorities, who are interested in social stability and, obviously, in preserving the integrity of the existing industrial structure, particularly of those enterprises which play a vital role in the economic and social life of the region. In practice the position of the arbitration management has been dictated by the need to compromise, which constantly reveals itself in the tactics of carrying out those policies which immediately concern production, managerial relations and their image, both their own and that of the reform process, in the eyes of public opinion and the regional administration.

CONCLUSIONS

The widespread practice of bankruptcy is the latest landmark in the development of reform in Russia. The Russian government is obviously disappointed that privatisation of enterprises has not brought fast positive shifts in management and in the growth of efficiency. The possession of shares has not brought radical changes in the behaviour of the new owners of industry — the existing managers (actual owners) or the workers (the nominal owners). The plunder of materials and parts has become a widespread phenomenon, factory management is rarely oriented to the market situation and acts short-sightedly, preserving old customs. The structure of enterprises changes only slowly, and is ill-adapted to new conditions, while the reconstruction of the social and welfare sphere of enterprises, a key aspect of the contemporary policy of the authorities in relation to the industrial sphere, lags.

Using the tactics and strategy of bankruptcy, the Russian government hopes to raise the modernisation of industry to a new level, hoping to play an active role in this process. Mass bankruptcy has already begun in Nizhni Novgorod and Orel. In Moscow, according to the mass media, a vitamin factory was declared bankrupt and sold at a ridiculously low price, 60 million roubles.

In principle the bankruptcy legislation is designed to achieve the transfer of former state enterprises to new owners, whether on the basis of secondary privatisation or through the forced privatisation of enterprises whose sale has hitherto been blocked by political obstacles. However, in Russia principle is always a very long way from practice. With its enormous economy and extremely undeveloped banking system, Russian industry and agriculture has faced a chronic shortage of working capital, which has been compensated by the growth of inter-enterprise debt, mediated through the banking system, the absence of control over which has freed enterprises from any predictable budget constraints.[11] The extended chains of indebtedness and low levels of liquidity make it almost impossible to define insolvency and bankruptcy unambiguously, since a large proportion of every enterprise's assets comprise potentially bad debts. This means that a declaration of insolvency or bankruptcy is essentially a political decision, even in the most chronic cases.[12]

It is important to distinguish the declaration of insolvency, which is the first stage of the process, from the formal bankruptcy and liquidation of the enterprise. There are several reasons why a declaration of bankruptcy for a large enterprise is an undesirable option from the point of view of the various interested parties.

11 The contrast between 'hard' and 'soft' budget constraints is misleading. The key point today, as in the Soviet period, is that budget constraints are hard but unpredictable. It is perhaps more appropriate to refer to this situation as the absence of 'firm' budget constraints.

12 Different sources give different estimates of the number of enterprises declared bankrupt. Belyaev was quoted in March 1994 as saying that not one enterprise had been liquidated (*Economist*, London, 19 March, 1994). In June he announced that a total of thirty bankruptcies had been declared, of which twenty were in Moscow (*Sevodnya*, 7 June, 1994), but in July Prime Minister Chernomyrdin announced that only six bankruptcies had been declared, with sixty cases currently before the courts and 1,500 to 2,000 cases being expected to be submitted by the end of the year (*Izvestiya*, 16 July, 1994). *Sevodnya* reported on October 15th that more than 200 enterprises had been declared insolvent, of which 50 were in receivership (*sanatsia*). In its first six months of operation the Vladimir oblast bankruptcy administration had looked at 68 state and 11 privatised enterprises and had taken control of about 30, of which one had already been declared bankrupt (Veronika Kabalina, interview with head of Vladimir bankruptcy administration, 16 November, 1994). See *Wall Street Journal* (12 November, 1993) for a report on the show-piece insolvency of an enterprise in Nizhni Novgorod oblast. However, as noted above, the Samara aircraft factory is still the only major bankruptcy in Russia.

First, the creditors of the enterprise stand to gain little from a declaration of bankruptcy because they are the last claimants to the assets of the enterprise, behind the existing employees, expenditure directed to the restructuring of the enterprise, and fiscal arrears, while their debts are frozen for up to eighteen months.

Second, the largest creditors are likely to be the enterprise's suppliers, who stand to lose a major customer if the enterprise is liquidated.

Third, a declaration of bankruptcy on the part of a large enterprise is likely to provoke a chain reaction as its creditors have to write off its debts. Such a writing-off of assets would have a devastating impact not only on commercial creditors, but also on the banking system. For all these reasons the creditors of the enterprise are unlikely to act, unless they have clear prospects of profiting by taking control of the enterprise, which in turn would normally imply that they have the support of the regional administration.

Fourth, regional and municipal authorities have a strong interest in preserving the large enterprise since, if that enterprise is liquidated, responsibility for the maintenance of what is often a very substantial infrastructure of health, education, welfare and housing provision falls to the local authority, which has no resources to meet such obligations. Moreover, large enterprises are the major source of municipal and regional tax revenues, the claim to which has priority over commercial claims.

Fifth, a declaration of insolvency of an already privatised enterprise immediately devalues the workers' shares, which they have so recently been induced with extravagant promises to buy, while liquidation implies widespread job losses. Although workers have long since lost all illusions about the benefits of privatisation, their expropriation could prove the last straw. This is perhaps one reason why privatisation through bankruptcy is being discussed primarily in relation to those large enterprises which have, for one reason or another, not yet been privatised.

While the liquidation of the bankrupt enterprise has little to offer any of the interested parties, a declaration of insolvency can play an important role in the struggle for control of the enterprise, since it is immediately followed by the dismissal of the general director and the installation of a new management team, nominated by the bankruptcy administration in consultation with the major creditors. Insolvency therefore provides a much more powerful lever for breaking the control of existing management than do any of the mechanisms of privatisation.

Insolvency proceedings are formally initiated by the creditors of the enterprise, and so formally provide a means by which commercial partners and/or banks can gain control over the enterprise. The procedure is channelled through the regional bankruptcy administration and is adjudicated by the regional arbitration courts, both of which bodies are normally associated very closely with the regional administration which is involved in the preparation of restructuring plans. However, the connections between financial institutions and the regional and national government bodies are even more important than the formal and informal links between judicial and administrative bodies in determining the course of insolvency proceedings. The largest and most powerful banks, and those who carry the highest levels of indebtedness to industrial and agricultural enterprises, are the former state banks which retain their traditional branch connections. However, the lever of state control over the banks is not so much these traditional and personal connections as the dependence of the financial system on the state. On the one hand, the banks rely for their bread and butter business (often liberally spread with butter) on channelling regional and national government loans, subsidies and remissions. On the other hand, most if not all of the banks are themselves potentially insolvent and so depend on government favour to remain in business.

An insolvency suit is therefore controlled by the regional government, through the banks, the bankruptcy administration and the arbitration courts, and provides a powerful means by which the regional administration can intervene in the management of state and recently privatised enterprises. Moreover, universal indebtedness creates a situation in which insolvency is a threat which hangs over all enterprises, up to 70 per cent of which are estimated to be insolvent. In this situation it is not difficult for the regional government to use the threat of insolvency as a lever of influence over all enterprises, to link up with a dissident faction within management, or even to replace the management team as a whole by its own nominees. Far from furthering the development of the market economy, bankruptcy provides the regional government bodies with a powerful means to re-establish control over enterprises which had been lost with the collapse of the administrative-command system.

Insolvency and bankruptcy provide a crucial means by which the state can re-establish control over industry and agriculture, mediated through its influence over the banking system. However, this does not mean that there is a simple restoration of the administrative-command system, since bankruptcy reinforces the shift in the balance of power away from the centre and towards the regional authorities, and so is a further element in the regionalisation of the economy. The centre cannot allow this regionalisation to proceed unchecked, but the only lever of influence available to it is its ability to create credit. Regional authorities can use debt as the means of creating and consolidating regional financial-industrial groups, but the central authorities have the power to release financial institutions and large industrial enterprises from the grip of regional authorities by issuing credits. During 1992–3, competition between regional and national government appeared primarily in the form of the issue of regional and national credits directly to industrial enterprises. During 1994, and particularly following the introduction of bankruptcy legislation, competition has shifted towards the struggle for control of the banking system, building on the existing tendencies within the banking system itself for regional affiliates to look towards the regional authorities to establish their independence from Moscow. During 1994, regional authorities have established tighter links with regional banks. We would therefore expect to see the dominant tendency in the next phase of this struggle to be the attempt to establish more systematic control over the banking system at national level, with the Ministry of Finance beginning to reassume the functions (and working practices) of Gosplan in a new guise.

These general conclusions are strongly supported by our examination of bankruptcy proceedings in the Samara region.

1. From the rather small number of facts at our disposal at this stage, it is possible to define three basic patterns of behaviour of local power organs in relation to insolvent enterprises:
   a) attempt of the local bureaucracy to change the management team (owners) in recently privatised industrial enterprises. The reason may be conflict with those in power or plans to reshape the enterprise.
   b) disagreements within the senior management of the enterprise, in cases in which one of the conflicting parties uses the support of local authorities.

c) if the authorities have no obvious intentions concerning the particular enterprise, the initiative of banks will be encouraged in relation to those enterprises which are obviously in an economic impasse and which do not play a key role in the economy of the region.

The new legislation, nominally oriented to the market and logically following the domestic policy of the Russian government, in its real implementation is a powerful instrument of influence on the economic processes in the region put into the hands of the local bureaucratic elite.

2. The circumstances of the bankruptcy of AO AVI.S show, in our opinion, the aspiration of local powers to participate more actively in the economic life of their regions. It appears that the process of bankruptcy of this enterprise was accelerated because of the risk of its transfer to the hands of influential external financial circles, expressing the interest of the regional bureaucracy in safeguarding the regional market from all expansion. The connections between the management of the factory and the local administration, established through the arbitration process, the composition of the team assembled by the new director, and the subsequent development of management strategy, all indicate the close co-ordination of the reorganisation of production with regional power structures.

3. In the example of the Samara region it is easy to see the levers of control, and the threads which connect various social institutions at the local level, which are hidden under normal circumstances. Those federal organs at the local level, the creation of which is perceived by some authorities as the formation of parallel power structures (*oblast* committees for the management of state property, privatisation, agency for bankruptcy and so on) are, in practice, organically linked to the *oblast* administration established in the region. Moreover, all the subjects of management act as a single team in those situations in which it is necessary efficiently to take decisions in the interests of the local leaders.

   The example of ZiM clearly demonstrates this. The local leaders had already interfered in the affairs of the enterprise a year before, having blocked the appointment to the post of general director of a person whom they did not consider congenial. The case of the halting of the hearing of the insolvency case in the arbitration court, mentioned above, shows the significance of a similar influence today. It was precisely the *oblast* administration which managed to convince the court of the need to carry on the business, and expressed its interest in changing the status of the enterprise, separating military production from it.

The bankruptcy of the aircraft factory also shows the confident control of the local banking system by the authorities. This is confirmed by the activism of the banks in bankrupting enterprises, which coincided with the change in the economic policy of the government. It is also symptomatic that the decision of the creditors' council, although formally autonomous, was taken in the interests of a particular circle. It is not clear to us how AvtoVAZbank succeeded in promoting the candidacy of Khasis to the post of director, having overcome competition from SVKB, the largest creditor of the factory, but on all the evidence it was not achieved without the influence of the regional power bodies.

4. It seems to us that these and other facts indicate that the formation of a new political elite in the region has been brought to a close. A kind of vacuum and indeterminacy, observed at the level of the regional power structures, has remained behind. People appearing at the helm in *krais* and *oblast*s created for themselves a favourable working environment, establishing collaborative relations with business circles and federal authorities, creating the necessary bodies, putting the necessary people in place there, and mastering the levers of influence.

   Most significant in this sense was the experience of management of industry in the region. For a long period, from the adoption of the Law On State Enterprise to the completion of privatisation, there was a widespread desire for the complete independence of the enterprise, which only gradually came to be seen as an error. Today both central and regional authorities have managed to adjust to new conditions, having mastered the means of influencing and controlling the activity and restructuring of factories. The tax authorities, arbitration court, various state-controlled and private banks, investment funds all became such instruments. We do not need to exaggerate the opportunities of the new bureaucratic elite, who are by no means all powerful. However, seeing them maintaining the tendencies to the concentration of power, legitimising their position through the Constitution of the *oblast* and other legal acts, it is also impossible to underestimate it. Some regret, however, has been caused by the relentless growth of the bureaucratic apparatus and this concentration of authority in the hands of a small circle of people, who are sometimes guided not by the interests of the state, but by private or sectional interests.

5. The position of the administration and its participation in the process of bankruptcy will be determined by its interests and its political position in the region, and also the character of its products and its size.[13] For those enterprises which find themselves in the worst situation, the law on bankruptcy can appear to offer a lifebelt. The top managers are in principle interested in the freezing of all their debts and receiving *carte blanche* to renew the technology. However, no less important for them is the preservation of their managerial posts and the protection of their own material interests. The preservation of the balance of interests between the regional administration, enterprises and banks is a delicate political process, over which Moscow has little influence.

13 Size is a very important factor. On the one hand, smaller enterprises find it much more difficult to continue trading as their debt mounts up. On the other hand, a declaration of bankruptcy does not have serious wider repercussions. The growth of indebtedness therefore provides a further powerful lever of monopolisation in the Russian economy by making smaller enterprises much more vulnerable to dismantling, sale or absorption by large enterprises, again with the active participation of the local or regional administration.

9. Privatisation and Restructuring of Enterprises: Under 'Insider' or 'Outsider' Control?

Veronika Kabalina

Privatisation in Russia abolished the state's monopoly in the ownership of enterprises and gave individuals and corporate bodies access to the ownership of shares and the right to share in the property of the enterprise. However, the result of 'spontaneous' and voucher privatisation in Russia was a form of 'insider' privatisation, which had its own specific features and which made the problem of corporate control particularly acute. Formally 'insiders', that is to say employees (managers and ordinary workers), became the owners of their enterprises. In practice the directors of the former state enterprises themselves managed to assert their control over their enterprises, using privatisation to legitimate their power within the enterprise and to oppose the challenge of 'external' owners — 'outsiders'.[1]

1 This chapter has been written on the basis of extensive research in Russian industrial enterprises over a period of many years, since 1991 within the framework of a research programme on 'the restructuring of management and industrial relations in Russia', involving research teams in the Komi Republic, Kuzbass, Samara and Moscow, co-ordinated by the Moscow-based interregional Institute for Comparative Labour Relations Research and in collaboration with the Centre for Comparative Labour Studies, University of Warwick. This programme has been funded by the University of Warwick Research and Innovations Fund, the ESRC East-West Programme and INTAS.
The empirical material for this article was collected within the project 'Owners, employees and corporate management in privatised Russian enterprises' which was undertaken in the second half of 1994 under the direction of Professor A. Schleiffer (Harvard University, USA) and V. Gimpel'son (IMEMO, RAN), with financial support from the Harvard Institute for International Development (HIID). The author began to collect material on labour relations and conflict in the enterprises in the spring of 1994 within the framework of a project on 'models of labour relations and conflict in privatised enterprises', financed by the McArthur Fund.
An earlier version of the chapter was presented to the conference of the British Association of Slavonic and East European Studies, Fitzwilliam College, Cambridge, 26 March,1995.

Neo-liberal economists consider that this pattern of 'insider' control is inefficient because of the lack of incentive and the inability of the 'red directors' to carry out the reconstruction of their enterprises. First, following the disintegration of the administrative-command system, the external and internal systems of Party control of the director's activities, from higher bodies and the factory Party committee, disappeared. Second, there was no internal opposition to administrative decisions on the part of the employees, as a result of the well-known ineffectiveness of trade unions as representative bodies. On the contrary, the general interest — fear of loss of their jobs on the part of both managers and workers — serves as a barrier to fundamental reconstruction of the enterprise. Thus the way out of this situation, in the view of some western experts, may be various post-privatisation measures to urge on microeconomic reforms, and particularly the establishment of external control of owners, especially financial institutions, as a counterweight to the internal control of management. Thus they believe that the further development of privatisation in Russia must be aimed at the formation of structures of corporate management with a leading role given to core owners — 'outsiders, who will fill the vacuum which has arisen after the removal of the state from the management of production, and who carry out the reconstruction of the enterprise and turn it into a firm whose aim is the maximisation of profits'.[2]

To what extent do these notions of the possibility of two models of control correspond to the Russian situation? There are now a few enterprises in which outsiders have become the principal owners, but in the overwhelming majority of privatised enterprises, despite the existence of a number of significant shareowners, management has preserved its insider control. Thus one can consider an investigation of Russian practice and the counterposition of the two models of corporate management as a research problem which can be broken down into a series of concrete questions. What are the essential features of insider and outsider control over the enterprise? How are the institutions of corporate management created and how do they function? Does the insider control of managers really obstruct the restructuring of the enterprise? The restructuring of the enterprise as a desirable

2 See, for example, Scott Thomas and Heidi Kroll, 'The Political Economy of Privatisation in Russia', *Communist Economies and Economic Transformation*, 5, 4, pp. 445–59.

result of privatisation is usually understood primarily as economic actions on four dimensions: the restructuring of internal organisation, and the recomposition of employment, production and investment.[3] The author of this article adheres to a wider interpretation of these terms, including, apart from economic aspects of the conduct of enterprises, changes in their internal and external relationships.

The problems considered were investigated by the author on the basis of research in two large enterprises of the mining sub-branch of the iron and steel industry.[4] The enterprise 'Ore' (the names of all enterprises, organisations and cities have been changed) employs a little more than 16,000 people, while 'Concentrate' employs about 14,500. Both enterprises dominate their small cities (each with a population of around 100,000) in two neighbouring regions of Russia. In the days of branch socialist competition, Ore and Concentrate were worthy contenders: both enterprises were considered to be among the strongest and comparable in their potential. They had the same advantages of geographical situation, producing iron ore by opencast methods, although the chemical structure of Ore's product is better suited for subsequent processing. Since they were both constructed at about the same time, at the end of the 1960s, they have the same type of technical basis. The management structure of both enterprises was that typical of the iron mining industry. Both went into the privatisation process at approximately the same time, although they made different choices: Ore chose the second variant, under which the employees could buy 51 per cent of the shares on privileged terms, while Concentrate privatised according to the first variant, which gave employees non-voting shares free of charge. This difference proved decisive in the subsequent fate of the two enterprises. The management of Ore was able to oppose the attempt of the Moscow bank Finance to break its insider monopoly control, while Finance managed to grab control of Concentrate. Thus, practically the same initial technical and economic conditions, with exactly the same external owner, provide a

3 W. Carlin, J.V. Reenan and T. Wolfe, *Enterprise Restructuring in the Transition: An Analytical Survey of the Case Study Evidence from Central and Eastern Europe*, European Bank for Reconstruction and Development, Working Paper 14, July 1994, p. 6.

4 Research in these two enterprises is only part of the project referred to above. The author would like to express her gratitude to her colleagues on the project, and above all David Kuenzi and Galina Monousova, with whom the author was fortunate enough to collect information in these enterprises and with whom the issues have been discussed in heated debate.

unique opportunity to investigate the influence of the structure of ownership and different models of control on the technical reconstruction of the enterprise, and also on the external and internal relationships of the enterprises.

The research used the methods of case study research, which are most appropriate for the investigation of processes of organisational change at the micro level. The author spent a total of five weeks over the spring, summer and autumn of 1994 at the first enterprise, formed as the joint-stock company Ore at the end of 1992. The main methods of collecting information were in-depth interviews, group discussions, observation of the production situation and of the meetings of the joint-stock company, but also analysis of available documentary materials (economic information, minutes of meetings of the Directors' Council, trade union committee, meetings of the labour collective, trade union meetings and also press publications). Apart from meetings at the enterprise, the author was able to meet with and interview several business partners of the enterprise, representatives of 'external' owners, and representatives of the local authorities. The same system of data collection was used in the second enterprise — the shareholding company Concentrate. However, the research in this enterprise was concentrated in the autumn of 1994, although, as in Ore, information was available covering a longer period, at least from the beginning of the process of privatisation of the enterprises in the second half of 1992.

PRIVATISATION: CONFLICTS AND COALITIONS OF INTERESTS OF INSIDERS AND OUTSIDERS

Both enterprises joined the privatisation process in the autumn of 1992, immediately after the adoption by the President of the package of decrees on privatisation. However, they made different choices. Ore privatised according to the second variant, under which the labour collective purchased 51 per cent of the shares, while Concentrate privatised under the first variant, in which the labour collective received a smaller package of non-voting shares free of charge.

Ore

There were no conflicts in the labour collective surrounding the choice of variant. The conference of the labour collective voted almost unanimously for the second variant, the choice of which was recommended by a working commission consisting primarily of representatives of management. The success of the enterprise meant that it had sufficient money in its privatisation fund, formed out of the profits of the previous year, to cover the cost of the employees' share purchase. The joint-stock company Ore was registered at the end of October 1992.

The management of the joint-stock company decided to adopt the tactic of freezing the movement of shares. So that shares held by insiders should not fall into the hands of outsiders, the Directors' Council proposed to include in the Charter an article which required employees who wished to sell shares to offer them first of all to the Council. To reduce the incentive for employees to sell their shares dividends were paid regularly. Two years after the registration of the company the employees still did not have share certificates, but only a simple receipt which declared how many vouchers and how much from their personal privatisation account they had invested. Many were convinced that it was necessary to have the share, or a certificate equivalent to it, to be able to engage in purchase and sale transactions, and none of the managers had explained to them that for this it was sufficient that there was a record in the shareholders' register. In any case the company management could monitor the movement of shares, since until October 1994 the register of shareholders was maintained by the company itself.

To limit the potential access of large external shareholders to the shares of the enterprise, the management sought to transform the voucher auction, at which the State Property Fund proposed to sell 29 per cent of the shares, from a national to a regional auction. For this purpose it secured the support of the regional authorities, which was promised a proportion of the shares to augment the funds available to support the socially unprotected strata of the population of the region. However, this attempt was unsuccessful. Given such an apparently strong desire to maintain control of the enterprise, the passivity of the management at the auction itself is difficult to explain: it did not use the money in its privatisation fund (created by a decision of the shareholders conference for the purchase of shares) to participate in the auction, as other enterprises had done, through a front company. Could it be that the management of the firm simply did not have any such front companies? True, the enterprise purchased about one per cent of the firm's shares at the money auction, subsequent to the voucher auction, at which the remaining shares were sold, so that the labour collective owned about 52 per cent of the shares. As a result of the voucher auction at the end of 1993 Ore found itself with a large external shareholder, one of the leading Moscow commercial banks, Finance, which held 22 per cent of the shares. The other 6 per cent were spread around in small holdings of small investment funds (including local ones), individuals and enterprises.

The appearance of the bank was a big surprise for the management of Ore. The struggle for control of the enterprise has led its management to take more active steps to establish alliances with other external agencies — local authorities and other enterprises. The formation of a financial-industrial group including Ore is on the agenda.

After the voucher auction 20 per cent of the shares remained in the hands of the state, of which 5 per cent were held in the shareholding fund of the employees' of the enterprise (FARP), and it was decided to sell the remaining 15 per cent through an investment competition. According to the rules of such a competition, the conditions of the competition are worked out by the regional property fund with subsequent confirmation by the higher body. But the feasibility report for investment projects is prepared by the enterprise. The idea is that an investment competition should attract solid investors who, in exchange for shares, agree to put money into the development of the enterprise. However, these two cases, together with other research carried out by the author at other enterprises, testifies to the fact that it is the struggle for control of the enterprise, rather than economic feasibility, that dominates the process of redistribution of property. So as not to miss the opportunity to acquire the last package of shares and to strengthen its control of the enterprise, the management of Ore directly participated in defining the conditions of the investment competition, so that it had already at this stage established a guarantee of its victory. The distinctive feature of these conditions was that the money was not to be put directly into production, but into objects which, on the one hand, would be very unattractive to a serious investor and, on the other, would considerably increase the cost to such an investor of getting control over a share of the property of the enterprise. The investment package was split into two parts: in one case the conditions of the competition included the investment of money in the development of the already established subsidiary agricultural activities of the enterprise; in the other case in the construction of a new stock-raising complex. The local authority was interested in precisely such conditions for the attraction of investment, since it wanted to resolve the problem of its own legitimacy, and was anxious about the problem of creating a local market.

The management of Ore used its alliance with the city administration to secure the approval of the conditions of the investment competition by the regional property fund. At this time direct contacts with the regional authorities were complicated by a conflict that had developed rapidly. The management of Ore invited a local voucher investment fund, Invest, which had already bought a tiny proportion of the shares (about one per cent) at the voucher auction, to participate in the investment competition. There is no doubt that this little local fund did not have anything like enough money to finance an investment programme amounting to around 8 million dollars, although for Ore, with a hard currency income of millions, this sum would not be a large burden. Conversations with representatives of Ore management and with the chairman of Invest left little doubt that the management of Ore itself provided Invest with the money to participate in the investment competition. The coalition of the three participants in the deal, the city authorities, chairman of Invest, and management of Ore, is tied together by informal connections, formed while working in a research institute in the years before perestroika. The friendly management of Invest emerged as victor in the investment competition. The bank, as one of its heads acknowledged in an interview, refused to participate in the competition, since it was not willing to pay a large amount of money to increase its shareholding, which would still not give it any chance to control the enterprise as its owner.

However, this struggle for control of the enterprise with the bank has not finished. The structure of ownership of Ore is now as follows (see figure one): 52 per cent is under the direct control of insiders. On my estimation the management of the enterprise does not have a majority of the insider holding, having not more than 40 per cent of the internal holding, or about 20 per cent of the founding capital. But when one takes into account the fact that the victor of the investment competition, Invest, is a friendly outsider, one can consider that its share is part of the insider holding. The 5 per cent held by the FARP can also be considered part of the insider holding. Thus insiders control at least 72 per cent, the bank 22 per cent, and the remaining 6 per cent is spread around. For the adoption of strategic decisions, including changes to the charter, the insiders have to secure the support of three quarters of the votes at a shareholders' conference. Therefore, as the shareholders' conference showed, the management needs to make further efforts to consolidate its position. The process of extending the borders of Ore has already begun, by amalgamating with two other joint-stock companies, former collective farms. In the near future the management of Ore plans a secondary share issue, as a result of which the share of the bank in the ownership of Ore can be reduced.

Figure One: Structure of Ownership of Ore

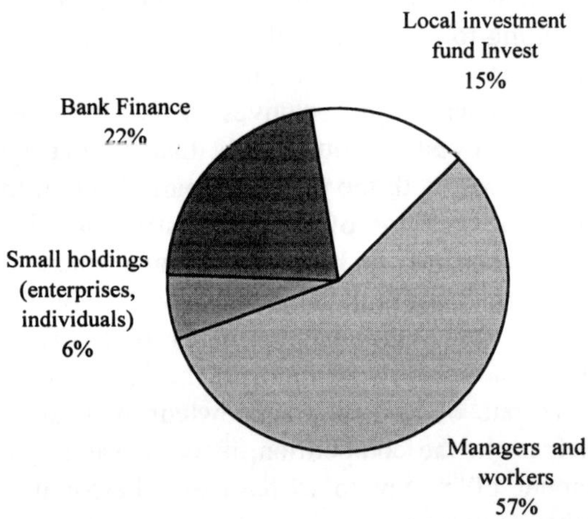

Concentrate

The privatisation of the enterprise began without any united point of view. A group of communists working at Concentrate, who were the nucleus of the city organisation of the Communist Party, conducted an active propaganda campaign against the privatisation of the enterprise. The bulk of the labour collective, including the workers and part of management, favoured the second variant, considering that 'the shares must remain with the labour collective'. However, despite the prevailing mood, the labour collective voted for the first variant. The supporters of the second variant could not justify its economic necessity and reality for the enterprise, while economic arguments became the trump card of the faction of management that favoured the first variant. It was the latter who were the organisers of the privatisation process; they dominated the structure of the working commission on privatisation, preparing the necessary documentation. Simultaneously with this paperwork the members of the commission on privatisation conducted an intensive propaganda campaign, organising meetings in all the industrial divisions of the enterprise. Their main argument in favour of the first variant was the economic impossibility of covering the payment for shares under the second variant, as the privatisation fund only had sufficient money to cover one eighth of the cost, so that the employees of the enterprise would have to pay the remainder in cash. The other argument they brought forward in their support was that the privileged shares with a fixed return would become a source of income in addition to their salary for the employees, and particularly for the pensioners of the enterprise. This argument met with a ready response since it appealed to the mass consciousness of the employees in relation to shares. Not the least important motive of the chiefs who favoured the first variant was their own share option. Reconstructing a picture of the mood at that time, I discovered from a number of interviews that, in fact, the management did not take into account the consequences of their choice: they did not really expect that there was any chance that there would be any serious interest in buying their shares, and hoped that they would have enough money to keep the situation at the enterprise under their own control. Other respondents expressed some doubt that the chiefs, all of whom were of pension or pre-pension age, had any serious interest in control or in the future fate of the enterprise.

The consequences of the choice of variant did not appear immediately. After the distribution of the privileged (non-voting) shares to the labour collective, amounting to 25 per cent of the authorised capital, 5 per cent of the shares were allocated to the chiefs, and 10 per cent sold by closed subscription to voting shares, while 60 per cent of the authorised capital remained at the disposal of the regional property fund. Because of resistance from the regional property fund, which hoped to preserve its influence over Concentrate on the basis of the significant shareholding that remained in state hands, the voucher auction was delayed. To unblock this situation members of the management team went to Moscow, where they tried to use informal contacts (and informal means) to secure support in their struggle with the regional authorities. They had some success: the auction was set for November 1993, where shares accounting for a little more than 20 per cent of the authorised capital were put up for sale. The results of the first voucher auction were unexpected: about 14 per cent of the shares were bought at the auction through affiliates and intermediary small-sized voucher investment funds of the same Moscow commercial bank, Finance, which had failed to carry through its hostile takeover of Ore. The other 6 per cent of the shares were bought by small voucher funds and individuals. After the first auction, Finance began intensively to buy up the shares held by the small voucher funds which had bought shares at the auction and by the employees through a local share shop, using the services of an intermediary. As a result of this activity it got its hands on virtually all the shares sold at the first auction and the proportion of shares held by the labour collective fell.

In the spring of 1994 a second voucher auction took place, at which 10 per cent of the authorised capital was on offer. Among the buyers were one Moscow and two local voucher investment funds. The shares which remained unsold after the voucher auction were bought at a money auction by Finance.

Finally, the remaining shares in the enterprise were sold in two packets, each amounting to 10 per cent of the authorised capital, through an investment competition in June 1994. (A further 10 per cent remained in the enterprise's privatisation account, and the shares were distributed among the employees of the enterprise in the summer of 1994.)

The situation which arose during the investment competition at Concentrate reflected the different array of forces compared with Ore.

Initially, as at Ore, investment in the development of the social sphere of the city was established as a condition of the competition. However, this had been introduced by the regional administration at the request of the city administration. The bank, which was not interested in making investments that did not generate an immediate profit, protested to the state property committee at the decision, where it found support. The administration of Concentrate, whose tense relations with the regional administration have already been remarked on, allied itself with the bank in this struggle with the regional authorities. But why did the enterprise have such a weak connection with the interests of the city?

Concentrate played and still plays no less a role in local economic and political life than does Ore, and urban problems still influence the decisions made by the administration of the enterprise. However, the head of the local administration has emerged as a more independent political figure, trying to strengthen his own position, than is his colleague in the neighbouring city. At the stage of the privatisation process at which the size of the authorised capital was defined it was still possible for the head of administration, against the resistance of management, to transfer a part of the social sphere, including housing, to the municipality. As the chiefs of Concentrate explained to me, their opponent had hoped to strengthen his position in the struggle for grants from the regional and republican budgets, while other city leaders hoped to extract personal and commercial profits. The chief of the administration also had a personal interest in this struggle with the top management of Concentrate. At one time he had himself been the General Director of the *kombinat*, until he lost an election to the present director, but he still hoped to return to the *kombinat* as one of the heads of the joint-stock company. In this situation, where the basis for informal relations was undermined, the head moved to a formal basis in his relations with the enterprise, having concluded a co-operation agreement with its management. At the same time he now also uses economic levers of pressure on the enterprise.

Thus, the final results of the struggle for the remaining packet of shares in Concentrate offered through the investment competition were determined by the balance of forces of the main participants and the coalitions into which they had entered: the bank and the enterprise management with the support of the central authorities against the regional and city administrations. As a result of its victory in the investment competition the bank acquired 20 per cent of the authorised capital of Concentrate, having undertaken to invest 20 billion roubles (about 6.5 million dollars) in the reconstruction of the enterprise. At first sight the behaviour of the new owner confirms its interest in the development of the enterprise. However, in assessing its motives it is impossible to overlook the fact that by participating in the investment competition the bank also resolved the problem of acquiring control over the enterprise.

At the beginning of 1995 the structure of ownership of the voting shares of Concentrate is as follows (see Figure Two). On my calculations, insiders hold about 28 per cent of the shares, with management and ITR holding 16–17 per cent, workers not more than 10 per cent and pensioners, former workers of the enterprise, 2 per cent. The bank holds a controlling interest amounting to 54 per cent of the voting share capital. The remainder of the shares are distributed among small outsiders: the two local investment funds hold about 5 per cent, the Moscow investment fund about 5.5 per cent, and other organisations

Figure Two: Structure of Ownership of Concentrate

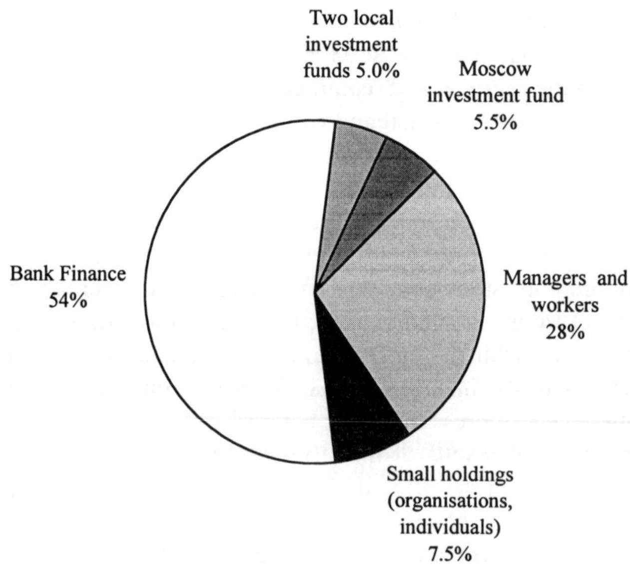

and individuals hold about 7.5 per cent. In the autumn of 1994 the turnover of shares slowed down, although it is quite possible that the policy of the bank of refusing to pay dividends and holding down wages will encourage the further sale of shares by the employees of the enterprise. Moreover, if the administration of the share register is transferred to one of the banks' own firms, as was proposed at the time I was carrying out my research, one would expect a further movement of shares in Concentrate into the control of the bank.

The tendency (noted by many researchers) to use established socio-economic networks formed under the conditions of the administrative-command system as a 'transformation shield', has additional characteristics when it comes to the struggle for control of the enterprise in the course of privatisation. All the participants in this network have difficulties in the period of transformation in their search for legitimacy and a new identity. The crisis of identity is an integral part of the 'transformation crisis'. Thus the configuration of this network is a result of the struggle for control over the process of transformation both at the macro level and at the level of the organisation and balance of forces of the participants in this process. The use of temporary coalitions to consolidate resources is a characteristic feature of these struggles. The basis of these coalitions is the temporary coincidence of interests. Thus the union of the management of the enterprise with the local authorities is not simply a legacy of the past as a part of cultural tradition, or an inseparable feature of the social organisation of Soviet-type society,[5] but is also a reality of the current processes of transformation. The institutional changes which are a result of this symbiosis of the past and the present are laying the foundations of the future social organisation. I am convinced that the institutional changes in contemporary Russia which are initiated from above, are corrected without fail by the actions of actors below — by enterprise directors, local authorities, banks, voucher investment funds, managers and even ordinary workers, realising their short-term and long-term interests.

[5] See Ed Clark and Anna Soulsby, 'Transforming Former State Enterprises in the Czech Republic', *Organisation Studies*, 16, 2, 1995, 215–242.

INSTITUTIONS OF CORPORATE CONTROL

The management bodies of the majority of joint-stock companies created on the basis of state enterprises have the same structure: a shareholders' meeting is the supreme legislative body, delegating its powers to the Directors' Council (*Sovet direktorov*), with the Board (*pravlenie*) as the executive body. However, this formal uniformity disappears completely when one contrasts the models of internal and external control of the enterprise, by management or by an outside owner. Only the analysis of the structure and real functioning of these bodies and of their evolution, can reveal these actual distinctions. Such an analysis is a necessary stage in the analysis of the relationship between the structure of ownership and labour relations, since the management bodies have become the main arena of the struggle for control and the taking of decisions concerning the development of the enterprise.

Ore

The composition of the Directors' Council of Ore changed three times from the point at which the labour collective decided to transform the enterprise into a joint-stock company, corresponding to the three phases in the struggle for control of the enterprise. The temporary Directors' Council (up to the first shareholders' meeting) included the general director of the enterprise, the chairman of the regional property fund, and the chairman of the city soviet; the interests of the labour collective were represented by the president of the STK (labour collective council), who was the deputy director for economics. He used this position to conclude a deal with a foreign partner that was very favourable for him, but unprofitable for the enterprise. As soon as he tried to use his position on the Council as the basis for opposition to the General Director he was immediately dismissed 'for financial crimes' and the STK was disbanded.

The new composition adopted at the first shareholders' meeting (at large enterprises these meetings, as a rule, take the form of delegate conferences, with delegates representing the interests of groups of shareholders) did not include any 'representative of the labour collective'. The Council comprised representatives of management (the

General Director), city authorities (chairman of the city soviet) and regional authorities (chairman of the regional property fund). The chairman of the city soviet was the next victim of the General Director in his struggle to establish a more uniform structure for the Directors' Council, being removed on ideological and political grounds. As an active supporter of the Russian Communist Party, he supported the Supreme Soviet and Rutskoi at the time of the events of October 1993. The General Director gave as the main reason for removing the chairman of the city soviet from the Council their 'ideological incompatibility'. He could not believe that it was possible to make commercial decisions with a Directors' Council that included somebody who was ideologically opposed to the market.

The exclusion from the Directors' Council was confirmed by a shareholders' conference held after the voucher auction at which Finance had acquired a proportion of the shares. At this conference representatives of the bank tried to get a place on the Directors' Council, but were unsuccessful, the conference voting almost unanimously in favour of the head of the local administration. Instead of a place on the Directors' Council, the bank got two places on the Board. In the present structure of the Directors' Council (see Figure Three) two people formally represent the interests of insiders (the General Director and the senior mining manager) and two represent those of outsiders (the head of the local administration and chairman of the regional property fund). It is interesting that the outsiders are not actually shareholders in the enterprise, but there are no doubts about the loyalty of the head of the local administration to the General Director. There is no direct evidence of a coincidence of interests of the chairman of the regional property fund with the interests of the management of the enterprise. However, one can assume that this is the case on the basis of the fact that he was not removed from the Council after the final package of shares in the possession of the state had been sold. The Directors' Council is not a body on which there are conflicts of interest and in practice it is under the control of the General Director. This position was formally endorsed at the shareholders' conference in November 1994, at which a rule was introduced into the Charter declaring that 'the Directors' Council will meet as necessary', instead of the former 'the Directors' Council will meet regularly once a month'.

The General Director also controls the work of the executive body, the Board of the joint-stock company. This could simply be called management by another name, since it includes all the executive directors (the former deputy directors for economics, commerce, foreign economic relations, former chief engineer) and the chiefs of all the production divisions of the enterprise. However, there are also places for the presidents of the trade union and of the youth organisation of the enterprise. The latter, far from disappearing with the collapse of

Figure Three: Governance Structure of Ore

The Directors' Council

GD	=	General Director
SM	=	Senior Manager
HLA	=	Head of the Local Administration
CRPF	=	Chairman of the Regional Property Fund

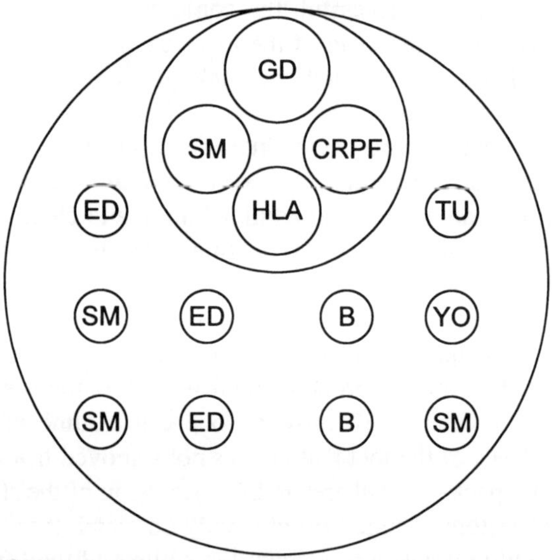

The Board:

B	=	bank
TU	=	trade union
YO	=	youth organisation
ED	=	executive director
SM	=	senior managers

the Komsomol, has been supported by the General Director. Certainly the participation of representatives of public organisations on this body is not very significant, reduced to the receipt of information, but it does set a precedent which might be further developed.

There is no clear differentiation between the areas of competence and jurisdiction of these two management bodies. Analysis of the agendas of the meetings of the Directors' Council over the period 1993–1994 (ten meetings) reveals that although the Directors' Council is mainly concerned with the distribution of financial resources, at the same time it also concerned itself with small-scale operational issues. For example, the agenda included questions of labour discipline, medical services for employees, and they reviewed a statement about financial assistance. However, it is hardly likely to be otherwise when it is quite obvious that both of these bodies are in practice merely formal covers for an authoritarian system of adoption of the decisions of the General Director, who keeps their work under his control so that he can maintain a relationship between the long-term strategic aims of development of the enterprise and its operational activity. Such a lack of differentiation of functions at this stage is a condition for the flexibility and efficiency of adoption of decisions and is a powerful factor in the effective work of the enterprise, but on one important condition, the competence and high degree of commitment of the General Director to the development of his enterprise.

Thus the Directors' Council and the Board of Ore are bodies through which is expressed the authoritarian power of the General Director, in which the possibility of conflict between insiders and outsiders is excluded. In this case the main channel for the institutionalisation of conflict becomes the shareholders' conference. Here the position of the director, who does not (and in a large enterprise cannot) hold a significant proportion of the shares, is at its most vulnerable. He can keep control of the enterprise and resist pressure from outsiders only if he can maintain the support of the labour collective.

With such a divergence between the formal and the real situations of these two management bodies of the joint-stock company, which are the channels of influence and control of the General Director, one might expect that their work would be secret. But, in contrast to the second enterprise, Concentrate, information about the work of the Directors' Council is regularly published in the company newspaper.

Concentrate

The establishment of new management bodies in Concentrate was delayed for some time by the fact that the main package of voting shares remained for a long time in the hands of the state. Before the issue of the controlling package of shares it was impossible to hold a shareholders' conference. The first shareholders' conference, at which the Directors' Council and Board were elected, was held in the summer of 1994. Up to this time the enterprise was governed by a temporary Directors' Council, comprising three people: the General Director, the senior mining manager (as representative of the labour collective), and the head of the city administration. Under the Presidential decree on privatisation the interests of the state on the Directors' Council should be represented by the chairman of the local soviet. However, the head of the city administration insisted that he should be the representative, since the enterprise dominated the city, and he was supported by the state property committee in this. In his words, he used his membership of the Directors' Council to press the interests of the needy strata of the city's population. In the absence of any other management bodies of the joint-stock company (shareholders' conference and Board), the temporary Directors' Council could be considered to be another bogus body, expressing the unitary power of the General Director. However, the very tense relations between the management of the *kombinat* and the local authority meant that the Directors' Council was in part the place where the balance of interests between the enterprise and the city was reached. And, before the participation of the external shareholders, all decisions concerning the technical and economic development of the enterprise and levels of employment were decided mainly by the management of the enterprise, with revisions put forward by the city authorities, so that a model of internal control of the enterprise was in operation.

As a result of the movement of shares a regrouping of the forces influencing decision-making took place leading to a radical change in the structure of the Directors' Council, which now reflects the structure of ownership (see Figure Four). Since Finance now owns a controlling interest, it dominates the Directors' Council, with six of the nine seats, five of which are occupied by heads of affiliated firms of the bank. The sixth representative of the outsiders on the Council is the chief of the joint-stock company, which had been created on the basis of the former superior body (*glavk*) of the *kombinat*, a man recommended to the bank by the *kombinat* as a person familiar with the problems of the branch. The former outsider on the temporary Council, the head of the local administration, tried to get into the new structure, using his control of two local investment funds which were also shareholders in Concentrate, but he was unsuccessful as he could not muster 10 per cent of the votes. A place was found for him in the auditing commission.

Figure Four: Governance Structure of Concentrate

The Directors' Council

B = Bank Representatives
GD = General Director
ED = Economics Director
TD = Technical Director

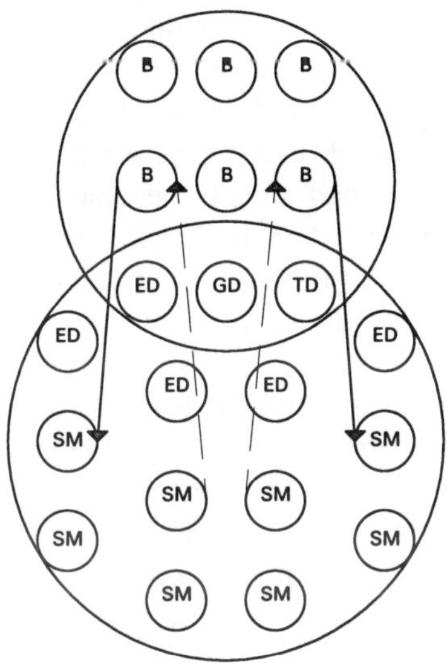

The Board

ED = Executive Director
SM = Senior Manager

The interests of insiders on the Directors' Council are represented by the General Director, the economics director and the technical director. It is notable that a struggle for representation on the Council developed not only between outsiders (the bank and the local administration), but also among the insiders. Four candidates were put forward for the three places available to the labour collective, as holder of 28 per cent of the shares, which showed the absence of unity in the senior management team. The person who failed to secure election was the senior mining manager who had been on the temporary Council. His removal probably symbolised a crisis in the fate of the enterprise — a shift in the model of control and a shift in the priorities for the development of the joint-stock company. Although he had received the support of the labour collective in the voting at the shareholders' conference, in opposition to the economics director, the latter prevailed since he was able to draw on outsider support, the Moscow investment fund, to secure election. This struggle over the membership of the Directors' Council has become an indicator, on the one hand, of the split in the management team, and, on the other, of the divergence of interests between the labour collective and those members of the management team represented on the Directors' Council. There are many signs that these managers are people loyal to the bank. The membership of the Directors' Council therefore seems to indicate its relative uniformity. However, during the rather short period that it has been working, it has become the main institution through which conflict between insiders and outsiders is expressed. Employees had already become well aware of the differentiation of shareholders when the shareholders' conference was being prepared in the summer of 1994. As one of the employees put it, they 'could already see a division of the shareholders into those who were purely shareowners and those who were simultaneously owners and workers, so that the shareholders were divided into workers and outsiders'.

It was equally obvious to them that the role of the conference was already ritual, with 'everything decided in advance'. On the eve of the conference the trade union committee of the *kombinat*, with the support of a part of management, tried to establish groups of delegates to vote in support of the interests of the labour collective, but the course of the conference convinced them of the uselessness of attempting to challenge the domination of the bank by coalitions of insiders.

The Board, established after the election of the Directors' Council, includes the General Director, executive directors (including the economics and technical directors who are members of the Council), and chiefs of all production divisions. The functions of the Directors' Council and the Board are divided: the Council decides strategic questions concerning the development of the joint-stock company, the Board deals with the operational management of the enterprise. Thus the bank controls financial administration and the selection of the management staff (the bank has not begun to change the management team, but the bank controls the recruitment of young specialists). The insider managers retain responsibility for technical policy and the organisation of production, but also for social relations within the enterprise.

The division of the spheres of competence of these two bodies raises fears among some members of the management team that there is no control over the activity of the owner of the enterprise, the bank, particularly on the part of the employees of the enterprise. At their insistence the shareholders' conference adopted a Code of Conduct for shareholders, which regulates the norms of behaviour, primarily of the outside shareholders, which they are not permitted to infringe. To reduce the tension that was aroused by fears of actions that might be seen as detrimental to the employees' interests, some concessions were made regarding the procedure for the consideration of issues by the Directors' Council. Before taking strategic decisions the Council is required to send them for consideration and discussion by the Board. However, the proposals made by the Board have no more than the status of recommendations. Thus the real link between insiders and outsiders is the three senior managers who are members of both the Board and the Council. Despite the fact that their work as members of the Board, with responsibility for economics and the realisation of the enterprise's investment programme, objectively unites their interests with the interests of the bank, at the same time they experience pressure from other colleagues — senior managers with responsibility for other parts of the activity of the enterprise which are of little interest to the bank. Thus, as members of the Council, they are required to articulate the interests of the labour collective. The Directors' Council of Concentrate has therefore become the arena for the conflict of interests between insiders and outsiders.

Given the short period during which the bank has controlled the development of the joint-stock company, it is difficult to evaluate the consequences of its management. However, the outsiders have already revealed their approach in the decisions taken by the Council. Thus, the representatives of the bank refused to provide money from the profits of the company to a branch fund for the support of weak enterprises. In concluding contracts for the following year they insisted on changing the terms to the advantage of their own partners. However, the calculations of one of the senior managers has shown that these probable contracts will be unprofitable for the company because of high transport costs. The managers are also afraid that the reorientation towards new customers may lead to a loss of markets. Some of the contracts proposed by the bank were quite simply unfeasible for technical reasons and not properly worked out, although the bank claims that it has qualified advisers in this field.

The bank's priorities in resolving problems that arise have already been clearly shown to be guided by criteria of short-term profit rather than the long-term development of the enterprise. This 'financial' approach of the bank collides with the 'social' approach of a part of the administration of the enterprise. The main disputes that have arisen have concerned the future fate of the subsidiary farms and objects of the social sphere, including housing, where policy is obvious: it is necessary to get rid of unprofitable facilities, everyone should attend to his own business, that is, industrial enterprises should engage in industrial production, agricultural enterprises in agricultural production for the food processing industry. The opinion of part of the management is that these subsidiary activities should be preserved for the long-term: the enterprise must concern itself with the needs of its workers, there must be restaurants and shops for the workers. The bank, however, wants to invest its capital, and does not think of anything else, knowing nothing of the reality of life in small cities such as Concentrateville. The management of the *kombinat* will continue to build housing for its employees, but instead of providing it free of charge it will be part-paid (leased with the provision of credit and loans).

The marked divisions of interest were resolved by compromise. It was decided to get rid of one agricultural subsidiary and establish a contractual relationship with the other. At the same time the decisions adopted in relation to the agricultural subsidiaries are not final the question of the construction of a meat *kombinat* to process the production of the agricultural subsidiaries, for example, is still being discussed. The decision about the fate of the welfare facilities in dispute has been postponed. The bank asked for one month to consider the issue of the future direction of housing policy, and then the Council of Directors accepted the proposals of the administration of the *kombinat* without amendment.

Thus, at an early stage in the realisation of its control the bank came up against limits which it is still taking into consideration since it is afraid of serious conflicts. An insider member of the Directors' Council commented on the bank's behaviour as follows: 'The bank Finance understands that at this stage it is necessary to take the interests of the employees of the enterprise into account. It does not want to face a strike of the labour collective.'

SURVIVAL STRATEGIES AND ENTERPRISE RECONSTRUCTION: THE BRANCH AND GENERAL ECONOMIC CONTEXT IN 1992–4

The branch and general economic conditions which developed in 1992-4 limited the freedom of manoeuvre even of these two fairly strong enterprises. The adaptation of both enterprises to the external socio-economic context was basically undertaken under insider control, since it was only in the second half of 1994 that the influence of the bank Finance as an owner over Concentrate began to be felt.

The General Director of Ore is a person 'on the inside'. He was recruited by the *kombinat* as chief engineer at the beginning of the 1980s and was elected General Director by the labour collective in 1988. Within a short time of taking the post of director he had managed to establish his authority among the chiefs of kindred enterprises and had established extensive contacts in government circles. During the years of reform he became a leading political figure not only at local level: he plays an active role in the Russian Association of Privatised and Private Enterprises and in Gaidar's party, Russia's Choice.

The present General Director of Concentrate 'grew up' in the *kombinat*, and became head of the enterprise on the eve of privatisation, following a period of instability in the management team and frequent changes of director. He is not a popular political actor even in his region and has a reputation as a fairly weak manager among the representatives of the bank Finance.

The fall in metallurgy production

The fall in metallurgy production as a result of the sharp fall in demand for its products was 18.9 per cent in 1992 and 20 per cent in 1993. By the middle of 1994 half of all Russian metallurgical enterprises were at a standstill, and many mines and mining *kombinats* had also suspended work. In the first half of 1995, despite some improvement of the situation in metallurgy, the ore mining sub-branch continued to experience an extremely acute crisis, which enveloped the majority of enterprises, many of which were only working at one third capacity. Concentrate stopped several times over 1993–1994, and production was halved compared with more prosperous times. The management of the *kombinat* decided to stop development work.

In 1992 Ore was a unique mining enterprise in the branch in reducing production by only 2.5 per cent. However, in 1994 this enterprise was also forced to reduce the volume of production by 20 per cent in comparison with the design capacity, although the *kombinat* did not once have to suspend work in this period. Management decided to produce for stock, and not to stop the combine. The enterprise also continued to carry out blasting to develop new production reserves. The management of the *kombinat* considers its production policy to be far-sighted and correct. If they had followed the example of other enterprises and suspended development work, they would not be ready in a year's time to take the niche in the market left by the other mining enterprises. By November 1994 the enterprise had already secured sufficient orders for raw materials for the following year.

In the first half of 1995 a favourable market situation developed for this enterprise, with a large demand for its product. The production programme for 1995 anticipated an increase in output of concentrate of more than 20 per cent and of pellets of 30 per cent, although demand was sufficient for an increase of production of 50 per cent, which was the limit of the planned capacity of the *kombinat*.

Although in both enterprises production fell, it was not catastrophic thanks to the fact that the quality of the product was fairly high, in relation to its low cost, so that it was in demand both on internal and external markets. Up to 1994 Ore provided half the Russian exports of iron ore, with Concentrate supplying about 10 per cent. However, the appeal of the external market for the ore mining industry has changed as a result of the increase in transport costs and the fluctuations in the dollar exchange rate.

Price restrictions

The most destructive factors destabilising the work of the iron extracting industry was the constant increases in cost imposed by the energy and transport monopolies. At the same time the kombinats had no opportunity to increase the price of their own production, which was restricted by the world market price. The price of electric power during 1994 rose by two to three times more than the price of iron ore.

Transportation rates exceeded the cost of the extracted ore by 1.4 times. Both enterprises reacted to the increase in transport costs by reorienting themselves to nearby consumers of their product. Export deliveries fell somewhat since, by the autumn of 1994, several export contracts had become unprofitable, with the CIS countries (Ukraine and Kazakhstan) being most attractive, while deliveries to the Urals fell.

At the same time the General Director of Ore organised political pressure, sending letters to the President, the government and other authorities in his own name and in the name of other directors of related enterprises. He tried to form a branch directors' council, but this body did not get off the ground. The trade unions were also involved in this activity.

More successful was the attempt to exert collective influence on the regional authorities to reduce the cost of electrical power, which was four times higher for this and a number of other large enterprises in the region than for the remaining industrial consumers of electric power because of the regional price monopoly enjoyed by the electricity generator. The pressure was organised by a regional association of enterprises in which the General Director plays a leading role. This association was created in 1992 and earlier was concerned primarily with the social problems of the region, but by 1994 a strong tendency to the politicisation of its activity had appeared.

In a similar situation the management of Concentrate entered into conflict with the regional administration on its own, supported, however, by the chief of the city administration, who also had an interest in reducing the cost of electricity for the enterprise, whose profits are the main source of revenue for the city budget. The trade union committee of the *kombinat* played an active role in this conflict, organising a city protest meeting against the inactivity of the regional leadership. However, the results achieved by this pressure were more modest than those achieved by Ore.

However, just as the market position improved, Ore and Concentrate used the revival of demand for their products to increase their prices. It is remarkable that even their old customers, the Chelyabinsk, Magnitogorsk and Novolipetsk metallurgical *kombinats*, were forced to agree to this.

Taxation

The other factor complicating the financial position of both enterprises was taxation, which was particularly onerous because of the royalties demanded from extractive enterprises. The share of taxes in net profits in 1994 amounted to 90 per cent. In the first half of 1994, when tax liabilities exceeded profits received, the management of Ore began consciously to withhold payment of taxes to the federal budget, and the enterprise accumulated debts for the use of electricity. At the end of 1994 it was forced to take a hard currency loan to pay off its tax debt and reduce its debt for electricity and rail transport.

Budget constraints

According to representatives of senior management of both enterprises neither of them receives privileged state credits. The receipt of credits through the regional administration was made complicated for Ore by the conflictual relations between the General Director and the regional leadership. However, the General Director of Ore used his connections in government and his political weight to get a series of preferential tax arrangements for his enterprise. In 1992 Ore was unique among metal mining and metallurgical enterprises in not having to pay two kinds of tax — customs duties and the compulsory sale to the government of half its foreign exchange earnings, although since July 1992 it has in practice sold the state half its foreign earnings. In March 1993 the head of the government signed a decree exempting the enterprise from import and export duties. In 1992 Ore used its export earnings to build an agricultural processing facility, purchased equipment and materials to improve production, purchased grain for the livestock industry of the region, and medical preparations and equipment. Most accounts estimate the benefit from the remission of export-import duties to amount to more than 20 million dollars.

Concentrate was also exempted from import-export duties, although for a shorter period of time, but it was not exempt from the compulsory sale of foreign currency. One can presume that the *kombinat* did not receive significant tax privileges because its management was less influential and politically less active.

Non-payment

Both enterprises were drawn into the circuits of non-payment between enterprises. At first the management of both enterprises (and particularly Ore) resolved the problem of a shortage of working capital, which was the effect of mutual non-payment between enterprises, by selling hard currency, although their currency reserves for this purpose were exhausted by the summer of 1994. At this time the management of Ore began to use intricate barter, receiving metal and automobiles from the metallurgical *kombinats* in exchange for ore, which they in turn offered in payment for rail transport. Having reviewed the profitability of these kinds of barter operations, the management of Ore decided to enter the business of selling metal and created a subsidiary to sell metal on Western markets. Having satisfied the demand of its own employees and the inhabitants of the city for various kinds of automobile, the enterprise signed contracts with firms specialising in selling automobiles throughout Russia.

One of the signs of the restructuring of the two enterprises was the tightening of their policy with regard to insolvent partners. In 1993 Ore stopped supplying its largest customer, a metallurgical *kombinat*, for a month, despite a long-standing partner relationship, and the result was that its large debtor paid its debts and began to pay in advance. In 1994 pre-payment became a general condition for all customers and, according to the General Director, by the end of 1994 the problem of indebtedness had been resolved. The management of Concentrate began to take a tough line with indebted enterprises rather later. With the appearance of the bank Finance this line became much stronger and began to be taken even with foreign customers.

Diversification of production

One of the consequences of instability in enterprises was the development of production of items unrelated to the core activity of the *kombinat*, but based on locally available resources. In 1995 Ore produced 60 different kinds of product.

In Ore production of chalk was begun with a Spanish-Russian joint venture, as well as silica bricks and synthetic granite. A construction trust was specially established to build industrial buildings and housing. Since the enterprise is in the black earth region and is surrounded by collective and state farms which cannot organise sales for themselves, the management of Ore decided to construct enterprises to process agricultural produce. In 1992–3 the foreign currency earned by the enterprise was used to buy equipment and to establish enterprises jointly with European partners for the production of cheese, vegetable oil, meat products, beer, bread and bakery products and so on. The products of these factories are sold to the employees of the enterprise and to the local population. Subsequently, in order to guarantee the supply of raw materials to the processing enterprises, two collective farms were invited to merge with the company. At the beginning of 1995 the production of agricultural raw materials, their processing and sale, were united organisationally in an agrofirm, which is still subsidised by Ore, but the management of Ore hopes that in future this activity will be profitable. They are also convinced that this is the way in which Russian agriculture should be privatised.

Concentrate has also gone down the path of diversification of production, indeed its establishment of agricultural subsidiaries provided the example followed by Ore, as the management of the latter admitted. However, in Concentrate they did not go on to establish processing enterprises to complement their subsidiary agriculture. At the time at which the enterprise began to receive foreign currency from the export of its products, management spent the money on buying consumption goods. Later brick and glass factories and a small shoe factory were built, small handicraft workshops were organised, but only the brick factory turned out to be profitable.

Technical reconstruction and investment

The attempts undertaken at the end of 1993 and beginning of 1994 to reduce production costs were a clear sign of market-oriented behaviour on the part of management of the two enterprises. The management of Ore planned to reduce production costs by 15 per cent in 1994, primarily through technical reconstruction and the installation of energy-saving equipment. In 1995 a tougher programme of resource-saving was undertaken, with an expected reduction of expenditure of 25 per cent. The enterprise has set itself the future task of increasing the quality of the product by increasing the iron content of the final product. These plans are being undertaken by the enterprise using its own resources. The main stimulus to this modernisation of production was the orientation, on the one hand, to strengthening its position on the internal market and, on the other hand, to winning a place on the world market, with its stricter quality requirements.

At the same time as conducting research on world market demand, the Ore management developed a large-scale plan to establish the production of higher quality types of product — metallised briquettes (whose price is of a different order of magnitude from the existing products of the *kombinat*) concentrate and pellets. The realisation of this plan will cost not less than one billion dollars. Naturally, the search for investment funds for the project is the most difficult point in the plan. Initially the management of the *kombinat* proposed to combine various sources of finance: its own funds and those of the enterprises which were its business partners, privileged state credit, and also credit from domestic and foreign banks. However, the government refused to participate in financing the project, while the largest domestic banks, to which management proposed partnerships, turned out not to have the resources to undertake a project of such a scale. In this situation Ore had to turn to foreign banks. The management proposed to attract the latter not with participation in capital but in profits. After three years of discussion with Western banks, in the summer of 1995 a framework agreement was concluded with a German firm to build the first pelleting plant, which will cost 200 million dollars. One of the six Russian banks which were included in the international classification of the world's largest banks has agreed to participate in financing the first stage of the project, and this decision played an important part in persuading the German banks to invest on their part. The conditions of the loan are favourable: the credit is for seven years at 7.5 per cent per annum and will be repaid from the sale of the product. The management of the *kombinat* believes that the project can pay for itself in two to three years. In the next stages it is planned to replace the consortium of German banks with a consortium of Russian banks.

Concentrate has also been taking steps to reduce the costs of production and increase the quality of the product through the modernisation of the technological processes and equipment. A programme and technical-economic basis for the reconstruction of the *kombinat* were worked out by its specialists, with the bank Finance as the investor in the project, having entered the investment competition with the condition that it will invest around 20 million dollars in this project over three years.

Participation of the bank Finance in the activity of Concentrate

Although it has not been long since the bank began to exert influence over the activity of the enterprise, one can observe the directions and priorities of that influence. For example, with the appearance of the bank the problems of inadequate working capital became less serious; at least, the bank made it possible to avoid delays in the payment of wages to the *kombinat*'s employees. The bank also took upon itself some of the financial problems arising from the payment for rail transport. As already noted, the bank is in favour of a tough line with insolvent customers.

INFLUENCE OF PRIVATISATION ON LABOUR RELATIONS

The new structure of ownership and control has already resulted in some changes in the internal relations of the enterprises.

Ore

As has already been noted, the General Director of Ore, in his struggle for control over the enterprise, paid a great deal of attention to questions of employment and the social development of the enterprise to maintain a strategic alliance with the labour collective.

Wages and employment policy

The level of wages of Ore employees remains one of the highest in the branch, and semi-annual dividends were regularly paid during 1993. During 1994 delays in the payment of wages were the exception rather than the rule. The enterprise, like many others, experienced difficulties with cash flow, but as a way out of this situation has developed various ways of making non-cash settlements. The most recent innovation was the introduction of magnetic bank cards, which at present are very rare in the provinces.

During this whole period, despite all the difficulties experienced by the enterprise in connection with the decline in production, the *kombinat* has not stopped work and has not sent the workers on compulsory leave. Even more surprising, until recently the enterprise had one of the largest increases in the number of employees in the branch. The statistical data conceals a rather complex situation with changes in employment. The growth of employment occurred against the background of a sharp fall in labour turnover (up to two or three per cent per annum), the practically complete cessation of recruitment in the area of basic production, and a reduction in industrial-productive personnel. Recruitment of new workers has been concentrated in the administrative services and new divisions of the *kombinat* — a building trust and subsidiary agriculture and food-processing factories. During the last months of 1994 the growth of employment took place through the unification of Ore with other joint-stock companies, two collective farms. In the spring of 1995 another closely related enterprise merged with the company.

Twice, in both 1993 and 1994, there was an annual reduction of staff of 10 per cent (each time involving the loss of 1400–1500 people). In 1993 the reduction involved the redistribution of staff from main production to objects of the social sphere and other new divisions of the *kombinat*, with all those wanting it being offered the opportunity of retraining. In 1994 the reductions took place under the slogan of the rejuvenation of the labour collective. The decision to reduce the numbers was taken by the Directors' Council, but it had previously been discussed with representatives of the shop trade union organisation. Together with the trade union committee, the administration has worked out a set of privileges for pensioners, to encourage their voluntary retirement from the enterprise.

Against the background of the fall in production and wages in many enterprises in the city, Ore has become an attractive place for the citizens to work. This contrasts not only with the situation in other enterprises, but also with that experienced by Ore in the years of stagnation, when workers literally fled the enterprise so that it had to use foreign labour imported from other socialist countries. The positive desire to work at Ore has only developed over the past two or three years. A competitive system of recruitment has been established in Ore. Thus the General Director supervises the recruitment of not only administrative but all personnel: even an ancillary worker cannot be taken on without his signature. He declared at the shareholders' conference that the rejuvenation of the labour collective is a priority in recruitment policy.

> We have protected pensioners socially and it is necessary to give way to young people, and for this we have to carry through redundancies and retraining of personnel.... We have to make the collective more healthy by bringing in young

people, therefore we want to give all our working pensioners the chance of a deserved retirement. And we will bring healthy young lads into the jobs freed, who now have no work. We are even ready to give the children of our own workers the priority right to join us.

Originally the General Director adopted a strategy of resolving the problem of employment by creating new jobs in construction and through the diversification of production. Recently there has been discussion of the possibility of resolving the problem through widening the joint-stock company by establishing connections with a range of new enterprises, initially those with existing connections with the *kombinat*. As the General Director declared at the shareholders' conference, he is convinced that the problem of employment has to be resolved for all enterprises, either adapting to the fall in demand, or carrying out technical reconstruction, so that it is necessary to be prepared in advance.

Social policy

Social policy plays a significant role in the strategy of the General Director for the development of the labour collective, as he puts it, for the 'care of people'. The enterprise, which had a weak social sphere in the years of stagnation, has in a short period and with its own resources not only strengthened it, but also significantly expanded it. The company now has its own cultural centre, polyclinic (equipped to the highest standards), country rest centre and children's pioneer camp, sports complex, stadium, swimming pool, and about thirty kindergartens. This is really a unique enterprise in the region in continuing to build housing for its employees, although it is true that the emphasis is gradually being shifted towards individual construction at the workers' own expense, but supported by credits from the company.

The dynamic development of the social sphere is in complete contrast to the general tendency for enterprises to get rid of the social sphere. Having privatised, the enterprise has not transferred a single item of its social apparatus to the municipality, having concluded an economic management agreement with it. A number of circumstances have been conducive to such a course of events. Above all, the economic situation of the enterprise has so far allowed it to allocate large sums of money to support the social sphere. A balance of interests with the local authority has been found in the resolution of questions concerning the social sphere. The head of the local administration is well aware of the advantages for the city budget, for which the additional costs would impose an insupportable burden, while at the same time it is able to profit from regional and federal grants. The management of the *kombinat* has an interest in preserving the enterprise's housing stock and other objects so as to be able to pursue a flexible employment policy and recruit the best experts not only from the region but from the whole of Russia. Not least, probably, is the hope that in the future the social infrastructure will become the property of the joint-stock company. It is impossible also to ignore what is referred to as 'social responsibility'. The General Director has no illusions about the fate of the social sphere in the event that it is transferred to the municipality. At the shareholders' conference he stated his position clearly:

> We will manage not to transfer anything to municipal ownership — kindergartens, polyclinics, housing. If we hand it over, the result will be the same as it is in the rest of the municipal social sphere, it will collapse.

The privatisation of the enterprise has not been an obstacle to the provision of support for pensioners and young workers. The General Director insisted that 10 per cent of the privatisation fund, established for the purchase of shares (including those bought through closed subscription) and financed from the enterprise's profits, should be reserved for pensioners, former workers of the enterprise, although not all the employees agreed with this proposal. The basic position of the General Director was that these people, who could no longer work and whom the state had stopped supporting, should not be abandoned in these difficult times. In the first year in which profits were distributed the participants in the shareholders' conference voted to allocate money to the society Charity, a public organisation which helps pensioners, the disabled, large families and the needy, and serves as the channel of communication between pensioners and the enterprise. The activity of this society has already developed beyond the framework of the enterprise and embraces a part of the city population. In addition to their pension, all former workers of the company receive a monthly allowance, which exceeds the state minimum pension by 1.5 times.

The company carries out an active youth policy. As already noted, a priority is given to youth in the recruitment of new workers. Young families receive interest-free credit from the company for the purchase of furniture, and have priority in the allocation of credit for individual house construction. The General Director supports the activity of the youth organisation, which looks after the organisation of the leisure activity of young people, but also questions of their professional development and careers, organising competitions around professional skill and identifying the most capable young workers for promotion to administrative posts.

How can one evaluate the General Director's youth policy from the point of view of the control of the enterprise? One can assume that besides the aim of developing the skill composition of the labour collective, the management could have one of two other purposes.

First, the recruitment of new workers, who are not shareowners, allows the management to strengthen its autonomy since the participation of the employees in taking decisions about the development of the company is reduced. However, such an assumption is contradicted by many statements of management about their intention in the near future to consider the problem of the allocation of shares to new workers.

Second, orienting itself to the recruitment of young workers and supporting them at the expense of the company helps the management to maintain its ambition of creating a body of shareholders loyal to management. In connection with the appearance of the opportunity to sell shares, various categories of shareholders have shown distinctive behaviour and intentions. The pensioners and those young people who have only a small connection with the enterprise are precisely those who have expressed an interest in getting rid of their shares, while the majority of young workers have expressed an interest not only in keeping their jobs and in maintaining their shareholding, but also in acquiring more shares. At the present stage the behaviour of the latter category of worker-shareholders corresponds to the tactical aim of the management to keep the shares within the company, and it is ready to encourage precisely these workers.

Trade unions

Formally the trade union committee is distinct from the joint-stock company — it has its own accountant, and its full-time workers are paid from trade union fees. The relative independence of the trade union committee of the *kombinat* is also demonstrated by its relations with the branch metal mining trade union and participation in branch trade union activities. However, in reality, when virtually all the employees of the enterprise, including members of the trade union committee, are its shareholders, the trade union leaders are not able to resolve the question of the place of the trade union in the company. In discussing the defence of the interests of the workers, the trade union leaders spoke about their common interests with the administration:

> Nothing separates us: we have a single business and have a single aim before us. That is how we work together.

The workers relate to the existing trade union as to a distributive body which serves the administration. In the view of the workers its influence on the world of the workers is insignificant, and the trade union as an organisation is dead. They do not consider it to be a body which defends their interests and do not trust those people selected by the administration to work in the trade union committees. They think that the only real body for their defence is the court. At the same time, ordinary workers do not see any possibility of using the trade union in the event of a restriction of their rights as shareholders. They also have no confidence that the present leadership of the trade union committee wants to interfere in the affairs of the company in defence of small shareholders.

At the same time, the management of the company has tried over the past two years to draw the trade unions into its strategy and incorporate it into the management structure of the company. In spite of the widespread impression of the contraction of the functions of trade union, we observe their expansion and their subordination to the aims of company management in the interests of the administration. Certainly the trade union retains the traditional Soviet trade union functions: health and safety, supplying the workers with the necessities of life and labour, supplying travel warrants to sanatoria and rest homes, providing garden plots, garages and homes. In a word, the basic sphere of activity of the trade union in Ore remains the social sphere and therefore it is easily incorporated into the strategy of the management of the company, based on an alliance between management and ordinary workers.

The management of the company also controls the conclusion of the collective agreement. It is interesting that changes in the collective agreement were confirmed at the shareholders' conference. The administration included many features in the collective agreement which allowed it to act against the interests of the workers within the framework of the law, including points about the possibility of short-time working, conducting a rigid employment policy which did not allow the workers recourse to the courts. In the collective agreement for 1995–6 the employer, in the form of the Council of Directors, assigned itself the right independently to define the system, form and payment of labour.

Subsequent events testify to the use of the trade union by management as a channel for the control of the worker-shareholders, and to the direct alliance with the union in its struggle against hostile outsiders. The common membership of management and workers in a single trade union gives them a legal basis to ensure that all trade union activity takes a direction which is favourable to them. It was the senior managers who initiated the resumption of the practice of holding trade union meetings. Senior managers of the company participated actively in the autumn campaign for trade union elections at shop level. They used these meetings, first, as channels of information through which they presented the workers with the information which allowed them to take decisions about how to behave as shareholders. Second, these meetings have allowed a release of the tension that was arising in the labour collective as a result of the delay in the issue of shareholding certificates and so prevented the expression of this discontent at the shareholders' conference. The shareholders' conference was conducted simultaneously with the trade union conference, and trade union questions appeared first on the agenda. This was a carefully planned step on the part of the General Director to resolve the problem of his struggle with the outsiders.

One of the foremen observed how the administration of the *kombinat* uses the trade union to maintain social peace in the enterprise. The workers were becoming increasingly dissatisfied because they had not received any documents confirming their share ownership, so the management of the enterprise, through the trade union, distributed lists to each shop on which workers could sign to obtain consumer goods at discount prices in the *kombinat*'s shops (cars, furniture, televisions and so on). The workers were drawn into this procedure, the problem of shares fell into the background, and social tension was reduced.

At the same time the unity of interests of the trade union committee and the management of the company persists in relation to that other outsider, the state. This was formally fixed in the collective agreement for 1995–6, in which it is stated that

> the trade union recognises its responsibility for realising the common aims and collaborates with the Directors' Council and management in the conduct of negotiations with state bodies of management and power on questions concerning the interests of the collective of the company.

Concentrate

There are more common features than differences between Ore and Concentrate in the wages and employment policies pursued in the period during which Concentrate was still controlled by management. The differences are, in my view, explicable in terms of the less stable economic position of Concentrate, and the smaller interest of its management in pursuing a more active policy designed to keep control of the enterprise.

Employment

The enterprise employed 14,450 workers in November 1994. There had been no mass redundancies, but neither was there any recruitment.

During 1992–1993, in connection with the transfer of the social sphere of the *kombinat* to the city, the staff should have been reduced by 1,350 but half of these workers (675 people) were recruited by the joint-stock company. In 1993 the rotor machines, which extracted the ore, were taken out of commission. Sixty of the 220 people were laid off, the others were recruited by the joint-stock company to jobs which had been created earlier: 80 jobs in glass production; 170 in a brick factory; 112 in shoe production, a total of about 400 jobs over three years.

Over the past three years labour turnover has fallen sharply, from about 9 per cent to 0.5-1 per cent. Latent unemployment has become obvious (production has been halved, but the level of employment has barely changed). Redundancies have become inevitable. The decision to lay off 1,400 people was taken early in 1994 jointly by management and the trade union, without any reference to the external shareholders. The decision provided privileges for pensioners who chose to leave, and many took this up, so that only 150 were made compulsorily redundant. Fifty per cent of those of pension and pre-pension age who left were replaced by young people, children of those who had left. In determining its employment policy the management took account of the situation in the city, and in particular the high level of latent unemployment amongst young people.

Thus, the management of Concentrate twice carried through redundancy programmes before the arrival of the external shareholders, which precisely repeated the sequence that we have already seen in Ore. Here also the questions were resolved with the support of the trade union. However, here, unlike the case of Ore, this was only after the trade union committee had sent persistent requests to management to take up the issue of the creation of new jobs. At the initiative of the trade union committee the question of the regulation of employment became central to the collective agreement which, in the opinion of the trade union officers, is gradually being filled with some real content.

Wages

The average wage of workers in Concentrate in the autumn of 1994, despite the relative prosperity of the enterprise in comparison with others in the branch, was below the branch average, and was only half the level of wages in Ore. Despite the fact that the approach to pay differentiation has not changed (skilled workers in the main trades still receive more than specialists), the workers complained that they worked as well as those at Ore, and so should be paid as much. According to one of the managers, the share of wages in production costs, 12 per cent, has fallen. By contrast to Ore, dividends have only been paid once, in the middle of 1994 (on the basis of the 1993 results). The bank, which at this stage was a large shareowner but did not have a place on the Directors' Council, spoke out against the payment of any dividend (the decision about the dividend payment was taken before the election of the new Council). Many are convinced that in future it will also refuse to pay dividends on voting shares.

Delays in the payment of wages are regular, to the displeasure of the workers, who blame management for using the money destined for the payment of wages for commercial objectives. The workers have also criticised the irrational use of foreign currency earnings from export sales by management. Contrasting their position with that of Ore, where foreign currency was spent on purchasing new equipment, the workers expressed their disagreement with the decision of their management to spend the money on importing consumer goods.

Social sphere

During the process of privatisation the housing stock, medical centre, sports centre, swimming pool and stadium were all transferred to the municipality. The *kombinat* retains hostels, the cultural centre, a children's sanatorium, and more than 20 kindergartens, which will be transferred to the municipality gradually. The bank has insisted that the children's sanatorium, which is extremely well-equipped, should either be transferred to the municipality or converted to another use, which the trade union is trying to oppose. Concentrate continues to build housing, but on a much reduced scale.

Trade union

The trade union was excluded from participation in privatisation. The labour collective was formally represented on the working commission on privatisation by the STK, which was disbanded immediately after privatisation. Members of the commission invited the trade union committee to participate only once, in relation to working out the procedure for the closed subscription.

During privatisation, with the transfer of a significant part of the social sphere to the municipality, the traditional field of trade union activity was cut back, and it concerned itself primarily with the distribution of goods. As in Ore, a society Charity was set up in Concentrate, which works with pensioners together with the trade union. However, whereas in Ore this society is separate from the union, at Concentrate it functions as a part of the trade union. Therefore in this enterprise there are more members of the trade union than there are employees, since the pensioners retain their trade union membership when they retire.

Gradually the functions of the trade union have begun to change. As my conversations with workers and managers showed, the workers in Concentrate express more anxiety about their jobs than those in Ore. The trade union committee has taken the initiative to make questions of the regulation of employment central to the collective agreement which, in the opinion of the trade union officers, is gradually being filled with real content. As one of the trade union leaders recognised:

> we are beginning to live under the collective agreement. The administration has its own interests, which are different from those of the collective.

However, ordinary workers ask themselves why they need a collective agreement in a joint-stock company, and support is growing for a refusal to conclude a collective agreement. In this situation the trade union committee uses the collective agreement to enhance its own status.

One can now observe a tendency towards the strengthening of the position of the trade union committee in the *kombinat*. It is gathering its forces for the time when some bright person with a public weight joins the leadership of the union. (The president of the trade union committee of the *kombinat* is a deputy in the regional duma and president of the city trade union council, while one of his deputies was a USSR People's Deputy.) The strengthening of their position is based on political activity beyond the limits of the *kombinat*, in the city and in the Russian metallurgists' branch trade union.

At the same time the trade union committee does not use the support of ordinary workers of the *kombinat*. In the working environment there is a feeling of alienation from the trade unions. In the words of the vice-president of the trade union committee, among the workers there is no desire and trust to use the trade union as the channel through which they could realise their interests as shareholders.

GROUPS WITHIN THE ENTERPRISE

Ore

There are no independent groups conscious of their own interests within the enterprise. A clear dividing line has appeared recently in the labour collective, but this is not related to the ownership of shares. This is the old division between bosses and ordinary workers which has been strengthened by the policy of the General Director, distinguishing those who are paid individually according to a contract and those who receive the traditional form of wages.

The introduction of the contract system by the General Director, initially for the heads of production subdivisions and specialists, aimed, on the one hand, to secure their support and, on the other hand, to increase the distance between them and the workers and to frustrate the possible formation of a coalition between managers and workers against the director. There is no clear differentiation within the group of those on contracts. At the same time one cannot consider this group to be homogeneous; it is more that it is atomised firstly, by the contract with its individual conditions of employment, and secondly, by the management style of the General Director. He is a leader who constructs his relationships with the management team and the labour collective on the basis of authoritarian paternalism.

Higher levels of management

According to my observations there is no harmonious management team of like-minded people at Ore; there are only individual people whose status depends on their distance from the General Director. One has the impression that the director does not trust any of his subordinates, they have very limited independence in decision-making, and the General Director keeps all questions of management of the enterprise and of personnel under his control. In their turn, those managers who are closer to the General Director than the others have been selected both for their personal devotion and for the significance of the subdivision which they head for the activity of the enterprise as a whole. There are three people who are more in the director's favour than the others. The head of the ore division, a member of the Directors' Council, has the support of the director as head of one of the key subdivisions of the enterprise, and as the director's son. The technical director is at present the president of the Board. This manager was simply a godsend for the General Director. First, he is a highly skilled specialist who knows production inside out so that the General Director can rely on him completely in matters of the operational management of production, and concentrate himself on strategic problems and on relationships with the external agents of the enterprise. Secondly, this person has authority both among the managerial staff and the specialists and among the workers. The third key figure is the director of external economic activity, who came to the enterprise three years ago from a scientific research institute. With his arrival the external economic activity of the enterprise really took off. Moreover, from my observation it is clear that he is the brains behind all the financial operations of the company.

The external economic department is the most dynamic and rapidly growing subdivision of the enterprise at present. In the process of widening the areas of activity of the external economic department, it is becoming obvious that it is duplicating the functions of the economic department and the internal economic department, with the clear aim of subsequently becoming the key economic subdivision and taking control of financial and material flows. But no open contradictions have arisen between these two departments, on the one hand because of the relative weakness of the position of the head of the economic department, and on the other hand because of the informal relations between the chiefs (until recently they had worked together for a long time in the same scientific research institute).

There are also no obvious signs of any contradictions within the administration between the production and economic departments, since at present they work autonomously and their interests do not intersect. The potential divergence between the interests of the heads of the company and the heads of the production subdivisions of the enterprise exist at present in a suppressed form. The management structure of the enterprise is strictly centralised and the large production subdivisions have no juridical independence, only having the status of shops. Two years ago the production chiefs raised the question of the decentralisation of management, with the managers of the subdivisions which were profitable for the *kombinat* showing a particular interest in acquiring financial independence. However, the General Director quashed their attempt to obtain independence, convincing them that they could not carry out the reconstruction of production on their own. The position of the General Director in relation to the small enterprises working on the base of large enterprises was also noteworthy: at no time was the rapid development of this form of activity in Ore observed. One can consider such a policy of the director as designed to prevent the appearance of a fraction within management which would have the relative independence and power to constitute an opposition to the top levels of management of the company. The conclusion of contracts with this group of managers, giving them much higher pay than in the past, emerged as the compromise.

There is a series of contradictions between various groups which exist in latent form within the management of the enterprise, which are based on the General Director's personnel policy. Firstly, from the very beginning the director protected those from his own district and from his previous place of work. Following the principle of supporting people from his own district (*zemlyachestvo*) in staffing the management apparatus, the director gradually forced out the veterans, that is to say, those who had worked in the *kombinat* since it was established. Tension between these two groups exists in latent form.

Recently, Ore has been actively recruiting specialists who very quickly (in comparison with the veterans of production) receive apartments, automobiles and other benefits. Such a favourable relationship to the recently arrived specialists provokes discontent on the part of old management employees, although this is not expressed openly.

The formation of opposition to the General Director on the part of the managerial apparatus is prevented, on the one hand, by the absence of group cohesion among the managers and, on the other hand, by the very harsh attitude of the General Director to those who are critical of him. More than once the director has sacked managers who demonstrated their independence. The most recent case, recounted by the vice president of the bank Finance, was the sacking of the economics director because the latter welcomed the representative of the bank, who had come to the shareholders conference. The General Director suspected him of contacts with the outside shareholders and of secret opposition.

Line managers

The transfer of senior foremen to the contract system increased the distance between them and the workers, and if in the past the workers could turn to the senior foremen with their problems, now they perceived them as part of management. Since the foremen have not yet been transferred to contracts, the tension between them and the senior foremen has also increased, although this is not expressed in the form of open conflict.

Groups of workers

At the moment there is no basis for differentiation among the workers. Differences between workers of various professions in their levels of pay, characteristics of their work, or the number of shares owned are completely insignificant. The workers themselves recognise this absence of differentiation. The sharpest distinction perceived by the workers is that between the earnings of managers and specialists, paid on a contract system, and ordinary workers.

Recently, as a result of management's policy of rejuvenating the collective there has been an intensive displacement of working pensioners by young people. However, no conflict arises between these two age groups since the sacking of one and the recruitment of the other do not coincide in time and also given the unlikelihood that they will work together for an extended period of time.

Although the opportunities to buy and sell shares have expanded recently, there is still only a very weak differentiation of workers in relation to share ownership. At this stage one can distinguish three groups of worker-shareholders:

1. Those who are ready to sell all their shares since they expect to have nothing more to do with the enterprise. This is mainly the pensioners who have been sacked and some young workers who have left to go and live somewhere else.
2. Employees who are ready to sell some of their shares because, believing the information about the high price of their shares, they expect to get a large amount of money to buy consumer goods (automobiles, television, furniture and so on) or apartments. These are, as a rule, employees whose relatives also work in the *kombinat*, so that they can be confident that even if they sell some of their shares, they will still be shareholders of the enterprise.
3. Workers who do not for the moment intend to sell any of their shares and who may even intend to buy additional shares. These are mostly young workers who have recently come to the *kombinat*. Their desire to increase their shareholding is not only due to their desire to receive more income in the form of dividends, but also to the need to consolidate their status. They more often than others spoke about their orientation to work in this enterprise.

Concentrate

The privatisation of Concentrate according to the first variant resulted in a division of the labour collective. Among workers there is a group of about 150–200 communists who have not accepted privatisation for reasons of principle. This group did not participate in the distribution of shares among members of the labour collective and so lost an opportunity to express its interests through the institutions of the joint-stock company, particularly the shareholders' conferences. The main part of the labour collective was expecting to 'be the owner of the enterprise' and to possess a controlling package of the shares, and for that reason was in opposition to that part of management which wanted to pursue privatisation according to the first variant. This line of division between management and workers has subsequently deepened since, on the basis of the conditions of the first variant, more than 150 managers received share options and have become the holders of 5 per cent of the shares, while the ordinary workers reacted negatively to such managerial privileges. Apart from the general discontent, that the chiefs have again received more than the workers, people also say that the labour collective has lost this 5 per cent, since if the chiefs leave they will either take them with them, or sell them. Some even propose that these shares should be taken back if they leave. Now the majority of the ordinary workers in the enterprise condemn management for the fact that it has carried out privatisation 'incorrectly' and has allowed in external owners. Thus the bulk of the labour collective has no confidence in the present management of the enterprise.

Management team

At the same time privatisation also turned out to be a watershed for the management team. The arrival of the external shareholder and new proprietor of the enterprise has deepened differentiation among managers of the *kombinat*. Within the administration of the enterprise there is a group that is loyal to the bank leadership, which is those with whom the bank now works (these are the people around the economics and technical directors). There is also a group of disloyal chiefs, who do not like the presence of the bank and who do not perceive the bank as the legitimate owner. These are those managers who at one time managed resources (such as social and welfare facilities, agricultural subsidiaries and some industrial subdivisions) which the new authorities cannot handle. Among those who have reservations about the participation of the bank in the management of the company are people who are inclined to oppose the bank within the rules. Earlier they had tried to persuade others that it was necessary to try to put together an opposition packet of shares with which to block decisions unfavourable to the labour collective. Now they have the idea of creating some kind of an association — a voting trust to consolidate the small packets of shares held by the local investment funds combined with shares held in the *kombinat*. At present their position has little support, and people who hold the position are not very influential.

These groups are concentrated in the top layers of management. The line managers are far from the problems of privatisation and corporate management and take a neutral position, as the policy of the bank at present does not touch on their interests.

The workers generally take a negative attitude to banks, and in particular to Moscow. They consider them to be parasites, against the workers who produce material goods. However, as I found in my conversations with workers, they are poorly informed about the activity of the bank, their new owner, and do not know the position of the bank concerning the social sphere. As an insider member of the Directors' Council remarked,

> the simple worker at the moment has no sense of the bank as the owner of the enterprise, but at some stage it is going to affect his interests.

What are the potential channels through which the labour collective of the enterprise can express its interests? As our analysis of the management bodies of Concentrate has shown, there is no place in those bodies for the trade union, or for any body that represents the workers. The bank prefers to work only with a part of management, not giving any thought to this question.

It would seem that the appearance of an outside owner should give a push to the transformation of the traditional trade union and the transformation of its role as defender of the interests of hired labour. And, certainly, through the decisions taken about the fate of the social sphere, the trade union has become one of the main opponents of the bank. However, as has been seen, in this situation it has become an ally of that part of the administration which is opposed to the bank, but so far not the defender of the workers. While the trade union continues to lack legitimacy, its main concern will be to strengthen its own position, either through political activity or through industrial conflicts. Thus, by neglecting the need to provide channels through which the interests of the labour collective can be represented, the outside owners will provoke conflicts.

CONCLUSIONS

At present in Russia there are two models of corporate control: of insiders (in the case examined of the General Director) and of outsiders (a commercial bank). While the basis of outsider control of the enterprise is the concentration of a controlling interest in the hands of outsiders, the basis of the insider control of managers is not their property, but their use of the former mechanisms of power and control over the management bodies of the company. Despite the differences in the sources of power and the existence of many owners, in both cases in practice the management of the resources of the enterprise is concentrated in a single pair of hands. And such a concentration and consolidation of control is a favourable condition for the reconstruction of the enterprise and the attraction of long-term investment.

Insider control does not prevent the adaptation of the enterprise to the external environment and its reconstruction. The comparison of the trajectory of the development of Ore and Concentrate, during the period when both *kombinats* were under the control of insiders, shows that the successful reconstruction of the enterprise depends first of all on the motivation and professional skill of a management team keeping control over the enterprise. The General Director of Ore, to keep a balance between the interests of the labour collective and the bank Finance, had to develop the enterprise. The maintenance of the high wages and employment of the workers compelled him to reconstruct the enterprise and to search for new ways of developing it. The basic method of maintaining full employment for this dynamically developing enterprise is widening the boundaries of the company both through the diversification of production and the construction of new enterprises and by merging with already existing enterprises. In this way, while unprofitable activities may be closed, basic production is rationalised and the workers freed are retrained and transferred to new jobs within the framework of the company. Thus, the common interest of insiders, both managers and workers, in saving jobs serves not as an obstacle, but as a stimulus to reconstruction. The other condition, and at the same time the result of the struggle of the General Director to keep control of the enterprise, is the strengthening of the old and the creation of new socio-economic networks. The result of the coalition of interests between the local authority and the enterprise was the preservation of the enterprise's social sphere and support for the socially disadvantaged sections of the local population. In my opinion, with the rapid pace of privatisation in Russia, such socially responsible behaviour on the part of management is rational, for without it there would be a significant increase in the risk of social disintegration.

The weak motivation of the leaders to keep control of the enterprise, as the development of Concentrate testifies, promotes a split in the labour collective that, in turn, increases the probability of the arrival of an external proprietor. External control on the part of financial institutions is established through formal procedures and the bodies of management of the company. Domination of them by an outsider can result in the adoption of decisions bringing short-term profit, which do not take into account the long-term interests of the development of the enterprise and its labour force. The emergence of an external proprietor promotes the formation of more conflictual relations inside the enterprise. However, the current situation provokes the formation of coalitions between workers and part of management, instead of the institutionalisation of labour relations between management and workers. The position of the bank Finance, which is not interested in the development of bodies to represent the interests of the labour collective, also promotes the engagement of trade unions in political activity and a struggle for control. The main effect of the financial control of the enterprise by the bank Finance is the promotion of a breakdown of the traditional industrial connections of Concentrate and the weakening of its connections with the community.

Index